BIRMINGHAM'S RABBI

Morris Newfield circa 1914.
(Birmingham Public Library / Department of Archives)

Judaic Studies Series

Leon J. Weinberger, General Editor

BIRMINGHAM'S RABBI

MORRIS NEWFIELD AND ALABAMA 1895–1940

MARK COWETT

THE UNIVERSITY OF ALABAMA PRESS

Library of Congress Cataloging-in-Publication Data

Cowett, Mark, 1951–
Birmingham's rabbi.
(Judaic studies series)
Bibliography: p.
Includes index.
1. Newfield, Morris, b. 1869. 2. Rabbis—Alabama—Birmingham—Biography. 3. Jews—Alabama—Birmingham—Politics and government. 4. Birmingham (Ala.)—Biography. 5. Birmingham (Ala.)—Ethnic relations. I. Title. II. Series.
BM755.N48C48 1986 296.8'32'0924 [B] 85-20897
ISBN 0–8173–0284–0

Publication of this book has been assisted by a grant from the Birmingham Jewish Foundation.

CONTENTS

ILLUSTRATIONS

ACKNOWLEDGMENTS

As all scholars are wont to do, I used to dream of the day that I could write a page of acknowledgment for the successful completion of a manuscript. I could never hope to thank everyone who nourished my dream, but I would like to recognize a few:

To my Mother, Sylvia Kazin Cowett, who has never failed to say "you can,"
To my brothers, Dr. Richard M. and Jon Cowett, who always encouraged me,
To my teachers, William W. Bremer, Roger Daniels, Peter A. Fritzell, Arthur Mann, Jacob R. Marcus, Harriet Russell, Thomas Sakmyster, and Anne J. Schutte, who taught me to appreciate and to write history,
To my students and colleagues at Keith Country Day School, with whom I have shared some wonderful times,
To two men in Birmingham, Alabama, Mayer U. Newfield, the rabbi's son, and Dr. Marvin Y. Whiting, who aided me greatly in the writing of this book,
To two very special women, Judith Casto and Linda Wantz Summerfield, for their love and friendship,
And especially to my Father, Allen Abraham Cowett, a native Birminghamian, who showed me love and told me to follow my dreams.

This book is because of, and for, all of you.

Mark Cowett
1–3–86

PREFACE

Since World War II, various commentators on American Jewish history have asked historians to present American Jewish history not as separatists chronicling events and experiences of Jews as they stand apart from the main currents of American history but as interpreters of how these are "part and parcel of American history." Complaints have been raised about the parochial nature of American Jewish history because it has consisted largely of chronicles of American Jewish life and has often failed to explore the relationship between Jews and other ethnic groups in America. This parochialism, however, has not been linked to American Jewish history alone but has been a hallmark of ethnic history.[1]

The present biography of Morris Newfield, a rabbi who led Temple Emanu-El in Birmingham, Alabama, from 1895 to 1940, is written, then, with a number of purposes in mind. It relates the deeds and thoughts of a significant Alabama rabbi who achieved importance in Birmingham, in Alabama, and throughout the South, and it explores the conflicts with which Newfield struggled to help his group maintain a sense of religious identity at the same time that he understood the Jews' need to develop close relationships with other ethnic groups in a somewhat hostile environment in Birmingham. American Jews and American Jewish leaders, in particular, faced the same task everywhere, not just in Birmingham and in the South.

Using Newfield's life and career as a vehicle, I explore the nature of ethnic leadership in America. The Birmingham rabbi must be seen not only as a leader of Jews but also as a Jewish leader in Birmingham and in Alabama, because, as I will demonstrate in the following pages, much like his contemporary Jane Addams, Newfield inhabited reality and understood that his success as a Jewish leader depended on his ability to comprehend the competing needs of a number of ethnic groups and to offer them meaningful leadership. His work, as a consequence, both affected and was affected by influences emanating from a fairly broad ethnic spectrum, from Orthodox Judaism to fundamentalist Protestant Christianity.

I will consider three questions: how and why did the rabbi become a leader of both Jews and Christians in Birmingham and in Alabama at this time? How did Newfield maintain his leadership in particularly stressful times? Does Newfield's style of leadership suggest that models of leadership might help us explain the activities of successful ethnic leaders?

The key to understanding Rabbi Newfield's work lies in the rabbi's sense of Jewish marginality in a largely Fundamentalist Protestant area, a sense that I shall seek to define. In particular, I will explore three reasons for Newfield's success as an ethnic leader: first, Jews needed a leader who could help them maintain a link with their tradition in a new and often threatening environment, but they also expected their leader to smooth the way for them with Christians in Birmingham; second, Birmingham Christians, exhibiting a distinct sense of religiosity, respected him; and third, and most significant, Newfield's own tactical style of leadership, stressing brotherhood instead of accentuating differences, overcame the ambivalent feelings that both Jews and Christians held toward each other.

Newfield's career, however, can also help us understand the essence of social welfare efforts in Alabama during the so-called Progressive era. Admittedly the chapter on his social welfare efforts differs from the other six chapters in this biography; I have emphasized the "atmosphere" of social reform in Alabama rather than concentrating solely on Newfield's actions and responses. Lest readers be puzzled by this shift in emphasis, I shall state my reason: many previous historical efforts on the South have either ignored or underestimated the humanitarian impulses in the South in general and in Birmingham in particular during the Progressive era. A study of Newfield's work can increase our insight into this problem.

Finally, Morris Newfield's life is important simply because his work makes him, contrary to the statement made by sociologist

Kurt Lewin regarding ethnic leaders in general, a reliable spokesman for the dilemmas confronting many southern Jews and Christians. Inasmuch as the problems, styles, and expectations of a particular ethnic group can be illuminated by a study of the life of any one member of that group, Newfield's biography can help explain the situation of many southern Jews who, in the early years of the twentieth century, hoped to remain loyal to their ethnic group but at the same time to develop successful relationships with southern Christians. For Newfield and for many southern Jews, the task was sometimes extremely challenging.

BIRMINGHAM'S RABBI

ONE

The Early Years: From Hungary through Hebrew Union College

On an early afternoon in June 1895, twenty-six-year-old Morris Newfield heard the Reverend Washington Gladden deliver the baccalaureate address to his graduating class at the University of Cincinnati. Five years had passed since Newfield had come to Cincinnati from Hungary to study at the Hebrew Union College with Isaac Mayer Wise. But Newfield had escaped from Hungary too, bringing with him keen memories. One was his father's unbowed commitment to Talmudic scholarship and his hope that Morris would carry on the family tradition in the rabbinate. Another was the great pain that the family's poverty had caused him, first as a young boy in Homanna and then as a student in Budapest. Morris's father, although revered as a learned man, was very poor. Morris would become a rabbi but not in Hungary. He would work in America, where he would earn not only the respect that the rabbinate endowed but also the security of a pulpit, which had been denied his father.

Mór Neufeld, as he was known in Hungary, was born on January 31, 1869, in Homanna, county of Zemplén, a German-speaking area in northern Hungary. He was a younger son of Seymon Shabsi Neufeld and his second wife, Lena (Klein). Mór's father was the last of a line of Orthodox rabbis who had moved eastward in Europe after the expulsion of the Jews from Spain in the wake of the Inquisition in 1492. His grandfather, Rabbi Jehudah of Berlin, Germany, had emigrated southward to Bonyhád, Hungary, looking for a congregation. Seymon Shabsi, the name given to all firstborn males in the Neufeld line, studied Talmud, as his father had asked him to do, under Meyer Ash, the chief rabbi of Ungvár (Uzsgorod). After receiving his "Morenu" diploma in 1842, he, like his father before him, had gone searching for a congregation, but he had not found one. As a result, the rabbi was forced, as were many of his fellow Orthodox scholars, to open a business, in his case a yardage goods store in Homanna, and to study the Talmud simultaneously.[1]

Seymon Neufeld's family had a difficult time making ends meet during Mór's childhood. For one thing, Seymon Neufeld, as was the custom among scholars, studied most of the time, hunched over a huge wooden desk that would later be used as his casket. He read and also received other scholars from various parts of Hungary. His wife, Lena, a small, intelligent, and industrious woman, ran the business. Unfortunately, their home on the main street (*fö-utcā*) attracted few customers, although there were many visitors because of Seymon Neufeld's reputation. Then, too, Seymon had married twice—his wives were sisters—and had fathered eleven children. By his first wife, there were five offspring, and by Léna, his second and Mór's mother, there were six, three boys and three girls.[2] The family had many mouths to feed.

Because of the poverty, Seymon's sons had to leave home while they were in their teens to find their places in Hungary or elsewhere. Emil Neufeld, one of Mór's elder brothers, left Homanna when Mór was quite young and in the 1880s came to America, where he developed a flourishing coal business in New York City. Frida and Teréz, two of Mór's sisters, lived in Homanna and helped with the family business. Mano, another brother, became a teacher at one of the gymnasia in Budapest.[3]

Such upward mobility, which was displayed by Hungarian Jews in general, indicated that some conditions were improving by the time of Mór's birth. As a result of newly won social and political freedoms after 1867, Hungarian Jews faced prospects of wider social opportunities. Actually, Jews had already been living in Hungary for nearly a thousand years, having moved there after the dissolution of the Frankish empire of Charlemagne and before the Magyar conquest of Hungary in A.D. 896. For the next 800 years, like Jews in most of Christendom, they were subject to the whims of the conquering peoples of the Danube basin. In 1239 the Magyar emperor Béla IV wanted Jews to help him raise money for his court, but a century later, after the Black Death, they were expelled from Hungary after refusing to convert to Catholicism. The Turks, who reigned in Hungary for 150 years after subduing the Magyars at Mohács in 1526, also persecuted the Jews. Although the Turks protected Jewish traders in the main commercial areas, the traders were forced to pay special taxes in the royal territories. There Jews were also impelled to curry favor with the pompous Hungarian landowners, who used them as managers of their farms but abused their right to act freely.[4]

By the end of the eighteenth century, the fortunes of Jews began to improve with the rule of Joseph II, the enlightened despot of the Habsburg empire. Although his mother, Maria Theresa, despised Jews, Joseph II was determined to turn them into "useful subjects" by allowing them to rent property and to settle in towns. In 1839, Jews were granted the right to live anywhere in Hungary except in a few specified mining towns. The new Jewish communities that sprang up in towns and cities included the twin cities of Buda and Pesth.[5]

In the three decades before Mór Neufeld's birth in 1869, discussions in the Hungarian Diet about economic and social equality for Jews became particularly intense. Joseph Eötvös (1813–1871), a fervent Hungarian nationalist and liberal whose ideas were expressed in his book *The Emancipation of the Jews* (1840), urged complete and unconditional equality for Jews because he hoped that they could play a significant part in the rebuilding of a great Hungarian nation. Other Magyars as well, including Louis (Lajos) Kossuth, recognized that the Magyar element in the Hungarian part of the Austrian empire was weak; if Hungary was to achieve the hoped-for goal of independence, other cultural groups willing to identify with, and to be assimilated into, the Magyar nation had to be cultivated.[6]

In 1848, when the Magyars revolted against the Habsburg dominance, many Jews, including Seymon Shabsi Neufeld, embraced the cause of Hungarian independence and volunteered to serve with Kossuth's army. This loyalty induced Kossuth to adopt a more favorable attitude toward Jews, and in July 1849 a bill for Jewish emancipation was submitted to the National Assembly in Budapest. The bill was stillborn, however, for the revolution was crushed in the summer of 1849.

Only with a partial restoration of Hungarian political life in the early 1860s, when the Emperor Franz Josef recognized that he needed Hungarian help to maintain his empire, did the question of Jewish emancipation again arise. Ministers Gyula Andrássy and Kálmán Tisza, as well as Ferenc Deák, the foremost political leader of the period, were favorably disposed toward emancipation. Following the Compromise of 1867, the Law of Emancipation was passed, granting full civil and political rights for Jews as individuals.[7]

Respect for Jewish rights in Hungary grew at this time because the Magyars needed Jewish assistance in developing an industrial state and in subduing other cultural minorities in Hungary, such as Romanians and Slavs. Native Magyar aristocrats, preferring the leisurely life of land ownership and civil service to the dirty task of building a firm industrial and financial base in Hungary, allowed Jews to operate in almost every branch of industry and trade. The Act of Trade of 1859 abolished religious discrimination and decreed that nobody could be excluded from the practice of either trade or commerce on account of religion. Because the first large industries in Hungary would necessarily work with agricultural products, Jews in 1860 were able to aid in the development of mills, distilleries, and sugar factories. According to István Végházi in "The Role of Jewry in the Economic Life of Hungary," Jews founded some of the great industrial concerns in Hungary and also made significant contributions in the world of finance.[8]

Jews could also study for the "free professions" such as medicine, law, and journalism. In fact, by the end of the period 1867–1914, they formed a majority of Budapest's lawyers and doctors, owned and edited most of the Budapest newspapers, and were generally very visible—disproportionately so—in the gymnasia and universities across Hungary.[9]

In 1884, Mór Neufeld, at age fourteen, went to Budapest to take advantage of one of the new opportunities for Jews, the Jewish Theological Seminary in Budapest. This liberal, or as they called it in Hungary, Neolog, seminary had opened seven years earlier as a rabbinical school and center of Jewish learning. It offered rabbinical degrees and doctorates in advanced studies in Jewish learning.[10]

Although both Orthodox and more liberal Jews attended the seminary, it was a symbol of a growing tension among Hungarian Jewry. The school had been started after a split had opened between the Orthodox Jews, who continued to accept past traditions, and the Neologs, who acknowledged Enlightenment influences and wanted fuller integration into the Christian society around them. While many Orthodox Jews continued to study Talmud in the cheders and yeshivas in Hungary, the Neologs, led by the Hungarian Jews from Slovakia, or the area where the Neufelds lived, sought a more secularized education.

In 1869 the internal struggle within Hungarian Jewry reached a high point at a Jewish congress at Pesth, which had assembled for the purpose of organizing the Jewish community on a local, regional, and national basis. The Neologs advocated a centralized system, while the Orthodox Jews were in favor of a large measure of independence for the individual communities, thus thwarting reformist tendencies from above. When the Neologs refused to consider an Orthodox demand that the congress not consider any statute or regulation which was not in accordance with the written and oral law as codified in the *Shulchan Aruch,* the Orthodox delegates left the congress. With governmental encouragement, the Neologs adopted a constitution for the Jewish community of Hungary and Transylvania and also established a seminary to train liberal rabbis.

Family tradition holds that Seymon Shabsi Neufeld, although trained in a yeshiva in strict accordance with Orthodox ritual, was not an extreme traditionalist and wanted his son to attend the Neolog institution. Mór began his studies in the high school section of the seminary in 1884. His first- or freshman-year report card, however, indicates that he did not do very well. While he studied the Scriptures, the Talmud, Hebrew, Jewish history, the Hungarian, Greek, and German languages, math, science, and singing, Neufeld missed fifteen lecture hours, an extraordinary number. The reason for his absences is not recorded, but he did finish the year. According to his family and his own records, Neufeld spent five years at the seminary and earned a B.D. in 1889.[11]

While he was a student at the Jewish Theological Seminary in Budapest, Mór Neufeld studied with three of the great Jewish scholars in Europe, David Kaufmann, Wilhelm Bacher, and Joseph Bonoczy. He also attended classes with a few students who would later attain illustrious careers. Lajos Blau became a teacher and director of the seminary in Budapest, Gyula Fischer became the chief rabbi of Budapest from 1921 to 1943, Morris Feuerlicht later moved to Indianapolis and served as a secretary of the Central Conference of American Rabbis, and Samuel Kraus achieved renown first as a professor and director of the Jewish Theological Seminary of Vienna, 1905–1933, and later at Cambridge, 1937–1948.[12]

Young Neufeld also matriculated at the Royal Catholic Grand-Gymnasium in Budapest, from which he graduated in 1889. This opportunity to study with boys of other faiths was also a result of the Emancipation Law of 1867. At least one other Jew graduated in the class of thirty-seven in 1889.

The Budapest Gymnasium was a training ground for future Hungarian leaders. Many of Mór's classmates achieved some distinction in the government of Hungary in the twentieth century. Béla Jakobb was a police commissioner in Budapest, István Kemény became a general counsel of finance, Aurel Knapp was an undersecretary of defense, István Marky served as a colonel in the Hungarian army, Albert Stoffer became a judge in the Royal Supreme Court in Budapest, Béla Szendey was a director of the Credit Bank, and royal Hungarian general counsel of the government, and János Szilárd (Schramar) served as the general counsel of finance of the Ministry of Commerce.[13]

The two years following his graduation from the Royal Gymnasium were terribly unhappy ones for young Mór Neufeld. He had very little to eat and was pursuing a career in medicine without telling his father. He could not admit to his father that he had chosen not to finish his rabbinical studies at the Jewish Theological Seminary and that he had instead enrolled at the Medical College of the University of Budapest. Feeling that this decision would hurt his father deeply, he kept it a secret. But Mór was paying dearly for his independence; correspondence from a friend spoke of his "uncomfortable and desperate life" in Budapest in 1890.[14]

After Neufeld had started at the Medical College, his father became very sick. Before he died, the elder Neufeld asked Mór to promise him that he would complete his rabbinical studies, and Mór agreed to please his father. He gave up his dream of a medical career, and a year later, on September 20, 1891, Mór Neufeld (now Morris Newfield) sailed from Rotterdam, Holland, with money that his brother Emil had sent him from New York. He landed at Ellis Island ten days later.[15]

Morris Newfield came to the United States to attend the Reform rabbinical seminary in Cincinnati, the Hebrew Union College. Isaac Mayer Wise had founded the school in 1875 to "train" modern rabbis because he felt that upwardly mobile Jews of German heritage were losing interest in maintaining traditional Judaism in America. From the beginning he hoped to develop rabbis, not in the traditional role as legal scholars, but after the model of Christian ministers. His rabbis would be pastors to their flocks, preaching and teaching. They would also be scholars, but their scholarship was expected to embrace secular learning as well as Jewish studies, so Hebrew Union College students took a degree at the University of Cincinnati as well. Wise wanted rabbis who could operate both as representatives of modern Jewish communities in the larger society and as synagogue leaders nurturing the minds and spirits of their congregations.[16]

Although there is no evidence bearing directly on the subject, there were probably several reasons why Newfield decided to come to America and Hebrew Union College rather than remain in Hungary and attend the Jewish Theological Seminary in Budapest. On the one hand, the struggling young student was attracted by the free tuition that Wise offered him. The reformer was having trouble at that time finding students who could pay; a rabbinical career lacked the prestige in America that it would later have. Well-to-do Jewish parents were not allowing their sons to enter a profession that was poorly paid and seemingly unglamorous. As a result, Wise was forced to turn to students such as Morris Newfield to whom a free education seemed very appealing. In addition, Newfield was encouraged to come to America by the example and the support of his half brother Emil Neufeld, who had done very well for himself in the coal business in Brooklyn.[17]

Although his four years at the college were terribly difficult for him financially, Newfield's correspondence indicates that he was happy, perhaps because he understood the necessity of sacrificing in order to secure his future. In 1892 his old friend Albert Markovits in Hungary replied to Newfield's news:

> Accept, my dear friend, my congratulations for that which you have accomplished in Cincinnati within so short a period of time. Your choice, due to your uncomfortable and desperate life in Budapest, led you in America to a beautiful, noble, and happy future. I am not only happy for you as a sincere friend, but happy for me, [because] you serve as an example . . . that I do not need to be in desperation. From suffering can come a better fate.[18]

Yet this letter sharply contrasts with the emotional and financial stresses that Newfield was facing. When he first arrived at the college in 1891, he knew very little English. Undaunted, he learned the language by living with a family on a farm outside Cincinnati in the summer of 1892. Although his half brother Emil gave him occasional financial help, and Wise gave him food and lodging, he still had very little money. Nevertheless, by 1894 the young rabbinical student had impressed Wise enough in his work at the college to earn the right to teach a course in Talmud at Hebrew Union College and to act as superintendent of the John Street Temple Sunday School. Evidently Newfield's commitment to his future prevented him from minding that he had little time for anything other than his studies and his jobs. Of the twelve students in the 1895 graduating class at the University of Cincinnati, only he did not participate in any extracurricular activities.

George Solomon and Seymour Bottigheimer, his two rabbinical classmates, did join clubs at the university.[19]

Newfield qualified for the collegiate department at the Hebrew Union College because he had already had some theological training. His studies in Budapest in Hebrew, Bible, rabbinic literature, and Jewish history apparently stood him in good stead. Morris did very well in his work at the college. The grade book of 1895 indicates that he was a better student than either Solomon or Bottigheimer and that he passed the requirements a year early, in 1894. He studied theology with Wise, Jewish history and theology with Gotthard Deutsch, and Bible with Max Margolis, doing especially well with the first two.[20]

Unfortunately, no letters written by Newfield during his student years survive. We can perhaps be instructed by the biographies of some of his contemporaries at both Hebrew Union College and the University of Cincinnati. At the college there were students like David Marx, Class of 1894, Abraham J. Messing, Class of 1897, Joseph S. Kornfeld, Class of 1899, Emil W. Leipziger, Class of 1900, and Henry Englander, Class of 1901. Marx, a close friend, eventually became one of the South's leading rabbis in Atlanta at the Hebrew Benevolent Congregation. He served the Central Conference of American Rabbis as a member of the executive board, as corresponding secretary, as treasurer, and as editor of the "Yearbook." He was secretary and vice-president of the Southern Rabbinical Association and president, vice-president, and director of the alumni association of Hebrew Union College. Like Morris Newfield later on, Marx gave much of his time and effort to charitable organizations, serving as a trustee of the Community Chest of Atlanta and as a board member for the Georgia Child Welfare Society, the Atlanta Tuberculosis Society, and the Children's Home Finding Society of Atlanta. He also helped organize and direct the Crippled Children's Hospital, the Boy's Club, and the Atlanta Art Association.[21]

Joseph S. Kornfeld, after graduating from the college, did graduate work in Semitics at the University of Chicago in 1905 and went to B'nai Israel Temple in Columbus, Ohio, from 1907 to 1921. There he also served as a member of the Charter Commission of Ohio in 1913. In 1921 he was appointed by President

Warren Harding as envoy extraordinary and minister plenipotentiary to Persia, where he served for three years. From 1925 to 1934, he was rabbi of the Collingwood Avenue Temple in Toledo, Ohio. Beginning in 1934, Kornfeld lectured as a forum leader for the Federal Office of Education (in the Department of the Interior) until his death in 1943.[22]

Emil Leipziger, another friend of Newfield's, was born in Stockholm, Sweden, in 1877. After graduating from Hebrew Union College in 1899, he went to Temple Israel in Terre Haute, Indiana. There he served until 1913, when he became the assistant to Isaac Leucht at Touro Synagogue in New Orleans. A year later he became the rabbi. Leipziger's career in New Orleans was to parallel Newfield's in Birmingham and Marx's in Atlanta in the commitment to social service that it reflected. In 1916 Leipziger became president of the Louisiana State Conference of Charities and a year later vice-president of the National Conference of Social Work. From 1937 to 1941, he would succeed Newfield as president of the Central Conference of American Rabbis.[23]

Henry Englander, a fourth classmate, was, like Newfield, Hungarian born. After graduating from the college in 1901, Englander earned his M.A., and in 1909 his Ph.D., in Bible studies from Brown University, where he then began to teach. A year later he began a long career as a professor of medieval Jewish exegesis at Hebrew Union College, writing treatises on biblical and Jewish history and the first detailed biography of Isaac Leeser.[24]

Abraham J. Messing, five years Newfield's junior, was a member of a great Prussian rabbinical family. He and Newfield were never close friends, and he met an unhappy fate in America. His grandfather, Joseph Messing (1812–1880), had been a Talmudic scholar. Aaron Messing, his father, had studied under the German reformer Leopold Zunz and was the rabbi of congregations in Mecklenburg, Germany, from 1859 to 1869, in New York from 1869 to 1870, and in San Francisco from 1871 to 1891. He helped to start many synagogues in California and in the Northwest.

After graduating from Hebrew Union College in 1897, Messing, over the objections of Morris Newfield, became rabbi of Kahl

Montgomery in Alabama, a hundred miles from Newfield's Birmingham congregation. He had difficulties in Montgomery, however, as his wife was reputed to have been unfaithful. After leaving Montgomery in 1906, he became a part-time rabbi in Champaign, Illinois. He also became a lawyer and wrote a legal textbook. In 1921 Messing was convicted for swindling various clients, and he died shortly thereafter in the federal penitentiary at Leavenworth, Kansas.[25]

Morris Newfield did not like Messing very much, as he indicated in a letter that he wrote on May 12, 1897, to a friend when he was asked to recommend Messing for a position as a rabbi at Kahl Montgomery. Newfield was, he explained,

> surprised to learn of this application. . . . I know Messing very well, only too well, and would I give Mr. Mohr my perfectly honest opinion of Messing, I am sure it would not be favorable to his candidacy. . . . it is not right, perhaps, that I should presume to judge over a colleague, especially when the result of such a judgment might prove to his disadvantage. . . . Messing is an able young man, is a good and forceful speaker and good writer. As to his intellectual worth, he is above the average graduate perhaps. . . . Where my objections to him center is his moral worth. I boarded in the same house with him for two years and consequently had a good opportunity to study his character. He was "one of the boys" . . . , loves all the sports from poker and horse races down to billiards and pool, [that] every respectable man ought to shun. . . . Messing is a good boy otherwise, but the trouble is, he has no strong will. . . . As to his principles—well he is about unprincipled.[26]

The young rabbi's thoughts about Messing are harsh, but they say a great deal more about Newfield than about the younger man. Evidently Newfield was a very serious and disciplined student, shunning many of the escapades that other students more fortunate than he might have enjoyed. Second, the transplanted Hungarian had a strongly developed sense of responsibility. He admitted in the same letter that he "scolded him [Messing] frequently, and for a time succeeded in keeping him in a purer atmosphere." Third, Newfield exhibited a keenly defined moral stance. This is the letter of a strong-willed individual who did not hesitate to speak his mind to people who he believed could appreciate his sense of principle.[27]

After five years in Cincinnati, Newfield received his B.A. from the University of Cincinnati at the same time that he graduated from Hebrew Union College, as was the custom in Wise's time. There he finished with twelve other students, including Solomon and Bottigheimer. John Howard Melish, one of his classmates, became rector of the Holy Trinity Church in Brooklyn, New York, and one of the leading proponents of Social Gospel theology there with his friends John Haynes Holmes and Rabbi Stephen B. Wise. All three were acquaintances of Newfield's.[28]

Social Gospel theology, emphasizing man's responsibility to others in society, was a leading concern of the day. As the Reverend Washington Gladden told the University of Cincinnati's Class of 1895:

> Change them that are rich in this present age that they be not high-minded, nor have their hope set on the uncertainty of riches, but on God . . . , that they be good, that they be rich in good works. . . . Mere power of gathering the good things of this world, and getting satisfaction out of them is not life for the sons of God; it may be life . . . for swine.[29]

Young Morris Newfield, who would be going to Temple Emanu-El in Birmingham, Alabama, accepted these words, making them an integral part of a consistent message of social responsibility to his congregants: he would claim that the attempt of any man to separate himself from his fellows is a dehumanizing one. Newfield believed that men are beings, united by ties of sympathy and helpfulness, and through others can fulfill themselves.

By June 1895, then, Mór Neufeld, the son of a Hungarian Orthodox rabbi, had become Morris Newfield, a Reform rabbi in Birmingham, Alabama. His early environment had been crucial in determining his choice of career. Perhaps the young man in the midst of medical studies at the University of Budapest had not wanted to be a rabbi as dearly as his father might have hoped; after all, he had not pursued ordination from the Jewish Theological Seminary, deciding rather to take advantage of opportunities in the free professions that were open to Jews in the late nineteenth century. Still, after his father died, Mór Neufeld could have continued to pursue a medical education or could have found a job in the civil service, as did many of his classmates at the Royal Gymnasium. But following the deathbed wish of his father, he accepted the aid of Isaac Mayer Wise. In fact a free education was more than Budapest was offering, and Neufeld believed that opportunities for rabbis were greater in America than in Hungary. At Hebrew Union College Newfield was one of the best students and achieved a status that had possibly been beyond his reach at the Jewish Theological Seminary because of his mediocre grades.

What did a career as a rabbi mean for a young man like Morris Newfield? It signified his loyalty as a son to a fiercely devoted Talmudic scholar. But it meant more: Newfield understood that a rabbi trained by Wise could earn not only a comfortable living but also, more important, the ability to influence people both within and beyond the Jewish community.

TWO

A Leader of Birmingham Jews, 1895–1914

In June 1895 Morris Newfield boarded the train for Birmingham, Alabama, where he had just accepted a job as rabbi of Temple Emanu-El. He was moving to a city that was, like him, young, ambitious, and eager for professional success. The city and the rabbi would develop together in the years 1895–1914. Birmingham would evolve from an unpopulated frontier town in the antebellum South that was rich in the natural resources of coal and iron, becoming a flourishing metropolis, the fourth largest city in the entire South. Newfield, a poor but hopeful graduate of Hebrew Union College, would attain financial security and a position of eminence as a leader in the Birmingham Jewish community.[1]

Incorporated in 1871, Birmingham, Alabama, was less than a quarter of a century old when Newfield appeared on the scene. Jefferson County, the area in which Birmingham lay, had originally been settled in 1815 by soldiers who had fought with Andrew Jackson against the Indians in the War of 1812. Although many stories had been told about its coal, iron, and limestone deposits, the area had been largely ignored by men with money to invest in land. Antebellum Alabama society had been captivated by the vision of a cotton culture and mesmerized by the image of the gentleman planter.[2]

In the post–Civil War era, commercial and industrial interests grew increasingly dominant in the United States. Businessmen in the North, equating progress with smoking factories, copious industrial production, and rapidly increasing wealth, convinced their southern counterparts that the future of the South lay in the exploitation for industrial production of mineral resources, for instance, the coal and iron resources of Jefferson County. The war had scarcely ended when, in 1866, the Alabama legislature passed a law to provide state subsidies for railroads.[3]

Ambitious men began to devise schemes to exploit the wealth of Jefferson County by building adequate railroad lines. But competition was fierce between local investors, including John T. Milner, who sought to develop a great new industrial center to manufacture pig iron within the mineral region itself, and the planter interests in southern Alabama, who wanted a competing Montgomery-to-New York railroad to ship their cotton, and still other investors in Chattanooga, including John Stanton, who wanted to monopolize the iron ore and coal traffic from the mineral district. The result was the building of two roads, the Alabama and Chattanooga Lines, completed from Chattanooga to Birmingham, and the South and North Road, which was eventually absorbed by the L & N Railroad, running from Louisville to the Gulf Coast ports and including Birmingham.[4]

The actual impetus for the settlement of Birmingham in the Jones Valley came from a group of promoters from both groups, including James R. Powell, Milner, Henry Caldwell, Josiah Morris, and William S. Mudd, who organized the Elyton Land Company with $200,000 for the purpose of land speculation at the point where the two roads crossed. By December 1871, a hundred houses and stores had sprung up and some 800 settlers had come to share in the fortune to be made from the rising land values. In the next two years, Birmingham grew extensively, causing speculation that "in less than ten years, Birmingham would be the Atlanta of Alabama." In 1873, Birmingham became the county seat, and prospects seemed very bright for its continued growth.[5]

Unfortunately for the speculators, a cholera outbreak in June 1873 and the failure of Jay Cooke and Company, which slowed the wheels of industry throughout the country, nearly destroyed the little town. Cholera and the resulting panic caused the population to fall from 4,000 to 2,000 citizens. Because of the financial failure and the fact that Birmingham had no established industry to create sufficient jobs for the residents, Birmingham remained only a real estate boom town at a railroad crossing.[6]

Had it not been for the initial successful large-scale production of cheap coke pig iron by one Northerner, the mining engineer Truman H. Aldrich, and two Southerners, the promoter Henry Fairchild DeBardeleben and James W. Sloss, who had made a fortune in land speculation, the mercantile business, and railroads, the little town might have collapsed permanently. Aldrich, a graduate of Van Rensselaer Polytechnic Institute in Troy, New York, was the first trained engineer to work in the Alabama coalfields. In 1880 DeBardeleben, who has been called "the most picturesque and dramatic character in the coal and iron history of the South" and a "savagely energetic, restless, and impatient man," built the first iron furnace. Birmingham became the leading pig iron and steel producer.[7]

By 1890, Birmingham produced more than 800,000 tons of pig iron a year, the fourth highest annual output in the country. The leading manufacturer was the Tennessee Coal, Iron, and Railroad Company (TCI), which bought out Enoch Ensley and the Pratt Coal and Iron Company in 1886. TCI in 1898 would build Alabama's first open-hearth steel plant in nearby Ensley, Alabama, ensuring further financial stability.[8]

Beginning in the 1880s Birmingham also began to develop a major cotton textile mill, a by-product gas plant, and numerous bakeries, printing companies, breweries, cottonseed oil mills, soft drink and mineral water companies, and factories producing brooms, furniture, paints, wagons, mattresses, fertilizer, cement, clay pipe, bricks, ice, soaps, cigars, and boxes. By 1910, the city had become the acknowledged financial center of Alabama, one of the largest producers of coal and pig iron, the hub of the cast iron pipe industry, a railroad nexus, and also the headquarters of the lumber trade in Alabama—in fact the second largest market in the country for yellow pine.[9]

The push to make Birmingham a major industrial area caused

the population to increase from 3,086 in 1880 to 26,178 in 1890 to 38,415 in 1900, but it also brought a number of serious social problems in the early years. As late as the 1880s the city had the reputation of being much like a Wild West mining town with a saloon and a brothel on almost every downtown street. It was common practice to carry firearms because police protection could not be counted on. In 1885, with a population of nearly 20,000, the town had only twenty policemen. The water supply was inadequate, and because the fire department was undermanned and poorly trained, burning houses were lost. In the 1890s, citizens began clamoring for increased city services, but they were slow in coming because of low tax assessments.[10]

Ethel Armes in her article "The Spirit of the Founders" suggests that in the 1890s "the game of self-interest got considerable headway. At times, nobody stopped to think of the place as a city. It ran wild, grew in any old way." This spirit of self-interest was reflected in the plight of the coal miners. In 1894, the coal miners struck in Birmingham, complaining about the miserable working conditions. Industrial leaders, including DeBardeleben, resisted any participation by labor in determining wages or rents. Coal workers, who were led by Eugene V. Debs' American Railway Union, finally capitulated, leaving behind a legacy of unresolved strife that was further complicated by racial conflict, because most of the coal miners were black. The leasing of convicts to private industry also continued unabated.[11]

By the mid-1890s, when Morris Newfield arrived in Birmingham, citizens had begun to leave the center of town to escape from the crime and grime engendered by industry. The once-fashionable Fifth Avenue North was abandoned in favor of South Highlands, a new residential area on the higher ground at the foot of Red Mountain. Victorian gingerbread mansions and pseudo-Athenian temples later stretched along Highland Avenue, and Birmingham claimed the most imposing residential avenue in the South. Upper-income residents would eventually erect copies of Tudor or Mediterranean mansions on the crest of Red Mountain, overlooking the city.[12]

Religion was very important in Birmingham in the first few decades, even if it was overshadowed by tales of saloons and fistfights. The Elyton Land Company donated city lots to churches. From the beginning there was cooperation between pastors and congregants of different churches and even different faiths. Free Bibles could be obtained as early as 1894. Sunday blue laws prohibiting card playing, sports, or hog and cattle driving were enacted by the city. Different Protestant faiths included Presbyterians, Methodists, Episcopalians, and Baptists as well as a large number of Catholics, mostly Irish and Italian railroad construction workers and miners who had settled in Birmingham in the first decade of its existence. Church activities were important social events as well as religious duties. Sunday was the day for family reunions, including the gathering of the clan for a big dinner. Sunday night was a popular dating night. The favorite place of amusement in the county was the so-called Crystal Palace at Naber's Spring, to which crowds came for political rallies, barbecues, dramatic performances, skating parties, and band concerts.[13]

A case can be made for the idea, expressed by James Bowron, the treasurer of TCI in 1895, that late nineteenth-century Birmingham experienced much social mobility. In that year, Bowron, himself an immigrant from England, was impressed by the city's society, which he felt was "based more upon what an individual accomplished than who his parents were . . . I found in coming to Birmingham that . . . the question was 'What does he do?' "[14]

At the turn of the century, acquisition of wealth continued to be a prevailing value. The important industries were still coal and iron, and TCI, the leading company, in the first decade of the twentieth century consolidated its hold on the country's economic life. Faced with a slump in the pig iron market, the Tennessee company had built its first open-hearth steel plant in Ensley in 1899 and in 1907 received an order which "riveted the attention of the entire steel world on the new Ensley plant." E. D. Harriman wanted 150,000 tons of open-hearth rails to supply his entire railroad network. Birmingham was now competing with giants such as Pittsburgh, Cleveland, and Chicago.[15]

But Birmingham's competitive posture was not to continue. In 1907, when panic threatened the American financial network,

J. P. Morgan, Elbert H. Gary, and Henry C. Frick purchased all but a fraction of TCI's stock from an ailing New York bank firm and took over the company. U.S. Steel had seized an opportunity to acquire for $35,317,632 the tremendous ore and coal deposits of TCI, which one authority conservatively estimated to be worth a billion dollars. Nevertheless, there is some question as to how much Birmingham benefited from this move. Some historians argue that U.S. Steel's corporate decisions saved Birmingham's underfinanced steel industry and added 25 percent to the value of all property in Jefferson County. Others claim that added transportation costs made Birmingham's steel no longer competitive. But few objections were raised at the time; U.S. Steel had a monopoly and brought an increased standard of living to Birmingham through its continued investment in TCI. With its new leader, George Gordon Crawford, a Georgia Tech graduate who had been born in the South, United States Steel's TCI division was the largest employer, the greatest landowner, and the most politically and economically powerful corporation in Jefferson County, with clout that the corporation was never shy about wielding.[16]

Coincidentally, during the period 1890–1910, civic boosters of the city of Birmingham were engaged in a struggle to annex the surrounding areas. Two reasons were given for Birmingham's desire to attach East Lake, Woodlawn, and North Birmingham as well as the Highland Avenue area at the base of Red Mountain: first, the need to broaden the city's tax base; and second, the desirability of increasing the city's population. The two reasons were equally significant. On the one hand, a large population would suggest lucrative possibilities to future industrial tenants. On the other hand, annexation would mean challenging existing industrialists like TCI in Pratt City, which did not want to pay city taxes on its property.[17]

In 1908 the fight for "Greater Birmingham" took place. It was led by Jefferson County representative Jere C. King and culminated on New Year's Day, 1910, when Greater Birmingham's boundaries took effect. The new population of 132,685 made it the fourth largest city in the South, following New Orleans, Louisville, and Atlanta. The population increase was glowing testimony not only to those leaders who had developed a larger tax base for Birmingham but also to the primacy of material needs in this city of the New South: much of the city's political life would be determined by the city's desire to ensure economic stability.[18]

Morris Newfield came to Birmingham in the fall of 1895 for a number of reasons. First, he had always claimed that he had a chance to make a start in a relatively new but developing city, where Jews had abundant opportunities. Second, a job was available at Temple Emanu-El, the congregation where many German Jews worshiped. Third, he had prior experience working in the South. In 1893 Isaac Mayer Wise had sent the young rabbinical student to Jacksonville, Florida, to officiate at the Jewish high holiday services. On this trip, he met a future friend, Adolph S. Ochs, editor of the *Chattanooga Times* and soon to become publisher of the *New York Times*. Newfield evidently performed well, because the Jacksonville congregation offered him employment after his graduation in 1895. But he accepted the Birmingham pulpit in April 1895 on the recommendation of David Marx, his close friend at Hebrew Union College. Marx had served at Emanu-El for the year 1894–1895 before moving to Atlanta.[19]

There may have been a fourth reason for Newfield's arrival in Birmingham. Although there is no evidence bearing directly on the subject, we may speculate that the young rabbi's Hungarian background had prepared him for the assignment. In the multi-ethnic Austro-Hungarian empire, Jews were a distinct minority, yet they had been capable, as we have seen, of achieving significant positions in the Hungarian government and business world. In Birmingham, Jews were in a similar position, and the young rabbi may have believed that he could minister to such a flock.

The Birmingham Jewish community which Rabbi Morris Newfield entered in 1895 consisted largely of Jews of Central European or "German" background, with a smaller number of Eastern European Jews. Robert Corley, who has traced the history of Birmingham's Jews, argues:

> Like so many of the others who came, these Jews were drawn by the prospect of a booming urban economy. But unlike many other

ethnic and immigrant groups, the Jews of Emanu-El did not come primarily to work in the mines and mills. Instead, they came to be merchants, bankers, educators, lawyers, and political and civic leaders. . . . In short, it was clear from the beginning that the Jews of Emanu-El had come to Birmingham not only to find prosperity, but also to help build a city.[20]

These German Jews believed that the newly emerging industrial town needed their assets and talents, and in a short period of time, their beliefs were borne out. As a result, they gained a respected position in this community. Not enough information is available about the Eastern European Jews for us to reach the same conclusion, but it is known that a small number came after 1882 and that they were strong enough to develop an Orthodox congregation, K'nesseth Israel, in Birmingham in 1889.

From accounts written later by Morris Newfield about the early settlers, it is also known that the first three Jewish families in Birmingham were headed by Henry Simon, Samuel Marx, and Isaac R. Hochstadter, all of whom were merchants. Simon, who had come from Selma, Alabama, opened a general merchandise establishment and built a splendid business. Marx, born in Bavaria in 1824, had emigrated to Montgomery, Alabama, where he lived until 1872. A year later, he relocated in Birmingham, and he, too, established a successful mercantile business. Hochstadter, according to Newfield, was born in Fayette, Mississippi, in 1852, came to Birmingham in 1873, and was "considered one of Birmingham's most energetic and respected citizens and participated in the days when the prospects of Birmingham were brilliant as well as when its best interests seemed doomed to failure." Hochstadter dealt in dry goods until 1880, when he opened a wholesale and retail liquor business with S. Wise. He also became a director of the Alabama National Bank.[21]

Other German Jews prospered too. Marcus and Ben Weil came to Birmingham in the 1880s and became owners of a clothing house. E. Solomon and E. H. Levi arrived in 1883 from Cincinnati and jointly operated a wholesale and retail dealership in wines, liquors, and cigars. Joseph Beitman operated a cigar jobbing house after he came to Birmingham in 1886. Ben Jacobs and his brother Bert, who would become two of Newfield's closest friends, ran a successful furniture company. Jacob Fies developed the Livery and Feed Stable Company, while Emil Lesser operated a German-language newspaper after he came to Birmingham in 1883. Morris Adler, a resident of Birmingham since 1886, became one of the most prosperous coal business executives with the Tutwiler Coal, Coke, and Iron Company.[22]

German Jews also competed among each other and with Eastern European Jews for the retail trade. Adolph B. Loveman and Moses V. Joseph joined forces with Emile Loeb to create the department store of Loveman, Joseph, and Loeb in 1889. Loveman, a native of Hungary, had made his start after the Civil War as a peddler in Tennessee and Alabama. After initial failures in Shelby, Tennessee, and Greensboro, Alabama, he came to Birmingham in 1886. Joseph, a native of Alabama, later became president of the Chamber of Commerce. The firms of the Caheen Brothers, J. Blach and Sons, and the Parisian Company were also vying for the trade along with the Louis Pizitz Dry Goods Company. Pizitz, a native of Poland, received rabbinical training there but came to America in 1889 and worked as a peddler in Georgia. In 1898, he moved to Birmingham and a year later opened his store, which still stands today.[23]

Probably the most influential of all Jewish businessmen at this time were the Steiner brothers, Siegfried and Burghardt. Born in Bohemia in the 1850s, they came to Alabama, where they became cotton factors. In 1888, the two men started the Steiner Brothers Bank in Birmingham and developed a reputation for attracting foreign capital to Alabama in the next decade. The Steiner brothers also helped the city survive the depression of 1893 by persuading the holders of city bonds to defer payments on the interest of the city's indebtedness until the Alabama legislature had agreed to increase Birmingham's tax rates.[24]

The period after Birmingham's founding, from 1871 to 1910, when the city annexed its predominantly Protestant suburbs, was both politically and economically the time of greatest activity for Emanu-El's Jews. Many of the Jewish merchants found themselves with a strong competitive advantage because the Old South had not fostered a strong merchant class. Politically, Jews were stronger in this period, since elections to the Board of Aldermen were designed to permit representation by wards throughout the city. Until 1896, all voters in the city cast ballots for nominees from all wards; after 1896, only voters in each ward voted for their representatives. In either case, Jews were well represented on the Board of Aldermen because their names were well known (they were merchants in the at-large districts) and later because the Jewish population was concentrated in the Second Ward. This political clout also meant that prominent Jews were selected for positions on city boards and commissions, such as the Board of Education and the Police Commission. Isaac Hochstadter served as an alderman from the First Ward in 1875–1878 and 1884–1888 for a total of four terms, as a member of the Board of Education, and also as a captain in the Fire Department. Simon Klotz won election four times to the Board of Aldermen from 1894 to 1896 and from 1905 to 1911. He was also appointed French consul for the Alabama district in the same year. Emil Lesser served as police commissioner from 1897 to 1899, as did Jacob Burger. Burghardt Steiner, Samuel Ullman, and Ben M. Jacobs were members of the Board of Education in Birmingham.[25]

Similarly, German Jews became members and officials of many of Birmingham's civic, commercial, and fraternal organizations. Samuel Marx, Moses V. Joseph, Jacob Burger, Simon Klotz, A. B. Loveman, and Ben M. Jacobs as well as Morris Newfield were high-ranking Masons. Joseph was president of the Commerce Club, the forerunner of the Chamber of Commerce, and Joseph Beitman, Burghardt Steiner, and Simon Klotz were members. Joseph is credited with having attracted Avondale Mills to Birmingham in March 1897, creating the city's first major industrial link to Alabama's treasured cotton economy. Under his leadership, furthermore, the Commerce Club helped to raise funds to build the city's first commercially successful steel plant at the Birmingham Rolling Mills. In 1899, Joseph helped organize the Board of Trade, an association of downtown merchants, some of whom were elected to the Board of Aldermen between 1900 and 1910. The Board of Trade campaigned vigorously for increased fire and police protection in the downtown area and for such progressive reforms as stricter building codes, underpasses for downtown rail crossings, municipal ownership of the waterworks, and the merger of the city and county health services.[26]

Many of the German Jews were members of Temple Emanu-El when Newfield came in 1895. Temple Emanu-El had a rather colorful history. It had begun in the informal worship services conducted by German Jews at the residence of Henry Simon on the north side of Birmingham in 1881. The congregation officially became a Reform one in 1891, hired three rabbis in turn, and nearly disbanded, owing to the controversy surrounding one of them. Often the temple shared its buildings with Christian churches in the neighborhood.[27]

Much of Temple Emanu-El's early history was compiled by Morris Newfield. In an article that he wrote on Birmingham Jewry in 1911, he traced the formal organization of the temple to June 26, 1882, when sixteen Jews, under the leadership of Isaac R. Hochstadter, met at the Masonic Hall in downtown Birmingham. The first service was conducted in September 1882 in the Cumberland Presbyterian Church on the north side, by Joseph Stolz, then a junior student at Hebrew Union College. Stolz was so impressive that he was reengaged for the holiday services in 1883. Significantly, Frank P. O'Brien, an Irishman, aided in the development of the services by bringing together the choir. It consisted of one Methodist, one Roman Catholic, one Baptist, two Episcopalians, and only one Jew. This interfaith cooperation was to become a hallmark of Temple Emanu-El in its activities in Birmingham.[28]

When a few hundred Jews came to Birmingham in the years 1883–1889, the congregation, being the only one in town, acquired land from the Elyton Land Company, free of charge, for the creation of a temple. The land company had donated land to Methodist, Episcopal, Presbyterian, and Baptist churches, but the new location of the Jewish temple was on North Seventeenth Street, a long way from the then-existing elite downtown district. This fact should not be overlooked. We can speculate that Emanu-El's Jews were considered an important but still marginal group in Birmingham: their land as well as their collective social standing in 1886 placed them on the "outside limits" of the community.

On July 13, 1886, the cornerstone for the new temple was laid in impressive ceremonies conducted by Isaac Mayer Wise. At this time, there were eighty-five families, most of them of German background, but there were some Eastern Europeans too. As a result, the congregation employed as its first rabbi Rev. Alexander Rosenspitz, who served only four months, from September to December 1886. Unfortunately for the congregation, the progress on the building was slow because many of the newly arrived members lacked the money to complete the work. Not until January 1889 was the temple completed.[29]

The lack of money in the 150-member congregation was not the only problem. The second rabbi, Rev. Maurice Eisenberg, found himself in trouble. In the spring of 1890, after Eisenberg had been at Emanu-El for nearly three years, he was accused of making improper advances toward a female member of his congregation whom he had offered to instruct without informing anyone else. Thirty to forty members led by Joseph Beitman, convinced of Eisenberg's guilt, left Emanu-El and formed a separate temple, B'nai Israel. The difficulties provoked concern in Samuel Ullman, the temple president. He wrote his friend Max Samfield, editor of *The Memphis Jewish Spectator,* "He ought not to have consented to give instruction . . . under the promise of secrecy." Ullman, one of the members of a four-man board established to investigate the charges, was disturbed by the rabbi's course of action. Although the president helped acquit Eisenberg of making any improper advances, he was clearly incensed by the rabbi's wish to make extra money for teaching: "If a rabbi desires to make any money he must give up the ministry; this exalted and noble calling is not intended for men of speculative tendencies." Only when Eisenberg resigned in September 1890 did members of the Temple B'nai Israel return to the fold of Temple Emanu-El.[30]

The four years preceding Newfield's arrival were also difficult because the congregation lost members in the depression of 1893 and could not attract a trained rabbi. Numerous congregants, including Hochstadter, left town. Aaron Hahn of Cleveland was offered the job in late 1890 but did not accept it.[31]

Emanu-El was able to survive because of the leadership of two men, Burghardt Steiner and Samuel Ullman. With the onset of the depression, Steiner was elected president of the board, and as a result of his efforts, the finances of the congregation improved considerably. Ullman, president of the board since 1886, was asked by his fellow Jews to become the lay preacher after Hahn refused, and he served Emanu-El creditably. In February 1894, after serving for three and a half years, Ullman resigned to enter the insurance business when the finance committee, headed by Steiner and Jacob Fies, refused to pay him $75 for services that he had conducted the month before. Two months later, Emanu-El obtained the services of David Marx, by then a trained rabbi. He was paid $1,800 a year. According to Newfield's account, Marx was eloquent and much beloved by his congregation during the year that he served, but he left to accept a call to a larger congregation in Atlanta. The minute books of Temple Emanu-El confirm Newfield's statements but also mention Marx's difficulties with the Board of Directors because the rabbi was solemnizing marriages without permission of President Burghardt Steiner.[32]

David Marx, hoping to help Emanu-El find a new rabbi and wanting his close friend Newfield to have the job, recommended Emanu-El and Birmingham to Newfield and Newfield to the congregation. On March 13, 1895, Steiner then wrote a short note to Isaac Mayer Wise, commenting, "We would like to have someone to officiate for us on Pesach and Shavouth. . . . I understand you have a young Hungarian, who will graduate this year, and if he is alright and speaks English correctly and fluently, he may be the one that would suit us." Two months later, after he had been interviewed by Steiner in Birmingham, Morris Newfield was elected rabbi of Emanu-El for a two-year term at a salary of $1,800 a year.[33]

The young rabbi tried very hard to please his congregation and to win the respect of the formerly quarrelsome Board of Directors of Emanu-El. After a short period of time, he succeeded. He won the admiration of Samuel Ullman, the former president and lay preacher of Emanu-El, and worked very hard with Steiner to put the temple on a secure financial footing. In addition he was aware that the lay leaders of the congregation wanted a spiritual leader who would stay and provide their religious community with some continuity.

When Newfield came to Birmingham, he moved into the home of Samuel Ullman because it was the custom for distinguished Jewish visitors to do so. Newfield also lived with Ullman because he was single, and single men did not live alone at this time. Ullman was recognized not only as an important Jewish leader but also as one of the leading lights of the Birmingham community. He had been born in 1840 in Hechingen, Germany, where his ancestors had lived for more than a hundred years. A year later, his parents moved to Alsace, then a French province, because his father wanted the equal rights that were denied to Jews in Germany. After 1848, his father feared a return of monarchical government under Louis Napoleon. The elder Ullman therefore sailed for New Orleans in November 1851. His family settled in Port Gibson, Mississippi, and ran a butcher shop. Samuel quit attending the public schools at the age of thirteen because he had to help his father in business.[34]

In 1861 Ullman volunteered for the Sixteenth Mississippi Regiment and served in the brigade commanded by Thomas "Stonewall" Jackson. In 1862, while he was in the Army of Northern Virginia under General Robert E. Lee, Ullman was wounded at Antietam. The injury cost him his hearing in one ear, and he carried a bullet for the rest of his life.

Ullman moved to Natchez in July 1865 and married Emma Mayer, the daughter of a merchant. There, at the age of twenty-five, he helped organize a Reform congregation and became the lay preacher and superintendent of the Sunday school. Ullman also served as an alderman for four years and as a member of the school board in Natchez for seventeen years. During his stay in Natchez, Ullman joined B'nai Brith and was elected grand president of District Grand Lodge Number 7 in 1878.

Largely self-educated, Ullman was a hard-working man and a born leader, as evidenced by his youthful activities in Natchez and his work in Birmingham immediately after he moved there in 1883. After opening a hardware business, Ullman was elected president of Emanu-El in 1886 and also served as the lay rabbi. He claimed that he did not want the job and was surprised that it was offered because his business was failing. He took it anyway because he was loyal to his congregation. From 1895 to 1897 he was also a member of the Birmingham Board of Aldermen.

Samuel Ullman, the father-in-law of Morris Newfield, championed black education in Birmingham and was an early leader of the community.

A self-styled democrat, Ullman's most conspicuous characteristic was his dogged persistence in the cause of quality education for the children of Birmingham. Only a short time after coming to Birmingham he was elected to the school board, where he worked diligently for nineteen years with his friend John Herbert Phillips, the superintendent of schools, to modernize the system. According to the minutes of the Birmingham Board of Education, Ullman drafted the standards for teacher certification in 1884, tried to obtain education for children of "nonresidents" of Birmingham in 1886, pushed for the hiring of women teachers in 1887, proposed the creation of a public library in 1889, suggested night school instruction for the children of working parents in 1891, developed a corps of substitute teachers in 1892, and helped Phillips to secure free education in Birmingham in the same year.[35]

But it was in the service of the Board of Education that Ullman suffered perhaps his greatest defeat. Refusing to accept prevailing southern notions that black students were not entitled to the same quality of education as white children, Ullman continued to battle other members of the Board of Education and the Board of Aldermen to appropriate more money for black schools and teachers. As early as 1886 he was cajoling the school board into negotiations with the Elyton Land Company for a black school in the East End of Birmingham. In 1894, he complained bitterly that the 2,095 black children in the public schools had only twenty-eight teachers, fewer than half as many teachers as the 2,793 white children had. After the *Plessy* vs. *Ferguson* decision, which legally sanctioned segregation in the South, Ullman argued that Birmingham's schools were anything but "separate and equal" and continued to champion the cause of black children.[36]

Ullman did have one great success. He urged that a curriculum more suited to industrial society be developed in white schools and in black ones as well. "Manual training," Ullman wrote in 1899, "ought to be a feature of those schools as well as our white schools. We should do this because it pays, both morally and pecuniarily. Schools can be maintained cheaper than penal institutions. An educated heart and hand is better adapted to overcome more than simple so-called book learning." As a consequence, Ullman urged the establishment of a black high school, which opened under the direction of A. H. Parker in the fall of 1900 with eighteen students in a small room at the Cameron School. By 1910 there would be nearly 200 students in the black Industrial High School.[37]

Between May 7 and September 26, 1900, however, Ullman fought to establish an eighth and ninth grade in the black schools and to add two more black teachers. In November he organized a mass meeting at the Commerical Club in Birmingham for his cause and enlisted the help of Mayor Melville Drennen. This move was to be his downfall. As a result of his action, some members of the Board of Aldermen so feared his persistence that they refused to reelect him to the Board of Education in December. Various members of the Board of Education, including Burghardt Steiner, supported the aldermen's decision.[38]

Ullman did have supporters in Drennen and John Herbert Phillips. They succeeded in having a new school, which opened in early 1901, named the Samuel Ullman Elementary School. Ironically, it was a school for white children. Ullman was finally reelected to the Board of Education in 1902 for one year, but he never regained the stature on the board that he had previously enjoyed.

In later years, before his death in 1920, Ullman began to write poetry, and a collection of his work, *From a Summit of Years—Four Score,* was published. One of the essays on youth, from which General Douglas MacArthur frequently quoted, outlined the Birmingham activist's view of the maturation process: "Youth means the temperamental predominance of courage over the timidity of the appetite, for adventure over the love of ease. This often exists in a man of sixty more than a boy of twenty. Nobody grows old merely by a number of years. We grow old by deserting our ideals."[39]

Morris Newfield and Samuel Ullman grew very fond of each other soon after Newfield's arrival in Birmingham. Perhaps the young rabbi saw many of his father's qualities in Ullman because Ullman respected learning enough to let his business fail while he became the lay rabbi of Emanu-El. His friendship with one of the leaders of Emanu-El could not but help the young rabbi gain quick acceptance with his congregation.

John Herbert Phillips, a close friend of Morris Newfield, was superintendent of schools in Birmingham from 1883 to 1921. (Birmingham Public Library / Department of Archives)

The Samuel Ullman School in 1935. (Birmingham Public Library / Department of Archives)

For his part, Ullman probably liked Newfield because the younger man was just as intensely committed as he was to Judaism and its teachings of justice. Nevertheless, the two men were a contrast in personalities: Ullman, an extrovert, was usually willing to speak out about issues that concerned him, while Newfield was more introverted and diplomatic. From the beginning of his career in Birmingham, the younger rabbi would combine a commitment to principle with a more pragmatic side that helped him accomplish things. While Ullman enjoyed doing battle with his enemies, Newfield would be recognized more as a negotiator and a tactician.

The friendship between the two men was enhanced when Newfield began courting Ullman's daughter, Leah. Born in 1874, in Natchez, Leah Ullman had attended the Birmingham high school that her father had helped build and was considered an accomplished pianist. As a young lady she was also very involved in the Council of Jewish Women and the Temple Emanu-El Sisterhood. When Samuel Ullman's wife died suddenly in 1896, Leah became mistress of the household in which Newfield still lived.

The letters from their courtship have survived and speak of the intensity of both people. From them we can see that Leah enjoyed the idea of becoming a rabbi's wife and Morris needed a person to whom he could confide his ambitions and anxieties. In one letter written in 1898, the rabbi spoke of what Leah now meant to him: "It seems there is in me a secret incapacity for expressing my deepest emotions and reproducing in cold type my true feelings. . . . I am timid, and distrustful of the future. I wish I could be otherwise and could satisfy you, my sweet darling, but also I have not attained much happiness. You must bear with me, and you will if you truly understand me." Morris clearly loved her very much and was testing her reactions to the anxieties that he felt. Family tradition holds that Newfield took a long time to ask her to marry him but that Leah was patient. The wedding took place in January 1901.[40]

As rabbi of Emanu-El, Morris Newfield displayed every willingness to please the members of his congregation. He worked diligently to enlarge the congregation, to build an effective Sunday school for Jewish children, and to develop the feeling among his congregation that, unlike the other rabbis, he was there to stay. He won plaudits from President Steiner of Emanu-El because the Sunday school was reported in "flourishing condition, the best school we've ever had." Three months later, thanks to his efficient work as leader of the Sunday school and as the preacher, the board was so successful in attracting new members that they could enlarge the Temple by two wings.[41]

Yet the correspondence between Newfield and the Board of Directors suggests that he was walking a thin line between his need to command the congregation and the board's need to control him. This particular kind of tension was symptomatic of the battles that were taking place over ministerial integrity in Reform congregations throughout the country. For example, Kauffmann Kohler and Emil Hirsch at various times conducted fierce struggles with their boards at Temple Sinai in Chicago, and Stephen Wise would develop the Free Synagogue, his own congregation in New York City, to maintain his ministerial freedom.

Newfield faced a very active board, led by Burghardt Steiner, that had forced the resignation of one rabbi in 1890 and had made life somewhat difficult for David Marx in 1894. The young rabbi at first placated his board by helping Steiner attract new members and by accepting rules that they laid down. One letter from Steiner, on January 13, 1897, read in part, "The Board unanimously agreed to the following rules and regulations. . . . Please announce this to the Congregation and oblige." In his annual report to the congregation eight months later, Newfield was soothing. "I am indebted to the Board for all the little successes my labors have been crowned with," he wrote.[42]

But the rabbi seems to have won the respect of his board—and consequently more freedom of action—after an incident that took place in early April 1899. He learned that a committee under Steiner's direction had issued a circular criticizing K'nesseth Israel, the poor, largely Eastern European Orthodox congregation in Birmingham, for its purported support of a particular candidate for political office. Newfield was furious with Steiner and other individuals who, he asserted, had wrongfully accused their coreligionists. As a result, he strongly suggested that Steiner issue an apology to the Orthodox congregation, and the banker complied. The new respect shown Newfield is apparent in the wording of Steiner's direction to his board on April 6, 1899:

> WHEREAS, Rabbi Newfield has denounced the action of the distribution of a certain circular, and WHEREAS, in said document, all un-intentional wrong was done to the Orthodox Congregation in assuming that this said circular emanated from the members of said congregation, and WHEREAS, Rabbi Newfield has stated that proper explanations or amends will be made to said Orthodox Congregation.
> Therefore be it resolved that the Board of Trustees of Congregation Emanu-El endorses the action . . . of Rabbi Newfield in the presses, and that this Board earnestly requests that no further mention be made of this matter.[43]

Newfield also won the respect of his congregation, since he convinced its members that he was committed to Emanu-El. In the few years before the turn of the century, the rabbi must have struggled considerably. He was eager to improve his circumstances, yet he was loyal to his flock at Emanu-El. As early as 1896, Morris's brother, Emil Neufeld, was pleading with him to try for a Reform pulpit in Brooklyn, a post that must have tempted Newfield. He could easily have refused to consider the offers of communities such as Montgomery in 1897 and Mobile in 1899 in that they were smaller congregations, but the invitations from Omaha and Dallas forced him to decide exactly what he wanted for himself; graduates of Hebrew Union College were at a premium to fill pulpits.[44]

There is evidence in his correspondence that Newfield was unsure about his future. In 1899, Samuel Katz of B'nai Israel in Omaha wanted him to become a candidate for that pulpit. Newfield wrote back on January 12 that he viewed the tentative offer as a compliment and liked the idea of more money, but "I have made a great many dear friends and have become largely established with both congregation and communal life [of Birmingham]." He also complained, "I should not need to rely on trial sermons to be elected rabbi." He seems to have been torn between his desire for a larger congregation with more prestige and money, and his satisfaction with and loyalty to Birmingham. But more significant, he felt that he had proven his mettle as a professional in the rabbinate and wanted his record in Birmingham to speak for itself.[45]

Newfield's struggle became even more pronounced in 1900 when Alexander Sanger of Dallas asked him to apply for the job at Dallas's Temple Emanu-El. The two men conducted a long and involved correspondence for a year and a half, with Newfield acting as he had while dickering with Omaha. He did not wish to be on trial again and would consider a call only if a definite offer was made. Furthermore, he was very concerned about hurting the people of Emanu-El in Birmingham. On April 3, 1900, he wrote to Sanger, "trial sermons are but seldom a reliable test of a rabbi's qualifications and . . . it places him in a most undesirable attitude toward his congregation."[46]

The ambitious rabbi seems to have wanted the position in Dallas, but he would accept it only if it was proffered without further risk on his part and if it was handled so that his congregation would not find itself without a rabbi. He finally turned down the Dallas job in June 1901. Thereafter, believing that he was now firmly entrenched as a leader of the Birmingham Jewish community, Newfield refused to entertain the thought of another position and assured the congregation that he would stay for good.[47]

As a result of his decision not to leave, Newfield found the first decade of the new century in Birmingham was very rewarding. He spent time with his wife and family and also secured his job as rabbi by making friends with the wealthier Jews of his temple and by playing a larger role in the affairs of the Central Conference of American Rabbis. Newfield began to participate in other affairs in the Jewish community by helping to develop the Industrial Removal Office—an immigrant organization—in Birmingham in 1905 and by helping the Orthodox Jews reorganize the Young Men's Hebrew Association (YMHA) in 1909.

On May 8, 1900, Morris Newfield was reelected to a third two-year term as rabbi of Temple Emanu-El, at the salary of $2,500 a year. This was considered a good salary for the times. The temple could afford to pay him well; many of his congregants—and Birmingham as a whole—had recovered from the depression of a decade before. As a result, many of them, including Simon Klotz, Louis Gelders, and the Newfields themselves, began moving away from the city's north side and the more crowded areas where the Eastern European Jews were now living to the south side and the beautiful trees and palaces on Highland Avenue. His congregants also erected a new building for their prestigious social organization, the Phoenix Club. Founded in 1883 for the moral, social, literary, and educational advancement of Jews in Birmingham, the club, which by 1909 consisted of ninety-seven men and their families, all associated with Temple Emanu-El, built a new clubhouse at a cost of $50,000.[48]

At this time Newfield's congregants were amassing wealth from their businesses, and their life-styles reflected their prosperity. The homes that were being built on the south side were often decorated by the Meyer brothers, and the stylish women bought poultry from H. Siegel, while on their walnut sideboards stood decanters filled with wines bought from Lowenthal and from Adler, Oppenheimer, Hirscher, and Simon.

The cultural tastes of Newfield's congregants reflected their particular interests and status. Many of them were faithful readers of the Jewish weeklies the *Memphis Jewish Spectator* and the *New Orleans Jewish Ledger,* which they ordered from out of town because they were eager to read on the society pages about friends in other cities or about distant relatives. Many of Newfield's congregants also enjoyed the Birmingham opera and the speakers that appeared on the Chautauqua circuit. Public speakers of national reputation, such as Theodore Roosevelt and Jenkin Lloyd Jones, addressed large audiences of Christians and Jews.[49]

The affairs of the Temple likewise reflected the prosperity of the Jews of Temple Emanu-El. In 1902, the congregation, led by Morris Newfield, could afford to organize a free kindergarten, one of three established in Birmingham because no state funds had been allotted for children between the ages of five and seven. Also supported by the Council of Jewish Women and B'nai Brith, the temple kindergarten was considered the largest and best conducted of the three. Chester G. Bandman served as assistant superintendent of the school, which had a student body of 150, a library of 500 volumes, and a corps of seven teachers. About a third of the children in the kindergarten were Christian.

One year earlier, Steiner had led a movement to liquidate the debt of the Temple by asking for voluntary contributions from the 200 members, and in 1904 the debt was paid. At the same time, the congregation displayed its approval of Newfield by re-electing him for the fifth time, for a five-year period at $3,000 a year. The next year, the sum of more than $10,000 was spent to improve the cemetery and to dedicate a chapel in the cemetery, the amount again being raised by voluntary subscription.[50]

From the letters Newfield wrote his wife when he was conducting services in other parts of Alabama, we can see that he was constantly preoccupied with his need to be a successful rabbi. On the Jewish holiday of Rosh Hashana Eve, in October 1902, he proudly told Leah, "Everything passed off very nicely. . . . crowds were very large, packed last night, and crowded this morning also. My sermons were, if I may believe the expression heard, well-received and appreciated." Two years later, on Yom Kippur Eve, he admitted, "I need not tell you that I am very busy. . . . am anxious to be thoroughly the master of my talk tonight." After the service, he crowed, "Crowds of friends were here last night, and all spoke in terms modesty refrains me from repeating."[51]

The service as practiced at Newfield's temple probably was not terribly different from that at northern Reform temples. The rabbi employed the *Union Prayer Book,* the standard text of Reform rabbis until 1980. Newfield led services on Friday nights and Saturday mornings. According to his son, Mayer, who attended services at his father's temple for twenty years, 90 percent of the service was conducted in English and the rest in Hebrew. Of the 400 regular members of the temple, approximately 100–125 people attended regularly on Friday nights, while there was always 100 percent attendance at high holiday services.

There were, however, a number of differences in the Reform Jewish ritual as practiced at Temple Emanu-El in Birmingham. First, as previously stated, the choir had the reputation of being the best in town, with the leading singers, Jew and non-Jew alike, led by Edna Goeckel Gussen. Mrs. Gussen was the leading organist and choir director in Birmingham and later the founder of the Birmingham Conservatory of Music, the forerunner of the Birmingham Symphony Orchestra. Second, Rabbi Newfield occa-

sionally employed guest speakers, including Protestant ministers, when he was conducting services. These ministers from neighboring churches spoke about the leading social issues of the day. Such speeches were probably more frequent than in pulpits of the North. Third, Newfield spent much time outside the pulpit because he had to travel throughout Alabama conducting services: Alabama had only three ordained rabbis—in Birmingham, in Mobile, and in Montgomery—and ceremonies in smaller towns such as Bessemer and Anniston needed officiating.[52]

In 1908, Newfield's congregation decided to build a new temple on Birmingham's south side, on Highland Avenue. This decision was a tribute not only to Newfield's popularity but also to the improved social status of Emanu-El's Jews. By 1908 Emanu-

View of Birmingham
and vicinity circa 1890.
(Birmingham Public Library / Department of Archives)

El was the largest congregation in Alabama, with 230 members, and these Jews had developed considerable economic and political influence in Birmingham. Newfield's congregants wanted a facility adequate in size and commensurate with their position. On June 14, 1908, the Temple purchased a lot on Highland Avenue from the Phoenix Club for $17,000. Unlike the first temple on the north side on Seventeenth Street, this one would be ensconced in the midst of the newly expanding Birmingham community. The new structure would be at Highland Avenue and Twenty-first Street, in the center of Five Points, the most fashionable area in Birmingham.

By 1911, the German Jews had sold the old site on the north side and had raised enough money to propose the erection of "a very handsome new Temple" at a cost of nearly $200,000, with a

Temple Emanu-El.
(Birmingham Public Library / Department of Archives)

seating capacity of 1,200 and "all the equipment that goes with a modern church plant." Under the leadership of Newfield and the officers of the congregation, Moses V. Joseph, Morris Adler, and Ben M. Jacobs, the cornerstone of the new temple was laid on June 25, 1912.[53]

The new temple opened on October 31, 1913. Less than five months later, on March 6, 1914, it was dedicated to the "service of God and Humanity." Participating in the three-day program that weekend were some of Newfield's close rabbinical friends and fellow graduates of Hebrew Union College. They included Leo M. Franklin of Detroit, David Marx of Atlanta, B. C. Ehrenreich of Montgomery, A. G. Moses of Mobile, and David Philipson of Cincinnati. The rabbi, who was now firmly established as a leader of Birmingham Jewry, was praised by Thomas D. Parke, one of the leading physicians of Birmingham, a Christian, and a friend of

Newfield's. "I think it quite a tribute to Newfield," he said, "that he has been enabled to bring about the erection of such a structure."[54]

That the dedication of the new temple came in recognition of Newfield's personal success was confirmed by colleagues and former teachers from other parts of the country. Kaufmann Kohler, president of Hebrew Union College, and Gotthard Deutsch, his former teacher there, sent their congratulations from Cincinnati. Joseph Stolz wrote from Chicago, "Having stood at the cradle of Temple Emanu-El thirty years ago, I rejoice with you and your congregation in the splendid success of your undertaking and congratulate you upon the great achievement." George Solomon, a close friend and classmate, wrote from Savannah, "May your handsome synagogue be a living monument to your splendid activities and genuine merit," while other prominent rabbis such as Stephen S. Wise, Max Heller, Moses J. Gries, and Emil W. Leipziger also sent their felicitations.[55]

Newfield's most treasured tribute, however, may have come from Burghardt Steiner, who had moved to New York City and Wall Street in 1905. On March 6, 1914, the man who had given the young Hungarian his first chance, wrote: "As your erstwhile President . . . have proudly followed developments of your congregation. . . . Be assured I shall continue to follow your career with affectionate interest and shall always covet the privilege of having been affiliated with your Congregation. I am proud of you."[56]

Now firmly entrenched as a leader of the wealthier Jews of Birmingham, Newfield began to branch out to acquire a role as a leader of the entire community. Although little is known about his feelings toward Orthodox Jews living on the north side of Birmingham, there is reason to believe that he treated them fairly. As has been indicated, in 1889, when Emanu-El was seven years old, a few Eastern European immigrants left the temple to found K'nesseth Israel, a new and more orthodox place of worship. By 1899 K'nesseth Israel had sixty members and an annual income of $1,500 a year, as compared with Emanu-El's 150 members and income of $4,000 a year.

In the first decade of the twentieth century, while the fortunes of the German Jews continued to improve and they moved to the south side and built a new temple, the Eastern European Jews remained on the north side and joined K'nesseth Israel in increasing numbers. In 1911, the congregation included 175 families and boasted an excellent Hebrew and Sunday school. Also, by 1917, of the 3,500 Jews in Birmingham, an overwhelming majority were Eastern European immigrants and their descendants.[57]

Yet by 1910 the German Jews on the south side and the Eastern European Jews to the north had very little to do with each other. For one thing, there was a great disparity in their standards of living. While many of the German Jews were established financially, the Eastern European Jews were just starting out in small shops or as peddlers. Second, while many Eastern European Jews remained attached to a religion that enveloped their lives, German Jews were far more interested in developing contacts with Christians in Birmingham.

Although antagonism existed between the two groups of Jews, Newfield's activities represented a conciliatory force because he tried diplomatically to bridge the cultural gap in a number of ways. In 1905, he became chairman of the executive committee of the Industrial Removal Office in Birmingham, an organization developed by German Jews to help settle their Eastern European coreligionists in less densely populated areas such as Birmingham where they would not bring disfavor on German Jews in New York. Although there is little information about the organization's work in Birmingham, Newfield's presence here gives the impression that he tried to aid his Eastern European coreligionists.[58]

Not only did Rabbi Newfield defend K'nesseth Israel, the Orthodox congregation, in the "circular incident" in 1898, he also spoke favorably of his coreligionists on other occasions. On Yom Kippur Eve in 1911, he chastized his congregants who sneered at Jewish immigrants: "The Jew is God's appointed preacher of spiritual democracy. What can be more absurd, or more self-contradicting, for instance, than a Jewish snob? . . . What right does the native-born American have to look down upon the immigrant?" At the same time, Newfield faced the prospect of having an Eastern European Jew as a neighbor. In a letter to his wife, he responded in an open-minded way: "Had an inquiry for your corner-lot and named $5000 as the price. Am not very sanguine as to sale of it. But if the prospective purchaser comes across with the money or equivalent, he can have it even if his native place is Suwalkis, Russia, and he boasts of being a 'mountain flower' or a 'flowery mountain.' "[59]

The rabbi and some of his congregants also helped the Orthodox Jews reorganize the Young Men's Hebrew Association in 1907 to provide an outlet for the physical, social, and educational needs of the less fortunate Jews in Birmingham. The Birmingham YMHA had been originally founded in 1887 by German Jews, including Moses V. Joseph and Samuel Ullman, but it had disbanded in the early 1890s probably because of the depression of 1893.

In 1906, the YMHA was reorganized by fourteen men, of mostly Eastern European origin, because they did not have a Phoenix Club. Their beginning was a troubled one because they had very little money, and by May 1909 the Orthodox Jews asked for help from their wealthy coreligionists. Early records of the YMHA note, "A general discussion was held regarding ways and means for the association to make further progress, and there seemed nothing left to do but to get the so-called 'German' Jews interested in our work." By October 27, 1909, Newfield, his father-in-law Samuel Ullman, Simon Klotz, Leo Steiner, and other individuals were members of the board of the YMHA. Newfield also asked his protégé, Chester G. Bandman, the assistant superintendent of the Emanu-El Sunday school, to take charge of the night school at a salary of $25 a month. Ullman became president of the Night School Committee and urged the entire community to support the YMHA. By 1910, Newfield was asking members of Temple Emanu-El not only to support the YMHA but also to join Eastern European Jews in a common organization as well. The common organization did not come into being.[60]

Newfield's interest in the Eastern European Jews seemed to increase after he had moved to the south side of Birmingham. Although the rabbi did not actively involve himself in political or legal efforts to prevent immigration restriction, he did inform his own congregants and other community groups in Birmingham, such as the Women's Club, of the need for work in this area. The rabbi provided impressive figures to prove that immigrants were capable of becoming useful citizens. Their literacy rates, he argued, were higher than those of native Americans. Immigrants took jobs that native Americans often did not want. Immigrants did not degrade the quality of American citizenship but rather promoted political reforms in the large cities where they lived. By his shrewd analysis the rabbi tried to allay the fears of both his congregants and his Protestant audiences while suggesting that immigrant Jews were citizens as capable as non-Jews.[61]

The strained relationships between the two groups of Jews that existed between 1889 and 1914 did not stop Newfield from serving in his accustomed role as a mediator between opposing forces. Perhaps the rabbi was more tolerant of his coreligionists than some of his congregants because his father had been a poor Talmudic scholar. The Reform rabbi's family history may have helped him to understand the problems of his coreligionists in Birmingham. There may have been a second reason as well. Newfield, as one of the leading representatives of the Jewish community in Birmingham in 1910, believed that Jews had to develop a united front in the face of a heavily Christian population in the city. His role, then, was consistent with his belief that men of different backgrounds could work together when they emphasized their similar needs and problems rather than their differences.

By 1914 Morris Newfield had come a long way from the poverty of his childhood and the years of frustration that he had felt as a student in Budapest. On November 15, 1909, he wrote to Leah from Ellis Island, where he had gone to visit, "Just examining the Immigration System as prevailing on Ellis Island . . . incidents occasionally tragic—Puts me back in mind to memories of 18 years ago. What I escaped—now you have to bear with me. Love, Morris." These years had found him pursuing the financial security that he felt he needed and, more important, winning the position that his father had not been able to achieve in the old country.[62]

By 1914, too, Morris Newfield was a leader in the Birmingham

Jewish community, firmly entrenched as the rabbi of the wealthy German Jewish congregation. Newfield's growing position of authority within this community was based on his ability to fit quickly into a new and foreign situation, and his strength of purpose helped him chart new directions for his congregants at Emanu-El. In a number of different areas, he aided his congregants: first, he gave them their first significant "professional" rabbi who not only listened to their needs but also formulated new agendas for them, especially with their coreligionists on the north side of Birmingham. Second, he presided over a time of transition for Emanu-El's Jews—helping them move socially from the outskirts of town in 1895 to a more respected position among the city's cultural and social elite by 1914. By accomplishing these tasks, he began to lay the groundwork for his work as a Jewish leader in Birmingham, for after 1915 he emerged as a leader in the entire community.

THREE

Newfield the Man

Thus far I have traced the developing career of Morris Newfield, the transplanted Hungarian who, by 1914, had made a successful journey, first to Cincinnati, Ohio, and Hebrew Union College, and then to Birmingham, Alabama, and a leadership position in the Jewish community. My first two chapters dealt with the "public" Newfield, the disciplined student who made sacrifices for future goals, and the resourceful young rabbi, who, by combining principle with diplomacy, began to lead a younger generation of Birmingham Jews. Succeeding chapters will also explore the "public" side of Morris Newfield. Now, however, I will look at the "private" or "personal" side of Morris Newfield, the man who lived in Birmingham from 1895 to 1940.

The task is difficult for two reasons. First, much of Newfield's correspondence and speeches pertains to his professional activities. Second, except in the letters that the rabbi wrote to his wife in the period 1896–1914, some of which survive, he did not express many of his innermost feelings. The "private" side of Morris Newfield, therefore, is apparent only in his most personal correspondence and from the recollections of his four sons and two daughters.

Newfield was, above all, a contented man: the fact that he remained in one pulpit throughout his adulthood suggests that he enjoyed his life and work in Birmingham. His contentment may have stemmed from Newfield's keen awareness of his alternatives in any situation in which he operated. The already quoted letters of courtship from the rabbi to his wife provide evidence of his heightened self-awareness and more important of his ability to adjust to the demands of different and often difficult situations. Perhaps this trait stemmed from Newfield's respect for flexibility. He must have learned early in his life that open-mindedness need not seriously diminish his strong commitment to principle.

In his professional activities, Rabbi Newfield exhibited his flexibility by practicing the art of diplomacy. He did not mind compromising, apparently because he viewed his leadership role at times as dependent on his ability to find consensus among his followers. This is not to say that Newfield did not maintain principle; rather I mean that he listened well and tried to develop moderate solutions upon which most people could agree.

The "private" Newfield was more authoritarian, more concerned with transmitting characteristics of self-discipline, personal warmth, and humane concern for his fellow man than with developing consensus at home. With his family and friends who knew him well, he commanded a sense of respect for the disciplined and humane life-style that he expected of himself and of the other people around him.

Newfield's children remember their father as a generally serious man who did not lack a sense of humor. Many of their anecdotes accentuate his deep commitment to self-discipline. The rabbi usually awakened at 7:00 A.M. and prepared to go to his study at the temple, which was six blocks from his residence on South Fifteenth Street, on Birmingham's south side. The Newfields had purchased this land and built a home on it in 1907 with the help of Leo K. Steiner, their friend and banker. They lived in this same house even after the rabbi's death in 1940. In the winter, after starting a fire in the coal furnace, Newfield ate breakfast, which the cook or his wife would prepare. He then spent three hours in his study, from 9:00 to 12:00, or went downtown to attend one of the many religious or civic functions in which he was involved. At noon, Newfield usually came home for the main meal of the day, as was the custom in Birmingham

Leah and Morris Newfield at home,
2150 Fifteenth Avenue South,
in Birmingham.

for many years. There was always soup at dinner or at supper because Newfield liked soup. At 2:00 he went back to the temple to receive visitors or to study. Then at 6:00 he would return home for supper, the one social occasion that the family shared on weekdays. After supper the evening activities varied. Sometimes the rabbi went to meetings at the temple or at other civic arenas throughout Birmingham. When he stayed at home, he would play cards with his wife or his father-in-law, listen to music with his wife, or read in his study.[1]

These evening activities were among the rabbi's favorite times of the day. He loved to read about many subjects, and at home in the evening he had time to do so. His son Mayer recalled, "Dad astounded the children with his comprehensive knowledge of various subjects like Geography, History, as well as current events." He was also a gifted linguist, conversing fluently in German, Hungarian, French, English, Hebrew, and Aramaic. He knew Latin "just like a teacher." Newfield also possessed a "phenomenal memory."[2]

Morris Newfield and his wife thoroughly enjoyed classical music. Leah Newfield was an accomplished pianist and singer. She often sang or played the piano at home, and sometimes the Newfields hosted meetings of the Birmingham Music Club, inviting many leading musicians from Birmingham and other cities into their home. One of their closest friends was Edna Goeckel Gussen, the Emanu-El choir director.[3]

Newfield was also an accomplished card player. His favorite card game was pinochle. Often Leah and Morris played with Samuel Ullman, and most of the time Morris won. According to Newfield's daughter Emma, "Grandfather was always aggravated that he could not beat Dad." Mayer recounts Newfield's card-playing experiences more explicitly, remembering his grandfather getting up from the table and sheepishly exclaiming, "Morris Newfield, you are incredibly lucky."[4]

Newfield was a disciplined man, too, when it came to his personal finances. He never borrowed money for anything except his home and as a consequence never owned a car until his congregation in 1920 gave him a Studebaker as an honorarium. Although by 1920 he earned $7,500 per annum, one of the highest salaries paid to any minister in Alabama, the Newfields never wanted to buy a car. The Studebaker, however, did not really change Morris Newfield's habits. He always enjoyed walking or using the trolley, and he was a terrible driver. After a few collisions, the rabbi asked his children to serve as his chauffeurs. Since the arrangement gave them free use of the car, they were only too happy to oblige.[5]

Other Old World traditions remained. Newfield continued to prefer Hungarian cooking which, according to his son, Leah never quite learned to prepare to his satisfaction. He could, however, enjoy good Hungarian food at the table of Ignatz Phillips, one of his best friends, at whose home he ate in the summer when his wife and children were visiting relatives in other cities. He loved Mrs. Phillips's goulash. He also favored sweet and sour dressing on many dishes, especially string beans, which he had grown to love as a child. Morris Newfield himself never spent a minute in the kitchen, regarding cooking, like dishwashing and cleaning, as proper work for a woman.[6]

Nevertheless, Morris Newfield adapted very comfortably to his new surroundings when he moved to Birmingham. He grew to love seafood of any kind, especially broiled fillets. His other favorite foods included Irish potatoes, steak, and sautéed onions. The rabbi also developed a taste for grits.[7]

Baseball and the Barons, the Birmingham minor league baseball team, provided the rabbi with his favorite pastime. Each summer he went faithfully to the games, often with his sons, Seymon and Mayer, and Joseph Gelders, the son of a close friend. Later, when he became one of the well-known community figures in Birmingham, the Barons gave him his own special free seat.[8]

The Newfields had a number of animals in their home. From time to time they adopted a stray cat, and in the rabbi's later years they owned a Boston bull terrier named Peggy, who caught rats and mice in the house. Mayer remembers the time when the rabbi let Peggy loose in the pantry to catch a pesky rat: "The dishes crashed and the food splattered but Peggy got the rodent."[9]

Although Newfield did not gamble, he and his wife enjoyed

going to the Phoenix Club for an evening of relaxation. On special occasions, such as George Washington's birthday ball, or just on nights when they played cards, checkers, or chess, Leah and Morris had opportunities to chat with friends from the south side of Birmingham.[10]

The Newfields were close friends of many of the leading members of the temple, including Louis and Blanche Gelders, Ignatz Phillips, Leo K. Steiner, and Bert and Ben Jacobs. The Newfield house was a half block from that of Blanche Gelders, Leah's closest friend, and was also near the Phillipses. On the same street lived two of Newfield's Protestant friends, Mrs. W. L. (Nellie) Murdock and Mrs. Patty Ruffner Jacobs, two prominent social workers in Birmingham. Newfield worked very closely with Mrs. Murdock through the years on various relief projects and greatly respected her for her devotion to her work. One reason for the rabbi's close friendship with Patty Jacobs was his support throughout the first two decades of the twentieth century for women's suffrage. Jacobs was president of a group that promoted women's suffrage. She was surely pleased when the rabbi strongly endorsed the Nineteenth Amendment in May 1919.[11]

Nevertheless, the Newfields were a close family, and their most intimate friendships remained within the family circle. Samuel Ullman lived with his daughter and Morris Newfield until his death in 1924, and many of the social occasions for the Newfields involved family gatherings when Samuel Ullman's other sons and daughters and their cousins from Natchez would visit. The Ullman and Newfield families rented space as well on a farm near Lake Michigan each summer, as did many southern and midwestern German Jewish families. Mayer Newfield recalls meeting and socializing with the Loebs of Chicago, of Leopold-Loeb fame, a relationship that continued because Seymon, the oldest Newfield son, belonged to the same fraternity as Dick Loeb at the University of Chicago.[12]

When the children were young, Leah and Morris Newfield took them to the farm in Frankfort, Michigan. On these trips the children came to know their father better. Morris took them fishing, on huckleberry-hunting trips, and on camping trips, during which they slept on hay in farmers' barns. This was probably the only time of the year when the rabbi could relax away from his official duties.

Yet much of the correspondence between Leah and Morris Newfield indicates that the rabbi had to spend many of his summers alone because of his rabbinical responsibilities. Either Newfield tended to his congregation in Birmingham or he was busy attending meetings of the Central Conference of American Rabbis in various cities throughout the country. From one letter that Morris wrote to Leah in August 1914, we learn that his summer schedule was not as tedious as that for the rest of the year:

> Worked in the yard after breakfast for a couple of hours until Louis Gelders came by and persuaded me to join him in a pool-match at the Club. Accepted and when finished had to get ready for dinner at Dr. Parke's. Enjoyed being with the Dr. and Mrs. and remained there until 4 P.M. chatting. . . . on going home nearly at six P.M., met Sidney and Retta [Leah's brother and sister-in-law]—was lured to walk home with them for supper—after supper went over to see Monte's folk [another brother of Leah's] and left them in time to see Jane and Bertha at the terminal before they departed for Natchez. [Jane and Bertha Lehman were cousins of Leah's.] Got home at a quarter past eleven, read till half past twelve.[13]

Newfield carefully taught his children his characteristic self-discipline and contentment. By 1915 Morris and Leah Newfield were blessed with six children. Eleven months after their marriage in January 1901, Seymon Ullman Newfield was born. He was followed by Emma Ullman in 1903, Mayer Ullman in 1905, Lena Jacobs in 1907, Lincoln in 1911, and John Aldrich in 1915.

A picture of an anxious, proud, and warm father comes through in Morris Newfield's early letters to his wife when he was away from his family. "Love, love, and love again mingled with many fervent hugs and kisses to both of my darlings sends your homesick and love-rich Husband and Father." He was a proud, doting father after Seymon was born in 1901. "Dearest," he wrote, "do you know that I am without a picture of our darling? And yet I hardly need one—Isn't he a prize in appearance? . . . How is his tooth, is it still a-coming?" A year later, the sentimental father sighed in a distant city, "How I wish I could see him crawling after his rubber ball or pulling your skirts. Dear and precious boy."[14]

Many of his letters were filled with questions and stories about his children. In 1908, when Leah went to Gulfport, Mississippi, to visit with her cousins, Morris wrote faithfully of their children's progress. He laughed over their pranks, "All well with us sweetheart. . . . Today our little ones have attempted to play April Fool's jokes on us and each other. Of course Seymon the schoolboy is the leader and has eager followers in Sister [Emma] and Mayer, although the latter does not quite grasp it. But he runs up to me anyhow with the cry 'Oh, Papa' and when I ask him what he wishes, he answers, 'April Fool.' "[15]

The rabbi may have been a hard-working man, but he was a father who was available to his children and not only on summer vacations. Besides taking them to baseball games, he helped buy their clothing and listened to them talk every night at the supper table. Every two months, Morris Newfield would also go to their schools and talk with the teachers about their development.[16]

But the children of Morris Newfield remember him most as a man who was not only self-disciplined but also a strong disciplinarian. Although Leah was usually responsible for disciplining the children, she was often so gentle with them that the children were not particularly mindful of their mother's strictures. On the other hand, "the rabbi's word meant something." The Newfield children were in awe of their father, and they knew that when there were "things you had to do, you better do them."[17]

Their stories of his authoritarian stance are legion. One of Mayer's earliest recollections of his father was being threatened with reform school at age six because "I had run away one sunny afternoon to the Birmingham Country Club with a number of Christian friends to get a highball." Mayer also tells the story about his father's expectations at the dinner table: "One night, when John was very young, he went visiting at 'Aunt' Blanche Gelder's house, which was down the street. When supper was ready, my mother called down there, and Blanche told John to go home, but that he could come back right after the meal to listen to records on the Victrola. John looked at her in all seriousness and said, 'No, I can't. I have to fold my napkin first.' "[18]

Rabbi Newfield also encouraged writing as a means by which the children could communicate with their mother and learn the necessary discipline too. He wrote for four-year-old Mayer on April 3, 1909, "Dearest Mama, I am sorry that I pulled some of your nice flowers and will not do it anymore. Sister [Emma] won't do it anymore either. . . . I will try and be a good boy all the time. Mayer."[19]

This sense of discipline was transmitted mostly by lessons in the value of education and strong study habits. Each night, immediately after dinner, the children were expected to go upstairs and prepare their homework before they did anything else. Bad grades in the Newfield household were forbidden. The rabbi's expectations of his children during services in the temple were similarly high. Mayer remembers, "He put the fear of God in you. He expected high standards of conduct at all times, and would not brook misbehavior."[20]

Although Morris Newfield wanted his children, and especially his sons, to pursue professional careers, he never encouraged his sons to follow in his path as he had in his father's. Instead, he told his children that as second-generation Jews in America they could develop careers in medicine, theater, law, or the arts—careers that had not been open to him.

Seymon Ullman Newfield (1901–1968), his eldest son, graduated from Howard College, now Samford University, in Birmingham in 1921, and from Rush Medical School at the University of Chicago in 1926. He became one of the leading obstetricians in Birmingham from 1928 to 1968, also serving as an assistant professor of obstetrics at the University of Alabama from 1946 to 1968 and as a founding fellow of the American College of Obstetrics and Gynecology. He married Leah Dessauer (a relative of Henry Horner, the Jewish governor of Illinois from 1933 to 1937) in 1928 and had two children.[21]

Emma Ullman Newfield (1903–1984) attended UCLA and received a bachelor's degree from the University of Chicago in 1928. In 1936, she married Bertram G. Minisman, the son of Jacob Minisman, one of the first Jews in Birmingham, and had two children. Like her mother, she was very active in Birmingham as a member of the National Council of Jewish Women and served as a manager of the Hillman Hospital in Birmingham, now the University of Alabama at Birmingham Hospital.[22]

Mayer Ullman Newfield, born in 1905, a graduate of Howard College in Birmingham in 1927, studied law at Harvard University from 1928 to 1929 and received a degree from the University of Alabama in 1931. After four years of private practice in Birmingham, he served as counsel to the Securities and Exchange Commission and as assistant regional administrator in New York City from 1935 to 1947. In this capacity he was the coauthor of Rule 10b-5 adopted by the SEC in 1942, which forms the basis for legal liability of persons engaged in fraudulent practices in the sale or purchase of securities. From 1948 to 1956, he was assistant city attorney in Birmingham and since 1956 has engaged in private practice there. He has served as Alabama state president of B'nai Brith in 1948 and as national commissioner and a member of the executive committee of the Anti-Defamation League. In 1938, he married Bertha Lehman, the daughter of Jannette Mayer, the first cousin of his mother, Leah. In 1978, five years after the death of his first wife, he married Loretta Schneiderman Ostrow. He has two daughters.[23]

Lena Jacobs Newfield, born in 1906, attended the University of Cincinnati for two years and graduated from the National College of Education in Evanston, Illinois, in 1926. She married Carl Forst, a lawyer, in 1928, and has a daughter.

Lincoln Newfield, born in 1911, graduated from Howard College in Birmingham in 1932 with a degree in music and later gave a vocal recital at Town Hall in New York City. He married Lea Halperin, who is a ceramics artist in Baltimore. He died in 1976.

John Aldrich Newfield, born in 1915, obtained a B.A. from Howard College and an M.A. from Yale University School of Drama, despite his father's initial misgivings. In 1954, he was an instructor of drama at Howard and also directed summer stock theater in Florida, supervising Katherine Cornell and other actors. At present, he is in public relations with Columbia Pictures in New York City.[24]

It is apparent that Morris Newfield enjoyed life in Birmingham, and he and his family prospered. The rabbi and his wife created a

NEWFIELD THE MAN

comfortable and warm environment in their home. In that environment, he championed a number of different feelings and ideas: first, life should be centered around work, because using oneself fully is of primary importance; second, recreation is also important. Newfield and his wife involved themselves in many varied pleasurable activities and encouraged their children to do likewise. Third, the rabbi stressed humanitarian concerns at home as well as in his professional life because he believed that caring for others was as important as giving to oneself. Finally, he transmitted a sense of pride in being Jewish. As a consequence, his children would later belong to many Jewish organizations.

Although the "private" side of Morris Newfield was very different from his "professional" side, the results of his actions in both areas were successful because he was not only a significant ethnic leader but also a warm and fulfilled person. In the public arena, he was more diplomatic and accepting of consensus—a man who created a following based on his awareness and acceptance of diversity. In his home, his style was very different and somewhat more authoritarian, but there too he remained aware of his many responsibilities and equally contented.

FOUR

A Leader in Birmingham, 1895–1920

Even as Temple Emanu-El's Jews were building their new temple in 1912, events in Birmingham were making the position of Jews somewhat anomalous. With the takeover of TCI by U.S. Steel in 1907, Birmingham's economy began to expand less rapidly than it had before, adversely affecting Jewish merchants, "who depended on the healthy wage earnings of area workers to keep their trade going." In the next decade, the number of Jewish establishments decreased and only the strongest survived. Financier Burghardt Steiner and Otto Marx left for the greener pastures of New York, while Ferd Marx's Dry Goods Company closed in 1913.[1]

More significantly, the political and social status of Jews in the years 1910–1920 was affected by the annexation of Birmingham's suburbs in 1910 and the subsequent change in the city government in 1911. The shift to a three-member city commission elected at large had a "predictable effect on the influence of ethnic or religious minorities in city politics." Election of the commission by a citywide vote meant that the concentration of certain groups in particular wards was no longer a factor in city politics. Consequently the political clout that had been enjoyed primarily by Catholics and Jews was dramatically diminished.[2]

The development of Greater Birmingham had still more far-reaching effects. Annexation brought a large number of pietistic Protestants from areas like Woodlawn and East Lake into the city electorate. As a consequence, the city was divided throughout the decade into two groups that called themselves the "Moral Elements" and the "Liberal Elements."[3]

As Leah Atkins has noted, "they fought over prohibition, prostitution, and Sunday blue laws." The pietistic Protestants pushed hard for antisaloon legislation, strict antiprostitution laws, and prohibition laws. The liberal elements of the city opposed the pietists heartily on their stands and usually lost. In 1908 liquor was prohibited in Birmingham, but three years later the law was repealed. By 1915, however, a statewide prohibition law had been passed. In 1918, too, 54 percent of Birmingham voters chose to prohibit Sunday movies in a referendum, owing to the

Supporters of the prohibition amendment marched along Twentieth Street on Sunday, November 28, 1909, the day before the vote. Photo by the Birmingham View Company. (Birmingham Public Library / Department of Archives)

successful mobilization of a pietistically minded Committee of Fifty of the Pastors Union.[4]

BIRMINGHAM LEADER

There was one attempt, by the Birmingham Chamber of Commerce, to bring together the disparate elements at the "Potlach" of 1913. The Chamber of Commerce publicly wanted the hostile men to overlook their differences. Invited were Alfred J. Dickinson, pastor of the First Baptist Church; city commissioners Culpepper Exum, A. O. Lane, and James Weatherly; park commissioner John Kaul; *Birmingham News* editor Frank P. Glass; and other prominent citizens. Although these men were Morris Newfield's friends and acquaintances, there is no evidence that he attended too. But the differences between the two groups were not resolved, and animosity remained.[5]

We could argue that these differences represented difficulties

On November 29, 1909, a crowd gathered
at the Jefferson County Courthouse
to support or oppose the prohibition amendment.
Photo by the Birmingham View Company.
(Birmingham Public Library / Department of Archives)

stemming from a continuing era of transition for Birminghamians. Because the city had grown so quickly with the 1910 legislation, disparate elements competed not merely for control of the city's political structure but also for the power to determine the cultural values of the city.

Although Birmingham Jews in this period found that their population of 3,500, or 1½ percent of the total community, kept them decidedly a minority, they had developed a leader in Rabbi Morris Newfield. His influence as a liberal grew steadily throughout the entire community. He accomplished his aims in a number of ways: first, he formed close working relationships with fellow ministers such as Dickinson and Henry M. Edmonds of the Independent Presbyterian Church; second, he joined various groups such as the Howard College faculty and the Quid Pro Quo Club, an intellectual circle consisting of leading businessmen, ministers, and politicians in Birmingham; and third, he began to speak out publicly on the social issues of the day, especially the 1918 controversy surrounding Sunday movies.[6]

Rabbi Newfield offered religious and social leadership to both Jews and Christians, proposing ways of reconciling and accommodating both groups. In searching for these solutions, Newfield confidently expected to operate as a leader of many diverse groups in the Magic City. He viewed himself as the conscience of Jewish businessmen, the spokesman for Jews among progressive Christians in order to effect harmony among open-minded religious types, and a representative of Jews among more traditional Christians who wanted to feel that Jews would not threaten their idea of moral and social order in Birmingham. An investigation of his ideas in this period can tell us not only about the style and content of his leadership but also about the nature of both society and ethnic leadership in Birmingham.

I Newfield's theology primarily reflected the tenets of classical Reform Judaism and of teachers such as Isaac Mayer Wise, who understood that Jewish congregations consisted of enterprising businessmen who wanted to be assimilated into the larger American society and also to maintain their Jewish identities. As a result, the young Hungarian-American perceived in the 1890s that the most important function of American rabbis of his generation was to redefine the relationship between Jews and their American environment.

Although historians of American Jewry disagree about the origins of Reform Judaism, it is accepted generally that the first five Reform congregations were Beth Elohim in Charleston, South Carolina, in 1841, Har Sinai in Baltimore in 1842, Emanu-El in New York City in 1845, Bene Jeshurun in Cincinnati in 1854, and Sinai in Chicago in 1858. Historians also accept the notion that German reformers such as Abraham Geiger were instrumental in developing a theology of Reform in Germany in the nineteenth century and that Samuel Adler, David Einhorn, Samuel Hirsch, Kaufmann Kohler, and Isaac Mayer Wise, a transplanted Bohemian Jew, developed the concept in America.[7]

Called the "Father of American Reform," Wise was probably the man most responsible for developing theological unity in the Reform movement in the nineteenth century. In 1854 he founded the *Israelite,* and a year later, *Die Deborah,* a German-language newspaper, to promote the dissemination of Reform principles in America. In 1855 he convened a synod of Reform rabbis in Cleveland to write *Minhag America,* a prayer book of Reform practices. Of this book Morris Newfield later wrote: "Judaism needed a reform prayer book, which should respond to the ideas of American Israel, eliminating dead hopes and exploding national issues, and giving expression not to lamentations over vanished glories, but to new and kindling expectations."[8]

Wise also helped organize a convention in Philadelphia in 1869 that was the first attempt of Reform rabbis to define the central issues for their movement. They suggested that American Jews no longer accepted the messianic goal of a national state of Israel and the physical return of Jews to Palestine. Rather they sought a spiritual fulfillment of this goal by propounding the oneness of God. Nor did these Reform theologians feel that Jewish people had been dispersed from Israel because they had sinned. They now regarded the Jewish diaspora as a tool which God employed to help Jews complete their mission "to lead the nations in the true knowledge and worship of God."[9]

In 1871 the rabbi from Cincinnati convened a third conference, in his hometown, to which twenty-seven representatives of congregations responded. It led in 1873 to the formation of a permanent union of Reform congregations, the Union of American Hebrew Congregations. Two years later, he and his friends founded Hebrew Union College.[10]

By 1885, however, Reform Jews were still not united on questions of dogma, and as a result, fifteen Reform theologians, led by Wise and Kaufmann Kohler (1843–1924), met in Pittsburgh in the fall. Kohler, formerly of Chicago Sinai and then at Beth El in New York, addressed the conference and tried to assess the needs of Reform Jews:

> We can no longer be blind to the fact that Mosaic-Rabbinic Judaism as based upon the Law and Tradition, has actually and irrevocably lost its hold upon the modern Jew. . . . Whether they have justificatory reasons for doing so or not, the overwhelming majority of Jews within the domain of modern cultures disregard altogether the Mosaic-Rabbinic laws concerning work or the kindling of light on the Sabbath, or any other ancient right. . . . Judaism is a historical growth, and we must find the focus for all its emanations and manifestations, the common feature in all its diverse expressions and forms. We must accentuate and define what is essential and vital amidst its ever changing forms and ever fluctuating conditions.

Their deliberations resulted in the adoption of the "Pittsburgh Platform," which remained the foundation of the Reform movement for fifty years. It repeated the ideas of mission and oneness of God that had first been set forth in Philadelphia. However, the rabbis moved beyond Philadelphia by insisting that their faith in God was not inimical to scientific discoveries of the nineteenth century and by acknowledging that Reform Jews had to confront actively the problems of the newly emerging industrial society.[11]

Morris Newfield was thoroughly trained in the principles of Reform Judaism at Hebrew Union College and accepted them wholeheartedly because he admired Wise and found that they offered him a meaningful career. The basis, then, of Newfield's theology was his insistence that Jews had a unique mission to develop a "Kingdom of God" on earth, or a society in which all men would live ethically. Because he wanted to give his congregation a reason to remain Jewish, he used the concept of mission to suggest that Jews were different from other religious groups. In a sermon that he entitled "The History of the Jew," he observed:

> Where the Jew stands foremost, where his particular genius finds its best expression is in the sphere of religion. By his guidance, the world has been brought to God and righteousness. His ethics have become the foundation of all moral laws and civilization. He it was who first brought the Fatherhood of God and brotherhood of man.

On the Jewish holiday of Shavuoth in 1896, he insisted that this mission was unique to Jews because they had accepted God's plea to spread His word after other nations had refused it.[12]

This concept of mission was sufficiently ambiguous to allow Newfield to preach that Jews were a separate group at the same time that he implied religious universality. A universal religion, he rationalized, might happen at a later time, but in 1900 Jews had to remain loyal to their faith to ensure their existence as a people. In 1894 he stressed this idea:

> The last word of Israel has not yet been spoken. Judaism, Christianity, Mohammedanism are not final truths, but phases of his spiritual life. The religion of humanity, the all-embracing faith of a universal religion is yet to come, and as of old, Israel is the forerunner, the preparer of that great Messianic time—out of their soul life must that future religion of humanity be born.

In this sermon, he seemed to use the concept of "Israel" in two different ways. At first he made it stand for a universalistic idea that had not been realized. Later, he implied that Israel consisted of Jews who had given the world the original idea of universality. A few years later, he repeated the more narrow use of the concept, "Go on then Israel. . . . Let it ring out and on until the distant future, when by thy perseverance, one humanity will rise from winter's night."[13]

Some historians who have studied the development of religion at the turn of the century have observed that an unprecedented ecumenical atmosphere prevailed. Although it would not have been farfetched for an intellectual historian of that time to predict a merger between Reform Judaism and progressive Christianity, such a union did not take place. It did not happen because Classical Reformers like Newfield were afraid that an ecumenical movement stressing the universal reign of God, regardless of race or creed, would lead to the religious assimilation of Jews and would therefore threaten the very existence of the Jewish people.[14]

As a result, the rabbi urged Jews to recognize that they were responsible for the mission idea. The Hebrew prophets, he claimed, were the first to reject formalistic concepts and to initiate the idea of a God unity among all men. They were the heroes who attacked the evil conditions of their civilization, challenged the powers that ruled, and pleaded for justice and equality. While he was still at Hebrew Union College in 1894, he carefully studied the fifty-third chapter of Isaiah and concluded that this prophet, and not Jesus, was the father of the mission idea. As a result he wrote, "Why should we accept Christianity? Why take a copy when we have the original?" Fifteen years later, he urged his congregants to recognize the significant Jewish influence in Jesus' teachings:

> They [Christians] and he [Jesus] teaches the Kingdom of Heaven. That phrase cannot be understood unless it be translated into the Hebrew of those times. What did those terms mean to the Jew of that day? The Kingdom of Heaven was not a kingdom beyond the clouds, not a heaven to welcome the weary wanderers after life. . . . it was therefore not of the life to come after this life that the Jew spoke. . . . [The Jewish prophets and Jesus] meant a new and better age which is to take the place of the present disturbed period. The Kingdom of Heaven meant the Kingdom of God. . . . In preaching the Kingdom of Heaven, Jesus had in mind the Messianic tense, as did other rabbis of his day, when righteousness will be and Justice triumph.

Newfield believed that Jews understood Jesus' message to them, "I go to prepare a place for you in my Father's house." As a Jewish teacher, Jesus was referring to the traditional prophetic ideal of a resurrected Israel and not to his individual resurrection in another world.[15]

Not surprisingly, Newfield also told his congregation of aspiring German-American Jews that their success depended more on deeds than on creed; they wanted to hear that they could achieve salvation through hard work and not through the outpouring of emotion or meaningless intellectual formations. "Our religion lays insistence upon the life rather than the belief," he explained; "it attaches the greatest importance to righteousness rather than to creed. . . . The burden of the Holy Scriptures is to Believe! Its battle cry is Do! Do!"[16]

Because he accepted the Reform tenet that Jews were unique in their historical commitment to a mission idea, he argued that the harsh, formalistic concepts and mass of creeds that had previously set Jews apart were unnecessary. Newfield equated blind acceptance of Mosaic laws with a continuation of the "meaningless sacrifices believed sufficient in the 8th century B.C." In 1914 he also explained:

> Religion has been made to suffer not by those who claim to be its most loyal devotees, [but by] those who could make it stand for all sorts of absurdities. . . . There are those who pose as friends yet are worse than the worst of enemies. . . . There is the ceremonialist who makes religion to stand for a mass of forms and rules, in whose eyes the chief occupation of God is watching and keeping books on the number of glorifications a man makes in his prayers. . . . how broad his phylacteries. [There is] the ceremonialist to whose mind the chief council of God is to persecute and punish men who neglect the ceremonies, no matter how upright his conduct.

Traditional Orthodox rituals, he further suggested, prevented Jews from fully exploiting their newly won freedoms in America. As businessmen, his congregants needed a religion that freed them from restraints of daily religious observances and offered them a meaningful substitute.[17]

Rabbi Newfield also warned his followers, however, that they could not afford to focus too energetically on individual accomplishments or material aspirations because they would lose sight of their missions, or their newly created raison d'être. In one speech he reaffirmed his central theme: "Israel's duty is to build an ideal city, not through armies or commerce, but through the principles of humanity and justice. Yea . . . , learning this lesson . . . is better than . . . struggling for gold and possessions, wet with the tears of our fellow-men."[18]

Here he acted as the conscience of Jewish businessmen in Birmingham, a role which he obviously relished, because he spoke out quite often. Many of his Atonement Day speeches ridiculed those Jews who never looked beyond the "music of the market place." On other occasions, he wondered whether some of his congregants could sit one day in temple "for solemnities promising no pecuniary compensation, holding out no proposals of reward exchangeable for income."[19]

From the frequency of his attacks, we might conclude that his congregation enjoyed them too. Perhaps the businessmen of Emanu-El wanted their rabbi to help them reconcile their material aspirations with their spiritual needs. The evidence indicates that Newfield understood their concern, because he often told them that their wealth entitled them to superior social positions but also forced greater responsibilities on them. Sounding much like Andrew Carnegie in his *Gospel of Wealth* (1900), in one speech Newfield instructed, "Men of thought do not protest against wealth as such. . . . I value the economic use of wealth. To it is largely due the favored stride of civilization. I honor as a benefactor the man who, possessing large means, puts them to proper economic use." In 1913, he further exhorted, "Tonight, ask yourselves whether what wealth you have gathered is being properly used, whether your social position is a responsibility—noblesse oblige—ask yourself whether your knowledge is a call to serve." To his congregation, he rationalized that the only justification for large accumulations of wealth lay in developing society or helping less fortunate people. Perhaps Newfield's congregants listened to his proposals for an ethical society because they could then feel less guilty for having more than other people.[20]

Rabbi Newfield also recognized that his congregants wanted a theology that reconciled Jewish faith in a God-centered universe with Charles Darwin's theory of evolution, which was popular in the latter half of the nineteenth century. Like the rabbis who wrote the Pittsburgh Platform, Newfield rejected claims of evolutionists who repudiated their faith in God, noting as late as 1907:

> But a few decades ago . . . it became fashionable for young men to devote themselves to science and to doubt everything. They doubted God . . . , but they had no doubt of one thing as to their descent from monkeys. . . . We clutched to our bosom the new cry of knowledge and left to solicitude the old faith and religion. This popular conceit has had its way. Today again, it is admonished that religion too has power and its warning flame is needed.

Because they did not believe in a God-centered universe, the Unitarians, the Free Religious Association, and Felix Adler's Ethical Culture Society held little attraction for Morris Newfield. These ethical systems, he thought, not only forced individuals to drift between selfish feelings and the always-changing "quicksand of public opinion" around them but also minimized the particular accommodation that Reform theologians had made for American Jews.[21]

Still, Newfield did not reject out of hand the theory of evolution. Instead he accepted it as a process but not as a force, or creator, or substitute for God. He chose to teach his congregation that an Infinite Power accounted for the process of evolution and that evolution was the work of the Power's procedure. Similarly, Newfield accepted scientific criticism of the Bible when it did not run counter to his belief that the Bible was divinely inspired and the source of divine revelation. An unthinking perusal of the ancient documents, the rabbi claimed, was as detrimental to the cause of truth as irreverent scoffing at them. He further reasoned:

> The former is stupid, the latter is unfair. In reading the Bible, we must not make our reason captive to blind faith. . . . On the other hand, the satires and ridicule of scoffers and infidels are altogether unjustifiable, and can be of no redeeming value. . . . Biblical criticism is not the product of skepticism, but the result of painstaking study of men devoted to religion.

The Birmingham rabbi believed that his congregants were going to think critically because they were aware of scientific progress in their day. If Judaism was to be meaningful, their faith had to be integrated with biblical criticism and study of the natural laws of civilization.[22]

Yet Newfield refused to compromise his faith by questioning

the existence of God. As a result, he believed that the Kingdom of God represented the highest level of the evolutionary process. In 1900 he observed:

> The race is not to the swift, nor victory to the strong. Not to Pharaoh, the powerful king, but to Moses, the spiritual leader; not to Goliath, the physical giant, but to David, the idealistic youth . . . in short, not the men of muscles have led their fellows . . . but the men of soul, the prophets of humanity. . . . with Israel's birth was born the conception "mind is more than matter."

In the synthesis that he proposed between Reform Jewish principles and evolutionary theory, Moses and Isaiah were exemplary teachers who had taught men to strive for an ethical society.[23]

Morris Newfield, then, preached the tenets of Reform Judaism because he felt that he had to offer his congregants a rationale for remaining Jews in an environment that threatened their identities as Jews. By rejecting many of the traditional laws he developed a set of religious practices that did not interfere with his congregants' quest for economic success in Birmingham. By accentuating the mission ideal, he asked them to remember that in their pursuit of worldly gain, they could not overlook their commitments to Judaism or to society.

II Morris Newfield's Reform theology also afforded him the opportunity of extending his leadership among Christians in Birmingham: he offered to both Jews and Christians at that time a rationale for peaceful coexistence. In doing so, the rabbi had help. We can argue that he became a member of an elite group of leaders, including Alfred J. Dickinson, Henry M. Edmonds, and Middleton S. Barnwell, titans all, who worked in many capacities to cope with the cultural changes brought about by the development of Greater Birmingham. The times called for and produced men who were both scholars grappling with theological issues and social leaders, who by the sheer force of their strong personalities heavily influenced the character of religious and social development in the city.

Until recently, historians of southern Protestantism, and more specifically, of the religious atmosphere in Birmingham, such as Charles H. Hopkins, C. Vann Woodward, and Samuel S. Hill, Jr., contended that southern Protestantism was largely evangelical in nature, concerned with sticking to the letter of the Bible and saving individual souls. Moreover, as Samuel Hill has eloquently stated, southern Protestants were unalterably opposed to social reform or to any liberal theology which sought to question the validity of the social environment, because they had never exhibited any desire to establish a "New Israel," unlike some of their counterparts in the northern states.[24]

One of the few comprehensive interpretations of Birmingham's religious life of the period is Martha Bigelow Mitchell's 1946 Ph.D. dissertation, "A History of Birmingham, 1870–1910." In it Mitchell has reiterated the claims of these more general treatises. Mitchell, too, claimed that many churches were characterized by Protestant traditionalism, espousing not only conservative theologies but also aggressive efforts to "evangelize" or impose their creed upon churches and schools in Birmingham. By 1910, she further argued, the three traditional southern Christian denominations, the Baptists, the Presbyterians, and the Methodists, had developed 74 of the 102 churches, emphasizing a myriad of activities relating to the saving of souls.[25]

More recently, other historians, including Kenneth K. Bailey, Rufus B. Spain, and Wayne Flynt, have demonstrated that industrialism in the South created "complex problems that demanded substantial modification of nineteenth-century pietistic Christianity" and that in response various ministers preached an increasing socialization of southern Protestantism. Flynt in particular demonstrated that "in religion, Birmingham was a city of paradoxes." Although a majority of churches and denominational newspapers emphasized fundamentalist concerns, "industrialization brought social distress to the working classes and alienated them from the church, forcing pietistic Protestants to begin dealing with the city's critical social problems."[26]

The attempts of Wayne Flynt and others to offer a more complete picture of the uniquely industrial habitat of Birmingham and the clerical responses to its problems in the years 1900–1930 are significant because they partially correct traditional stereotypes which have plagued treatments of Birmingham religious life. Nevertheless, in his attempt to paint a picture of social liberalism in Birmingham churches during the Progressive era, Flynt may have overstated these liberalizing influences; his assertions need to be further investigated.[27]

A treatment of Morris Newfield's ministry gives students of this period further opportunity to assess the nature of religious life in Birmingham in the years 1900–1920 and to test the validity of the above-mentioned generalizations. This analysis may be accomplished in three ways: first, by studying the rabbi's sermons to ascertain his perceptions of the religious issues of this time; second, by scrutinizing one of the important religious controversies of the decade 1910–1920—the fight over Sunday movies, which took place in Birmingham in 1917—to assess the strength of fundamentalist Protestantism; and third, by examining Newfield's work vis à vis other ministers in Birmingham to discover whom he perceived as his friends and opponents in clerical circles. Although he was Jewish, his ministry can shed light on the nature of Protestantism in Birmingham at this time.

Among his congregants Newfield often spoke in a straightforward fashion, leaving little doubt about his attitudes toward various social and religious issues in Birmingham. Morris Newfield understood that many evangelical Christians had accepted stereotypes that caused them to respect but also to fear Jews in Birmingham. Although historians of southern Jewry have suggested that many Reform rabbis in their eagerness to coexist happily with Christians often emphasized their similarities to, but not their differences from, Christians, Newfield does not conform to these general observations. He in particular wrote many sermons that directly confronted the ambivalent feelings of Christians.[28]

The tenor of his sermons indicates that Newfield spoke very defensively about Jews at times because he feared the extent of Christian power in Birmingham, but he also expressed a good deal of pride about religious traditions that, he felt, allowed Jews to be different from Christians. The rabbi established many contacts with ministers of the three largest evangelical denominations because he confidently expected that he, as a representative of Jews, could help them develop more informed attitudes toward Birmingham Jews.

Newfield recognized that evangelical Protestants in Birmingham had mixed emotions about Jewish merchants. He knew that they recognized contributions that Jews had made to commercial progress and industrial development. Christians, he reasoned, also appreciated the work of the Steiners, his congregants who had broken the hold of the injurious crop lien system by developing competitive credit facilities in rural areas outside Birmingham to finance their cotton crop. They also enjoyed shopping at Loveman, Joseph, and Loeb's department store and at Ben Jacob's furniture store or having their horses shod by Jacob Fies at his livery and feed store.

But the rabbi knew that Christians often viewed Jews as avaricious and cunning parasites because they were merchants or professionals rather than farmers. Each year, on the Jewish holiday of Succoth, he parried their attacks. In 1896, he suggested that Jews were not farmers because Christians had prevented them from tilling the land.

> There is nothing in his [the Jew's] religion that would arrest the inclination to be a tiller of the soil. To the contrary, the natural instinct of the Jew in Biblical days ran toward the plow. . . . The religion of the Jew, if it encouraged any tendency . . . , promoted the leaning toward agricultural life, and discouraged disposition to engage in mercantile pursuits. . . . And if we ceased to be farmers . . . , Medieval Christian Church and State must bear the blame. . . . I will not dwell on the picture of the dark night of tears when the Jews were huddled together in ghettos and all means were devised to degrade and humiliate them, to stifle their physical and moral growth.

There were also times when he went as far as to identify with critics of Jews. In 1897, when he proclaimed that Jews should be good farmers, he sounded like an evangelist with Populist sympathies:

> Yea, not merely the Jew should heed the lesson of the day. The whole of the American people may lay it to heart. There is something unhealthy in the growth of our city-centers. . . . City-culture is often fringed [*sic*] by shame and sin. The city is the house of

> learning, but also the cover of the slums. . . . These slums should be cleansed and out into the freer and nobler area of the country should the redeemed be sent. . . . We should remember the prophecy of Jefferson that "the American people will remain virtuous as long as agriculture is our principal object."[29]

We may speculate that Newfield dealt judiciously with the feelings of those who disliked Jews for their economic successes. He did not attack what he may have perceived as reasons for these outbursts—the jealousy of Protestant capitalists about Jewish business successes or the enmity of newly emerging working classes who disliked their Jewish bosses or co-workers.[30]

Similarly, the rabbi sensed that evangelical Christians had ambivalent feelings about Jews because Jews were not Christians. Judaism, suggested Newfield, was seen as both the mother religion of Christianity and a repudiation of its legitimacy. On the one hand, he suspected that evangelical Christians expected Jews to act as if they had inherited the mantle of prophets. As a result, he often warned his congregants that their attempts to stray from their faith only encouraged prejudicial attacks. In one speech he claimed, "Gentiles even today believe that Jew and Talmud go together and that every Jew knows the Talmud by heart." In 1897 he also cautioned them, "A faithless Jew is a faithless man; such men create prejudice and ill-will. The noble, devout, honest, and dignified Jew will not fan the flame of prejudice and intolerance." Although we can see that he used the threat of Christian intolerance to keep his congregants in line, he also reinforced the impression that Christians expected religious loyalties from believers, regardless of creed.[31]

On the other hand, the rabbi often tried to counter Christian beliefs that Jews were Christ-killers. In "A Jewish View of Jesus," which appeared in the Birmingham newspapers, Newfield gingerly attempted to prove to Christian audiences that Romans and not Jews had killed Jesus. Jesus was a threat, he suggested, not to Jewish law, but to Roman political authority:

> It may be a shock to conventional Christian thought to hear that the Jewish people at the time of Jesus were anything but impoverished in intellect and in idealism. The common view, issued in the average pulpit, is that the Jewish people were, at the advent

> of Jesus, socially, intellectually, and morally bankrupt. Nothing can be further from the truth than this. . . . Taking the reputed trial of Jesus, it is undoubtedly admitted that the entire procedure and method of the trial were against Jewish custom and Jewish law. I am sure only in a generation that was not familiar any more with Jewish law and Jewish custom, could such a trial as recorded here have been imputed to the Jewish authorities.[32]

After examining the powerful influence of Christians in Birmingham, we can see why the rabbi so readily accepted the mission ideal. Not only did he attempt to modernize Judaism for businessmen in his congregation, but he also rationalized Jewish separatism in an area that feared alien customs. Newfield sensed that a historical commitment to God was not threatening to Christians, because they expected it of Jews. Still, an attempt to emphasize Jewish racial characteristics would be misconstrued, because Christians feared their differences too.

Newfield worked very hard to explain to evangelical Christians that Jews were different because they were committed to their unique mission. "So that we may be better able to fulfill our mission, God has endowed us with wonderful faculties and abilities, which has made us proverbial. He has given us greater vitality to survive the storms of hatred and persecution, wealth, and wisdom to emulate in the solution of the greatest problems of mankind." Nevertheless, the rabbi also insisted that Jews were very loyal Americans. Making repeated allusions to Jewish love of the South, he suggested that "in such instances as our own, or England, Germany, Hungary—where the Jew is in possession of the rights of citizenship, he is not wanting in the feeling of kinship with his fellow citizens. . . . The Jew has always been patriotic."[33]

Although much of the evidence suggests that Newfield's theological response to evangelical Christians in Birmingham was a defensive one, designed to allay their fears, some of his work indicates otherwise. There was "another" Newfield who refused to accommodate evangelical Christians and who proudly proclaimed Jewish distinctions because he believed his people to be stronger and often more intelligent than Christians with whom they lived.

At times, Rabbi Newfield angrily rebuked Christians who tormented Jews and Jews who meekly accepted Christian harangues. Although Newfield did not share these feelings often or outside the confines of his temple, he did make some powerful statements. On Rosh Hashana morning in 1907, he lambasted his congregants: "I, for one, friends, am tired of this weak-kneed, weak-backed, characterless, toneless, spineless, and nerve-less prating of a brotherhood which is no brotherhood, or progress which is but veiled prejudice. I am wearied of giving up for the sake of the flattery of the non-Jew." In another speech he exhorted, "We want an aggressive Judaism today . . . that will not lie down and deny itself because of petty and social prejudices . . . , that can afford to be ostracized . . . because it is representative of a truer manhood. . . . We want men—men of strength."[34]

When Newfield castigated Christians, he suggested that their anti-Semitic outbursts were confessions of their own inadequacies. In a speech entitled "Dream of Temple," he exclaimed, "Anti-Semitism is the confession of bankruptcy of society; it is the admission of failure by the boasted philosophy of materialism on the one hand, and on the other, of the impotency of a religion which abandons the world for the sake of the next."[35]

Newfield also admonished evangelical Christians for believing that Jesus knew anything about concepts of original sin, transubstantiation, immaculate conception, and atonement, claiming that these were later doctrines of his disciples. In 1896, he argued that Christianity was a lesser religion than Judaism because "the antique world . . . was not yet ripe for the pure thought and lofty idealism of Israel. Christians spelled Israel's mind to the Gentiles by blending Jewish thought with heathen conception."[36] Two years later, the rabbi criticized evangelical Christians for accepting miracles, because he believed that they promoted weakness in men.[37] In 1908, Newfield, in turn, rejected Christian complaints that Judaism was a harsh religion: "Judaism is a cold religion because it does not hold out eternal fantasies of salvation to him who outraged the laws of humanity or those who violated God's most sacred precepts. . . . Judaism is an austere creed because it does not proclaim as saints, converted criminals and deathbed confessed hypocrites."[38] In these instances, the theological conciliator became outraged, and as a result, he lashed out at Christians who he perceived were preaching destructive messages about Jews.

From these sermons, it is clear that Newfield believed strongly in two ideas: first, evangelical Christian sects were very strong in Birmingham; and second, he, as a Jewish leader in Birmingham, had to parry their attacks. The frequency and intensity of his comments might lead us to question the extent to which the rabbi noticed the diminishing influence, as Flynt suggests, of evangelical Christians in social matters in this period.

Perhaps we can learn more about the period by looking closely at the controversy between Rabbi Newfield and the Committee of Fifty of the Pastors Union over the showing of Sunday movies in Birmingham. In 1915, after a four-year campaign, Birmingham's labor unions and several small theater owners had obtained permission from the city commission to show Sunday movies, suggesting that the movies provided worthwhile amusement to working men and their families on their day of leisure. But the Pastors Union, the Women's Christian Temperance Union, and several Sunday school organizations protested and launched an anti-Sunday movie drive which forced the issue to a referendum in 1918.[39]

During the referendum campaign the Committee of Fifty of the Pastors Union claimed in a newspaper advertisement that a petition that listed individuals who favored Sunday movies included the names of "every prominent Jew in the city." In a letter sent to all Jewish voters, the ministers claimed that Jews need not be concerned with this issue because it was a Christian matter and asked Jews publicly not to vote.[40]

Morris Newfield responded publicly to P. B. Wells of the Committee of Fifty that he considered the right to vote a political, and not a church, question:

> I was indeed grieved, very much against my will, to come to the conclusion that your letter contains a veiled threat, that unless the citizens who profess the Jewish faith abstain from voting in this election . . . , the fact of our participation you say "will undoubtedly create an undesirable and most unfortunate friction between some of the best Christians and some of the best Jews in Birmingham." My past experience with the rank and file of my Christian friends in your city does not permit me to agree with you. They are broader in thought, bigger in principle than to follow such harmful doctrine.

> You may not mean to do it, but your suggestion is equal to an attempt to intimidate. I have, in the past 22 years of my residence, refrained from entering into newspaper controversies or discussions over politics . . . , but your letter and advertisement was so startling in advocating a principle so foreign and prejudicial to our great American principles that I felt it my duty to reply.

He forced the Pastors Union to deny publicly their questioning of Jewish right to vote. But Wells's reply made what could be considered yet another veiled threat to the rabbi and the Jewish community:

> It is this same stalwart faith of their [Pilgrims] sons and daughters which have made this land what it is—a Christian nation where the weary and oppressed of every clime may find a refuge. You, my dear rabbi, are in a position to appreciate . . . the vitalizing power of the Christian Sabbath, as compared . . . with the blighting breath of the Continental Sabbath in Hungary. . . . You are today proud of your American Citizenship—and well you may be. We would not have you forget, however, that it is the Christian faith which is the secret of America's greatness.[41]

Newfield knew that he was provoking trouble by answering the Pastors Union but was unafraid because he believed that he had to speak for the Jewish community. Reactions of Fundamentalist Christians were generally not kind. One writer, calling himself "Yours for Fairness," sent him a note on May 7, 1918:

> You should realize that your people are here among us and do not produce enough from Mother Earth to feed one infant. . . . [also] you were not born in Free America, reared nor educated here but in Germany. Consider . . . and profit thereby. I feel that you owe an apology to the Pastors Union for having published such an infamous letter.

Another wrote, "Allow me to congratulate you on your failure to deliver our Christian Sabbath into the hands of our enemies—anti-Christians and non-Christians. Your reply to the friendly letter of Dr. Wells was unkind and unbrotherly."[42]

Robert Simpson of the First Christian Church, a member of the Pastors Union, also let Newfield know that he was treading on dangerous ground. Simpson was gracious but nevertheless suggested that Newfield had overreacted:

> As a local minister and a preacher of the Pastors Union, I wish to express my deep regret over the recent letters issued by the press. . . . I cannot believe, however, that any intentional discourtesy or injustice was in the mind of our fellow-pastors . . . , for I believe that every Christian minister in the city appreciates the great worth of you and the congregation to whom you minister, in the civic and religious life of our fine country.

Newfield's actions came to naught because Sunday movies were prohibited as a result of the election.[43]

This particular controversy, however, is more complex than it first appears, for a number of reasons. First, the Committee of Fifty did not represent the sentiments of the entire Pastors Union—Middleton S. Barnwell of the Episcopal Church of the Advent, the church of many of the city's social and economic elite, Henry M. Edmonds, pastor of the theologically liberal Independent Presbyterian Church, and George Eaves, a British Congregationalist pastor, all close friends of Newfield's, were a minority of the union that rejected this position and joined the committee favoring the Sunday movies. Second, one minute book of the Pastors Union has survived from this decade, detailing their concerns. It provides conclusive evidence for Wayne Flynt's assertion that Christian ministers were interested in social concerns as well as in saving souls and prohibiting alcohol. There were a number of discussions about strengthening the child labor laws of Alabama and helping the Anti-Tuberculosis Society in Birmingham. Nevertheless, the controversy over Sunday movies and the ferocity of Newfield's reaction to it provide compelling evidence for contrary assertions that the orientation of the Pastors Union was largely evangelical in tone and that its influence was extremely powerful in cultural matters in Birmingham, Alabama, in this decade.[44]

Morris Newfield's sermons about, and his subsequent public argument with, some of the activities of evangelical Christians, suggest that he believed their influence to be very strong in Birmingham at this time. His goal was to convince evangelical

Christians that Jews were different but acceptable. His tactics were twofold. On the one hand, he diplomatically rationalized Jewish similarities to, and differences from, Christians, in order to make peace with them. For the most part, he won respect from them for what he judiciously said and admiration from his congregants because he dealt successfully with these Christians. On the other hand, although he spent much time understanding evangelical Christian fears and accommodating their needs, he was not afraid, in other instances, to express his Jewish identity. In doing so, he played on evangelical Christian beliefs that Jewish representatives of the "Book" deserved respect.

III Wayne Flynt may have not only underestimated the influence of evangelical Christians but also overstated the importance of social gospel theology in Birmingham in this period. The ministries of Newfield and Christians such as Dickinson, Edmonds, and Barnwell suggest a different idea—while evangelical Christians maintained great cultural influence, a group of talented men, liberal theologians all, by the sheer force of their strong individual personalities promoted a following for a Social Gospel theology. They might be called the harbingers of a future liberal ecumenical society in Alabama.

Morris Newfield not only shared personal friendships with these Christian ministers but believed, as they did, that organized religion had become too closely concerned with enforcing piety and traditional dogmas. He joined them in urging that an ethical society be created. We might argue that he and they hoped to shift the emphasis in religious thinking from individual piety and dogmatic ritual assertions to the creation of an ethically based Kingdom of God on earth. The goals of these men were to create a religious atmosphere in America through a set of theological precepts that would transcend the values of growing materialism and the inflexible practices of Orthodox sects. Also the ministers confidently expected their theologies to reduce enmity that had developed between capitalists and laborers and could reconcile the laws of science with their faith in God and in the Bible.[45]

Newfield and these Christian theologians chose to pursue different paths toward the goal of a Kingdom of God, or a universal religion. While the rabbi was looking for a reason to justify the separate existence of Judaism, and therefore of Jewish people, the ministers also hoped to emphasize the particular contributions that Christianity, in general, and their sects, in particular, were making toward an ethical society. As a result, Newfield listened to Gladden and worked closely with Dickinson, Barnwell, and Edmonds in common religious forums, but he was not willing to concede the possibility of sacrificing his particular religion for the sake of an immediate religion of humanity.[46]

In 1895 Newfield had come to Birmingham, thinking that Reform Jews and progressive Christians could work together harmoniously because he was armed with the recommendations for an ethical society from his Jewish teachers and from Gladden. As a consequence, in 1898, he invited the Chicago Unitarian minister Jenkin Lloyd Jones to speak at his temple. Jones's speech, entitled "The Parliament of Religions and What Next?" marked the beginning of a long friendship between the two men, and his talk was the first of three that Jones made at Temple Emanu-El. In 1898 Jones lectured Newfield's congregants and progressive Christians of Birmingham on the importance of mutual understanding between religious groups and spoke of his hope for a universal religion. He came back in 1914 to address the need to appreciate various ethnic groups. Three years later, on March 26, 1917, he pleaded for peace and remonstrated against war. Newfield's iconoclastic friend Thomas Parke reported on the latter two speeches, and was very impressed with Jones's humanistic philosophy and with Newfield's efforts to promote a following for Jones at Emanu-El.[47]

Of more significance, however, were Newfield's friendships with Dickinson, Edmonds, and Barnwell, who not only helped him understand evangelical Christians but also treated him like a brother in a fraternity of socially advanced clergymen. All of these ministers developed large individual followings because they were charismatic figures, but they worked together because each was strong enough to see the others' ethnic or religious worth.

In 1899, Newfield was asked by Parke and Dickinson to join the Quid Pro Quo Club, an intellectual circle consisting of ten or twelve of the leading ministers and professionals in Birmingham. The level of discussions was very high, the topics ranging from biblical interpretation to analyses of political and social issues.

The diaries of Thomas D. Parke, one of the group's founders and a leading Birmingham physician, are a particularly good source for exchanges that took place between Newfield and these Birmingham Christians. Parke leaves us with the impression that religious topics were a main focus of their discussions. Newfield often delivered speeches about Jewish contributions to the modern world, or about various prophets, while evangelical Christians argued about evolution. After one speech on the latter topic, Parke retorted, "It was absolutely ludicrous if not pathetic to listen to such a crowd of far above ordinary intelligence taking positions as were taken there last night." Newfield, however, attended the meetings faithfully, probably viewing them in a more constructive fashion because he wanted to exchange religious views with evangelical Christians.[48]

The rabbi's close relationships with Alfred J. Dickinson and Frank Willis Barnett, two evangelical Christians of a more open-minded persuasion, suggest that he worked diligently to develop his associations with the Fundamentalist Christian community. Dickinson does not really fit into any neat category. He was, as Wayne Flynt has perceptively noted, the city's chief intellectual mugwump. Although he was the pastor of the First Baptist Church, a prestigious Baptist institution in Birmingham, he may have belonged to a respectable group of "Baptist Bourbons" who saw no conflict between evangelical concerns and academic challenges to the literal interpretation of Scripture and defended "higher criticism" against all comers, a position which they shared with Newfield.

The two men shared a common view that the modern-day church had to develop the Kingdom of God on earth, or work toward improving society. But even more significant, as strong-willed clergymen they believed that the task of the minister was to correct defects in society by encouraging their members to accept the necessity of civic responsibility.[49]

Their relationship took several different turns. In 1903, when Dickinson's church was in the process of building a new structure, the iconoclast preached his gospel in Newfield's temple. In 1918, however, when Newfield argued with the Pastors Union over the issue of Sunday movies, Dickinson, who had entered into an alliance with the "True Americans" or supporters of the prohibition of Sunday movies, carefully affirmed to the rabbi that Jews had the right to vote on the issue but that they also had to acknowledge the sanctity of the Protestant Sabbath. Dickinson's reason was clear: at this time, he argued a belief that white Anglo-Saxon Protestants should control cultural mores in Birmingham. His message to Newfield was implicitly worded to this effect.[50]

Similarly, Newfield boasted a close relationship with Frank Wills Barnett, a member of Dickinson's church and editor of the *Alabama Baptist.* It is not difficult to see why the two men were friends. Although Barnett did not share his pastor's theological liberalism, his editorials challenged liberalism while also defending the freedom of Baptists to take critical theological positions without fear of retaliation: "Let us shake off a false Baptist demagogy which, boasting of its own self-sufficing orthodoxy, becomes the worst of all tyrannies in striving to force its narrow tests upon all who are willing to receive with open minds truth from any source." The editor spoke his enlightened message at Newfield's temple a number of times. Moreover, in 1920, Barnett paid homage, as columnist in the *Birmingham Age-Herald,* to his friend on the rabbi's twenty-fifth anniversary dinner. After reading aloud various plaudits that other men had offered, Barnett spoke of Newfield's leadership as it extended throughout the whole Birmingham community:

> I haven't the space here for a eulogy of Dr. Newfield, and what's more, he does not need it at my hands, for with his own, he has builded for himself a lasting monument in the hearts not only of the Jewish, but the Gentile people of this great community, devoted to the uplift and the upbuilding of every worthy cause.[51]

Morris Newfield was asked as well to speak a few times at evangelical churches. When he did speak at the Southside Baptist Church or the South Highlands Presbyterian Church, he highlighted themes of brotherhood, declaring, for instance, that he could accept the teachings of Jesus as words that all faiths could understand. Not only were these sermons enthusiastically received, they were reprinted the following day in the newspapers.[52]

BIRMINGHAM LEADER

The rabbi was asked by one of the leading Baptist ministers, Rev. James M. Shelbourne, who was also president of Howard College, to teach Hebrew and Semitic languages at his college. Newfield agreed to do so without receiving a salary because the Baptist institution had financial problems. His sons later all received free educations from Howard in payment for his generosity.[53]

The implications of Newfield's relationship to Howard College are very important. Teaching Hebrew at Howard gave the rabbi a faculty-student relationship with many Baptist students, most of whom headed to seminary for ministerial training and many of whom were already pastors in churches in or near Birmingham. This relationship not only made Newfield aware of the ideas expressed in Baptist churches throughout Birmingham but also helped him develop contacts throughout these same churches.

Another one of Newfield's closest friends, Henry M. Edmonds, was pastor of South Highlands Presbyterian Church from 1913 to 1915 and, after 1915, of the Independent Presbyterian Church. They met after Edmonds came to Birmingham from Montgomery, where he had had his initial pastorate. Josiah Morris, Edmond's uncle, had been one of the early founders of Birmingham. Edmonds was considered a maverick by the Presbytery of North Alabama because he refused merely to "preach the gospel" but accentuated the social teachings of Jesus and the ideal of the Kingdom of God. His ministry indicates that some Christian clergymen in Birmingham were interested in solving social problems and in involving themselves in more than safe concerns such as individual regeneration.

In 1915, Henry Edmonds, who had attracted a large following at South Highlands Presbyterian, began preaching to his congregation and in the newspapers that he could no longer concur with the thinking of the Presbytery of North Alabama. He disagreed with the idea that Christians could receive salvation only when they acknowledged that God, through Jesus, could save

Henry M. Edmonds,
a close friend of Morris Newfield,
was pastor of the Independent Presbyterian Church
from 1915 to 1942.
(Birmingham Public Library / Department of Archives)

mankind. Edmonds reasoned from his study of the Old Testament that salvation was the result of good works and that Jesus was the perfect example to whom Christians could look to fulfill their ethical duties in society and unto God.[54] The differences between orthodox Presbyterians and Edmonds were clear-cut. The former suggested that men were born evil and that as a result they could do good works only when they accepted God. Edmonds, on the other hand, questioned the validity of Original Sin and believed that men could earn salvation by living ethical lives.

In October 1915, the Presbytery of North Alabama tried to censor Edmonds by telling him that he could not preach until a meeting of the presbytery had been called to examine his ideas. Edmonds quickly resigned from the presbytery and on October 21, 1915, issued a call to his friends to protest its action. At this meeting the next day, a new church, the Independent Presbyterian, was formed with approximately 200 members of the South Highlands Church as charter members and Edmonds as its leader.[55]

Charges were hurled by both sides, the presbytery suggesting that Edmonds was a heretic and Edmonds replying that the presbytery was advocating a Fundamentalist line that few churches in the North or in Birmingham could accept. While the presbytery accentuated the inadequacies and further passivity of man in the face of God, Edmonds reiterated his Social Gospel theology. In a pamphlet entitled *The Other Side of the Recent Case of Dr. Henry M. Edmonds and the North Alabama Presbytery,* Edmonds and his followers stated that men were not evil and further suggested:

> His readiness [is] to bestow His saving grace on all who seek it; . . . that men are fully responsible for their treatment of God's gracious offer. . . . We hold it to be the mission of the Church of Christ to proclaim the Gospel to all mankind, exalting the worship of one true God, and laboring for the progress of knowledge, the reign of peace and the realization of human brotherhood. . . . We work and pray for the transformation of the world into the Kingdom of God; and we look with faith for the triumph of righteousness.

Later, in his examination before the presbytery, Edmonds dwelt on the teachings of the prophets and suggested that leaders of religious thinking no longer "held the old mechanical theories with their medieval ideas" about a vengeful God and a sinful humanity. Jesus Christ, he contended, died to reconcile man to God, and not God to man, because men were capable of understanding His mind. As a result, Edmonds argued, the Kingdom of God on earth was a logical extension of Jesus' perfect example.[56]

When Edmonds was attacked, Newfield immediately came to his aid. On October 22, 1915, before the meeting that led to the formation of the Independent Presbyterian, he received a letter from Sydney J. Bowie, a fellow Quid Pro Quo member and a parishioner of Edmonds's church, which stated:

> The friends of Dr. Edmonds will meet tonight at eight o'clock for the purpose of organizing a new church. While they are not taking official action, it seems to be the universal desire that our first meetings should be held in the Temple Emanu-El and, if possible, that they should continue to be held there until we can make some other definite arrangement.

Edmonds, in *A Parson's Notebook,* relates that Newfield, the next morning, came to proffer his temple for Edmonds's use, "beginning immediately and continuing as long as was convenient to us, without money and without price. . . . The Sunday morning two days following, we met in Temple Emanu-El."[57]

Less than a month later, on November 25, 1915, Newfield and Edmonds organized a civic Thanksgiving service, at the Lyric Theatre under the auspices of the Birmingham Chamber of Commerce. In writing the Thanksgiving message, these ministers indicated their desire to promote interfaith harmony:

> Thanksgiving Day . . . is the one religious day which can be and is celebrated by the three major faiths of our diversified population. Ours is a nation which in one fundamental respect is different from the nations of the Old World, in that it is founded in neither race nor creed, but rather in the adherence to a common principle. From the earliest beginning of our national history, it was our need and our privilege to unite all mankind to come and work together toward the building of a new world conceived in liber-

ty. . . . No occasion is perhaps better suited for remembering the debt which America owes to Jew, Catholic and Protestant.

Because there was no newspaper article written about the event, there is no record of the attendance of the meeting or the reaction of the participants. Still, the attitude toward Jews in this message differed from the one offered to Newfield by the largely evangelical Pastors Union quite strikingly.[58]

Because World War I delayed the building of Edmonds's new church, the congregation of the Independent Presbyterian remained a guest of Temple Emanu-El for seven years. Edmonds further relates:

> During that time there was not one ripple of disagreement or even of uncertainty in our association. We had the building on Mondays for our Women's Organizations, on Wednesdays for our midweek meetings, and on Sundays for our Sunday school and regular worship services. . . . the two families lived together, using the same kitchen and all the rest, and made out of the experience a song without discord. The more I think of it, the wonder grows. And the more I feel that Dr. Newfield was the guide, philosopher, friend, and fine gentleman who made it quite possible.

The two groups had their annual dinners together, too, an occurrence that continued long after 1922, when the congregation of the Independent Presbyterian moved into its own building.[59]

Newfield and Edmonds also developed a close friendship because Edmonds showed the Jewish rabbi that some Christians in Birmingham were open-minded in their appreciation of Jewish ethnicity. When Newfield invited Edmonds and his wife to a Passover meal, the minister applauded the custom. Newfield, in turn, helped Edmonds understand that Jews and Christians could share not only life experiences but their mission ideals too. Edmonds relates the story of his finding Newfield one day in the temple, on a ladder, helping with the Christmas decorations for the tree by placing the star. He continues, "I introduced Dr. Newfield once, as he was about to speak to a group of our young people, as the best Christian I knew. He responded by calling me the best Jew he knew."[60]

Newfield, claims Edmonds, also took the time to explain quietly to him that stereotypes of Jews as moneylenders and commercial exploiters were not true. Instead of losing his patience with Edmonds, who may have retained some of the same stereotypes about Jews that evangelical Christians did, the rabbi later brought forth the results of a survey of *Fortune Magazine* and showed Edmonds that only one Jewish firm was prominent in national banking and that Christians, and not Jews, owned a majority of Hollywood, the automobile industries, and the steel industry. Only one line of manufacturing, he further insisted, "is controlled by Jews—the garment industry."[61]

The rabbi also suggested to his friend, as he had to evangelical Christians, that Jews had been forced by Christians into trade and away from farming. He told Edmonds:

> I admit that Jews are clannish. But again, that has been forced upon us. The one thing that we have desired above all others, is to be men among men. But we are denied entrance to many hotels . . . , to schools and colleges . . . , to marry a Christian. You say that we are clannish. Yet you have locked us up in ghettos and have descended upon us in bloody pogroms. How could we avoid being clannish?

He also rationalized the "noisy and self-assertive qualities" of Jews in speaking to Edmonds: "You pressed us down for centuries and then received us in this messianic land, where we have freedom. How could the ignorant and the newcomer among us escape some regrettable strutting up and down, some childish exhibitionism?" Perhaps Newfield's gift to Edmonds was his acceptance when the minister needed reassurance that he had friends. Together they learned that there were many theological roads toward the goal of an ethical society and that differences did not preclude respect.[62]

Newfield also became friends with Middleton S. Barnwell, the Episcopal minister of the Church of the Advent, who lived in Birmingham from 1913 to 1924. Barnwell shared Newfield's and Edmonds's belief that the sphere of religious activity was often both nonsectarian and societally based. As a result, Barnwell often worked with the other two ministers in his roles as county chairman of the Red Cross, in the Liberty Loan drives during World War I, in the organization of the Jefferson County Children's Aid Society, and as head of the Associated Charities. The *Birmingham Ledger* once wrote of him, "In the large field of usefulness in which he is engaged, his habits and personality exercise themselves potentially for the common good irrespective of creed or religion."[63]

In 1922 Barnwell was invited by Newfield to join the Quid Pro Quo Club. Barnwell's reply to the rabbi reflects both Barnwell's difficulties as a Social Gospel minister in Birmingham and his respect and affection for the rabbi:

> My dear Dr. Newfield,
>
> I have been thinking deeply concerning the invitation you extended to me the other day, and have been increasingly conscious of the affection and confidence which I know lie beyond it. Nevertheless, I think I must decline.
>
> As a matter of fact, I am far from a permanency in this field. Whether I stay in Alabama or not depends entirely on the outcome of the Council which meets in July for the purpose of electing a Bishop Coadjutor. If Bishop Beckwith succeeds in imposing his will upon the Diocese again . . . , I shall leave Alabama. I am not willing to spend the rest of my life breaking my head against a stone wall. . . . I think the two men in the city for whom I feel the deepest affection and greatest respect are Mr. Robert Jemison [a real estate broker, and a member of his parish], and yourself, and in my heart, you are his full equal. . . .
>
> You are the very first person in Birmingham to whom I have spoken my mind. . . . But I had to write you frankly.

Barnwell and Newfield both knew that the former was "breaking his head against a stone wall" because the Episcopal Diocese of Alabama was not favorably disposed to many of his outside activities, choosing rather to take an apolitical position on many of the public issues in Birmingham. As a result, Barnwell, in the course of his ministry, was forced to resign from fifteen of the seventeen civic organizations to which he belonged.[64]

IV Morris Newfield's theology, then, was shaped by four forces: his training in Reform Judaism with Isaac Mayer Wise at Hebrew Union College and subsequently his sensitivity to the needs of his congregants, who wanted to integrate their religion into their daily lives; his awareness of the mixed feelings which southern Christians held toward Jews; and his knowledge of the theological developments occurring in more progressive Christian churches that resulted in a Social Gospel movement.

The first two of these forces provided the basis for his feeling that Jews could be loyal Americans and also maintain their existence as a distinct religious group, the third sharpened his awareness of difficulties that Jews faced in Birmingham, Alabama, while the fourth helped him realize that Jews were allies with southern Christians in a quest for peaceful coexistence.

To recognize the extent of Newfield's achievements in developing a theology that not only helped Jews rationalize their group solidarity but also allowed them to feel comfortable about living with southern Christians, who often expressed mixed feelings about them, is to understand two very different ideas about the rabbi as an emerging ethnic leader. First, he had personally matured, changing from a transplanted Hungarian who had come to America with goals of financial security and a leadership role in a Jewish community into a man who was now sensitive to the needs of his entire community, both Jewish and Christian, in Birmingham. Second, in a period of continuing transition, as Birmingham moved from a frontier town into a complex metropolis and experienced the confusion of changing cultural standards, Newfield and others like him, the Social Gospel theologians, were agents of change. Armed with ideals but also with coping mechanisms that allowed them to persist in the face of both opposition and the social timidity that they noticed around them, they looked positively to a future liberal ecumenical society where men could be respected for their deeds and not despised because of their ethnic differences. Although he was not accepted fully on account of his Jewish background, or for his progressive hopes, he had become a representative ethnic leader in Birmingham.

FIVE

A Leading Social Worker in Alabama, 1909–1940

As Morris Newfield grew older and more established in Birmingham, he became involved in social welfare activities, hoping to translate his Social Gospel theology into practical efforts. Taught by his teachers at Hebrew Union College that his religious activities should in part focus on the problems of society, and assisted by Christian ministers like Edmonds and Barnwell who shared this belief, Newfield after 1909 participated in relief efforts in Birmingham and also in activities to aid children on the local, state, and national levels. The rabbi's career, then, can be used as a case study of social welfare efforts that occurred in Birmingham and in Alabama during the first four decades of the twentieth century.[1]

Social workers and historians who have written about social welfare efforts in Birmingham in this period have emphasized their private scope and elitist nature. Bessie Brooks, a co-worker of Newfield's in the Red Cross Family Service, identified the agencies that dealt with needy people in Birmingham and suggested that charity efforts were, in the main, privately funded. The Red Cross Family Service Agency that acted as the primary relief-giving body from 1925 to 1932 was largely funded by private donations through the Community Chest because there was no local department of public welfare at this time in Birmingham.

Only after 1933 did the city, county, and state governments unwillingly make provisions for poor families when they were forced by federal requirements to be eligible for public money. Anita Van DeVoort, a student of this period, concluded that private agencies and large corporations like the Tennessee Coal, Iron, and Railroad Company met the needs of poor families because the city, county, and state governments were lax in providing support. The research of Brooks and Van DeVoort, however, has not explained the reasons why public assistance was not readily available until 1932.[2]

Edward S. LaMonte has suggested that the concept of "privatism" explains why relief efforts were largely private in Birmingham until 1932. "Privatism," a term coined by Sam Bass Warner, Jr., is "the assumption that government should meet the demands of business and industry, attempt to provide services inexpensively to all neighborhoods of the city, and recognize that the business of the city . . . [is] business." More simply, city fathers were afraid that corporations would not develop businesses in Birmingham if they had to pay heavy taxes to support needy people. Before 1915 the prevailing assumptions were that "welfare was not a major responsibility of local government, and that the private sector would render most services necessary to cope with the perceived needs of the poor"; after 1915, attempts were made to develop public assistance programs, but local government services proved inadequate, still giving private activity the widest possible latitude.[3]

LaMonte also asserted that private relief efforts were elitist in nature. After analyzing the backgrounds of the directors of the Community Chest and its member agencies after 1923, he suggested that the leaders were primarily middle- to upper-class businessmen who were neither able nor eager to understand the viewpoints of the needier groups in Birmingham, such as blacks and unorganized labor.[4]

Students of this period, however, do not know much about the thoughts and actions of those leaders who sat on the boards or staffed the private welfare agencies in Birmingham or about those individuals who assisted in the sphere of child care activities or in the professionalization of social work in this region. A broader understanding of some of these efforts can be gained by studying closely the interests and motivations of Morris Newfield, who was one of the key leaders.[5]

SOCIAL WORKER

I An understanding of the nature of Newfield's personal motivations may help explain why he chose a secondary career as a social worker. Simply, the rabbi cared for others, and so part of his concern may be termed "altruistic." Similarly, Newfield may have chosen to develop a career in social work because he believed that it would enhance his career as an ethnic leader in Birmingham. A possible explanation for this choice lies in the idea of social work or "service to others." The rabbi may have believed that first generation Jews like himself could effect important leadership roles in Birmingham more easily through humanitarian efforts than through aggressive business careers. As has been shown, Fundamentalist Christians feared Jewish business successes and, as a result, often looked askance at Jews in their midst. But they also respected Jews as "people of the book" and expected them to serve humanity.

In Newfield's time, there were examples of southern rabbis who left their careers in the ministry to pursue other professional opportunities. Elliot Grafman of Tampa became a lawyer in 1930, while B. C. Ehrenreich of Montgomery became a camp director in Wisconsin. Newfield's path was different. Rather than leave the rabbinate, he built another career of service on the foundations of his eminence in the Jewish community and his stature as a religious leader.[6]

Another explanation for Newfield's decision to pursue his interest in social work may be a desire to emulate other rabbis in the American Jewish community. Although he came to Birmingham in 1895, he did not become involved in social welfare efforts until 1909. In that year, he helped develop the Associated Charities, a federative movement designed to bring rationality and stability to private relief efforts. His initial participation came at the same time that the Central Conference of American Rabbis (CCAR) formally opposed child labor.

Leonard Mervis, in a perceptive essay entitled "The Social Justice Movement and the American Reform Rabbi," suggests that

Reform rabbis, with the exception of Emil Hirsch of Chicago and Stephen S. Wise of New York, did not throw their energies into social ameliorative efforts until 1909. Previously, Mervis notes, they had not been prepared to confront immediate problems, choosing rather an approach based on the Pittsburgh Platform of 1885 that represented "a philosophical attitude rather than a dynamic call to action."[7]

The coincidence of the dates of Newfield's participation with the CCAR proposal is interesting and suggests that the rabbi was moved to act because other rabbis had begun to do so. We should not, however, overlook the progression of Newfield's rabbinical career. By 1909, he had established himself in the Jewish community and may have been ready, as were other rabbis of his generation, such as David Marx of Atlanta and Emil Leipziger of New Orleans, to pursue other interests.

Perhaps the impetus of Christian ministers in Birmingham encouraged him too. Mervis further suggests that Reform rabbis waited until 1908, a year after the Federal Council of Churches of Christ formally adopted a social creed, to take a stand against child labor. Although an older generation of Reform rabbis had claimed in the Pittsburgh Platform that Jews had a mission to promote social justice, they faced congregations of businessmen who wanted acceptance from Christians. Hence they were not eager to agitate for social change and, as a result, risk earning disfavor from the host society.[8]

Newfield had read about the work of Edgar Gardner Murphy, who founded the Alabama Child Labor Committee in 1900 and the National Child Labor Committee in 1904 from his pulpit at St. John's Episcopal Church in Montgomery, Alabama. Murphy, a Texan by birth, came to Montgomery in the same year that Newfield moved to Birmingham. Once settled in Montgomery, Murphy organized the first Conference on Race Relations in 1900 and the subsequent child labor committees. Although Murphy did not share the belief of liberal reformers that men were basically good, or that they had the capacity to create benevolent environments, he nevertheless believed, as did his liberal counterparts at the turn of the twentieth century, that institutions shaped man's character, and that by changing institutions, human actions and thoughts could be changed. More simply, fate, and not human ability, played a large role in Murphy's thought.

Murphy believed, however, that he should undertake efforts to improve working conditions of children employed in the cotton mills. With the formation of the Alabama Child Labor Committee, he attracted Alabama leaders such as John Herbert Phillips (the superintendent of the Birmingham Public Schools) to his cause. By 1903 he had persuaded the Alabama legislature, with the help of B. B. Comer, an influential mill owner and gubernatorial aspirant, to support a child labor bill. It prohibited the employment of children under twelve except those with widowed mothers or dependent fathers. A year later, in April 1904, he became the secretary of the National Child Labor Committee, and in 1907 Murphy directed the Alabama Child Labor Committee in their successful efforts to obtain a more stringent Child Labor Act. Under this legislation, all children under twelve were prohibited from working, and those under sixteen were prevented from doing night work.[9]

Although there is no record of any correspondence between the two men, Newfield's later participation on the Alabama Labor Committee indicates that he was aware of Murphy's efforts. For Morris Newfield, Edgar Gardner Murphy may also have been a model of a minister who did more than talk platitudes about social justice.

The influence of Newfield's father-in-law, Samuel Ullman, was probably also a reason for his involvement in social work. Although Ullman was much more outspoken than his son-in-law, he probably showed the rabbi that idealistic Jews, who persisted on a day-to-day basis in the face of traditional attitudes about self-help and the supremacy of property rights, could accomplish social change. Ullman's success and failures may have convinced Newfield that he could ameliorate the social order in a slow but steady fashion.

Newfield's associations with the other members of the Quid Pro Quo Club also gave a paternalistic flavor to his social work. Because the club consisted of conservative lawyers such as Sydney J. Bowie, Henry Upson Sims, and James Weatherly, and

Phillips, an educator who was not egalitarian in thought, it provided an environment for discussions of stewardship and of improvements in, but not substantial change of, the social order in Birmingham.

As a result of Newfield's personal motivations, a picture of a man who sought to extend his influence as an ethnic leader in Birmingham, and perhaps as a Reform rabbi in America, slowly emerges. But Newfield was also a socially concerned individual who believed that Jews and Christians would listen to his ideas about improving society because he was a minister. Comforted by cues given Murphy and other Christian ministers, the rabbi believed that Jews could take a far more active role in pursuing social justice than they could by simply preaching from comfortable pulpits.

Newfield, like Murphy and Phillips, two of his fellow reformers, may have believed that he, as a responsible professional, had a right to lead society. Newfield often used the concept of noblesse oblige; as a man concerned with justice, he would pursue the ideal of truth, defined as a rigid, unbending loyalty to the betterment of mankind. Newfield was not a "democrat" in the sense that he believed that the masses could govern themselves but rather a steward who felt that he could help create a more progressive society.

Newfield and others like him in the Quid Pro Quo Club were also not particularly emotional or warm public men. Rather they were principled individuals in the vanguard of their times. Reform to them meant neither seriously upsetting the established canons of the capitalistic society nor transcending the social mores of their day. Newfield, Murphy, Phillips, and other leaders were committed to the idea that they had inherited a world which, in the main, was good, but had to be reshaped to conform to their ideals of rational improvement for mankind. As a consequence, they, and not the rabble-rousers, had to lead because they alone were conservators of past ideals and harbingers of future progress.

II Morris Newfield first became involved in social welfare efforts in 1909 by helping to develop the Associated Charities. His efforts at that time were significant for two reasons. On the one hand, he agreed to help organize private relief efforts, although he had refused two years earlier to serve on the Board of Education because he did not believe in mixing church and state. On the other hand, the rabbi believed that private relief efforts in Birmingham were needed because he knew that the city, county, and state governments were not implementing publicly funded programs to help needy people.

Although he was a close personal friend of John Herbert Phillips and the son-in-law of Samuel Ullman, both of whom were heavily involved in educational reform efforts, he passed up a chance to join the Board of Education in 1907. He was afraid that his service would establish a sectarian influence in an area that he wanted to keep separate. In a letter to his wife on September 26, 1907, he made his reasons clear:

> Just had a long chat with Dr. Phillips. . . . You may have noticed that Ben Jacobs is now a member. I had him elected to that office, foregoing the honor myself. It was offered to me by . . . Parker [John, one of the city's leading aldermen], who assured me of a practically unanimous election if I would accept. While I appreciated the honor offered, I nevertheless would not accept—I was afraid that once one minister would get on the board, the way would be opened to other ministers in the School Board—which I consider dangerous to the welfare of our schools. You understand what I mean.

Newfield refused to serve on the board because he feared that once a minister was elected, evangelical Christians would try to dominate the Board of Education.[10]

Since Morris Newfield understood that private agencies bore most of the brunt of relief support, he lent aid to efforts to help needy citizens in Birmingham. The rabbi knew that public assistance was minimal even though legislation had been enacted as early as 1803 in the Alabama Territory which obligated each county to care for its poor. He had also read that another state law of 1883 had specifically directed counties to budget annually for the care of its poor citizens. Before 1909, however, the only relief that the Jefferson County government offered was an unspecified amount of support for an almshouse. Although the city government had provided cash subsidies or "outdoor relief" to needy people at various times, by 1897 the city commission, realizing that it had not developed any supervisory procedures to investigate cases or the outlay of cash, refused to distribute any more cash for relief and simply directed black and white paupers to the county almshouse.[11]

As a consequence, between 1883 and 1909, most of the relief work was organized and implemented by agencies such as the United Charities of Birmingham, founded in 1883 by Mr. and Mrs. W. T. Underwood, the brother and sister-in-law of the future senator from Alabama, Oscar W. Underwood. Other private institutions included the Mercy Home for orphans, Hillman and St. Vincent's hospitals, and the Boy's Industrial School.[12]

Rabbi Newfield agreed to help when a group of businessmen and ministers decided in 1909 to reorganize the United Charities, believing operations to be often unreliable and haphazard because it was a private charity. They also knew it had failed to cooperate with other social agencies in Birmingham. On March 23 and 24, 1909, Newfield and other community leaders, including Phillips, William Henry Sims, and George Eaves, a Congregational minister, started their work. In a letter to his wife, the rabbi indicated that the leaders were primarily businessmen and that the newly developed "Central Council, consisting of two delegates from each of the philanthropic organizations of the city," would bring order to relief efforts in Birmingham. When the Associated Charities was incorporated in 1910, the individuals who signed the papers included Robert Jemison, Sr., a real estate developer, and two Jews, M. V. Joseph, the department store owner, and Samuel Ullman.[13]

The Associated Charities launched various activities such as milk stations, work rooms, and day nurseries for the needy. Since there was no public-supported health clinic, a trained nurse was secured to visit the homes of sick clients. With the help of two doctors, R. M. Cunningham and Thomas D. Parke, the charities also established a committee for the study and prevention of infant mortality.[14]

Although the Associated Charities was directed mainly by businessmen, and the scale of charitable activity increased significantly, it failed to raise large amounts of money. During one month in 1911, the Board of Directors tried to secure $12,000 and collected only $5,000. During the recession of 1914–1915, the Associated Charities was forced to close its woodyard, where men could earn lodging and food.[15]

Consequently, Newfield and other directors of the Associated Charities and a public commission of 159 business and religious leaders, on which the rabbi and a few of his congregants also served, urged that the city take responsibility for supporting relief efforts. They favored local government action for two reasons: the charities had incurred a $10,000 debt with little hope of paying it off through private donations; and the business leaders were tired of the inconveniences of unsuccessful charity drives.[16]

In 1916, the Birmingham Social Workers Club, which had been founded in 1901, and which Newfield had joined in 1913, made a separate study and suggested that the county and the city assume responsibility for the debt and provide services for the destitute using tax funds. But their plan was not followed because the city, unable to extract county funds for the care of the needy, established the City Department of Relief and Correction, with the stated purpose of eliminating the inefficient system of private charity.[17]

As LaMonte has so ably shown, the services provided by the private welfare agencies by 1917 were not adequate in many cases. Both poor whites and blacks found no stable institutions offering health and welfare services. Private donations simply could not sustain the services needed, especially in times of economic recession such as 1914–1915.

Significantly, when the city accepted the responsibility of caring for its needy in 1917, the new head of the Department of Relief, Walter Brown, was not a professionally trained social worker but a Congregational minister in Birmingham. Until the third decade of the twentieth century relief efforts were often managed by nonprofessional social workers because there were very few trained workers in Birmingham and in the South. As a consequence, there were many opportunities for humanitarians like Brown and Morris Newfield to become involved not only by sitting on the boards of the private agencies but also by participating in the day-to-day operations of both private and public agencies.[18]

The activities of the City Department of Relief and Correction consisted of giving relief in the form of cash payments, developing a sewing department that was run by clients, and operating the Pisgah Welfare Home, a residential facility which housed and served meals to needy individuals. The department's services, however, were terribly inadequate. In one year, it spent $8,000 for relief, which was less than the Associated Charities spent. The department also issued relief in such a haphazard fashion that it "sank into a sea of almsgiving."[19]

Owing to the department's mediocre performance, the League of Women Voters, with the help of the state Child Welfare Department and the Jefferson County Red Cross, made a survey of existing welfare institutions in Birmingham in 1921. The league found that the Department of Relief was poorly organized, that case and worker supervision was inadequate, and that the Pisgah Home, which housed people with all types of problems, was a health hazard where inmates were thrown together without supervision, work, or recreation of any kind.[20]

It is difficult to explain why the department was so poorly organized, because their records were destroyed in a fire at City Hall in 1925. One reason for the department's failure, however, might be the strongly negative attitudes of the public and their leaders toward subsidizing needy people. Not many people wanted to establish a welfare department in 1914, and fewer wished to maintain it adequately after 1916. Corporation leaders who had given little to private relief efforts before 1915 paid out even less money in taxes because their corporate taxes were very low. The League of Women Voters thus suggested in 1921, despite its awareness of the poor showing made by the Associated Charities before 1916, that private charities be encouraged to provide funding for relief institutions. The women recommended to the city that businessmen organize a Community Chest to raise funds in a systematic fashion for welfare work.

Newfield's involvement in many successful private relief activities, which were connected with his membership in the Associated Charities, can explain the recommendation of the League of Women Voters. The rabbi helped develop and maintain two agencies, the Anti-Tuberculosis Society and the Jefferson County Red Cross, which offered valuable services even though they suffered from a lack of community support.

In 1910, Newfield was one of the founders of the Anti-Tuberculosis Society, whose purpose was to study and prevent tuberculosis in Jefferson County. Led by George Eaves, a Congregational minister who had survived the disease himself, the Anti-Tuberculosis Society and its twenty-four-man board of directors included Newfield, M. V. Joseph, Samuel Ullman, John L. Kaul, a lumber company executive, and Thomas D. Parke, the latter two being Quid Pro Quo members. In 1911, they organized the first successful Christmas Seal campaign to collect money for victims of the "white plague." A year later, they developed the first TB "camp" in Alabama, on land donated by the city of Birmingham. Although the camp's beginnings were meager—it started with only four surplus army tents and no running water—in the next few years it expanded to forty patients on a hillside retreat. In 1915 the camp erected its first building, and soon after, five more were added with Christmas Seal funds.[21]

By 1916, the Tuberculosis Society, as one of the few agencies that dealt with both blacks and whites, opened a fresh air school that served children as a preventive measure and also built a sanitarium for blacks as a supplement to the mountain camp. More than 1,200 persons were reached by the society's various programs that year. The organization was commended at that time by the city health officer, R. M. Cunningham, who said that the society was responsible for a reduction of the tuberculosis death during the past five and a half years of from 108/100,000 among whites to 74/100,000, and from 519/100,000 among blacks to 360/100,000.[22]

Newfield also helped form the Alabama Anti-Tuberculosis League in 1914. Although many of the league's records no longer exist, we can speculate that Morris Newfield was highly respected for his part in the league's efforts throughout Alabama, because he was elected to serve as its president from 1919 to 1921. In this capacity he worked very closely with the state health officer, Samuel Welch, who wanted to develop a local health unit in every county, to make the Tuberculosis League's preventive efforts a part of the county's health activities.[23]

Thanks to the successful work of the Jefferson County and Alabama anti-tuberculosis leagues, the privately funded sanitarium in Birmingham waged a spectacular campaign to treat victims and to educate citizens about tuberculosis. By 1920, the Birmingham Board of Revenue, with no public institution for the treatment of tuberculosis, had contracted with the Anti-Tuberculosis Society for the care of indigent tubercular patients. As was the case with its Department of Relief, the city of Birmingham found it cheaper and, as a result, more advantageous to depend on the work of a successful private agency led by ministers than to develop its own public institution.[24]

A third private relief agency in which Newfield was actively involved was the Birmingham Red Cross. It was founded in February 1909, was formally organized in April 1910, and was chartered by the national organization seven years later. As was true for the Associated Charities and the Anti-Tuberculosis Society, the Red Cross leadership in the first decade consisted of businessmen and clergymen, including Richard Massey, president of the Massey Business Colleges, Robert Jemison, Jr., Paschal G. Shook, a coal and iron company executive, Middleton S. Barnwell, Henry M. Edmonds, and Newfield. Mary Parke, wife of Thomas D. Parke, was credited with its original development.

In 1911 the Red Cross chapter worked closely with the local tuberculosis society to sell Christmas Seals and collected $2,730 under the leadership of John L. Kaul. By Christmas, 1917, sixty-six Red Cross branches and fifty-five auxiliaries had been established throughout Jefferson County. In the same year, George Eaves, secretary of the Anti-Tuberculosis Society, organized the Civilian Relief Committee through the auspices of the Red Cross and initially used the staff of the Anti-Tuberculosis Society for this effort. Its function was to provide help to indigent Birminghamians and their families. Significantly, this committee was managed by the Red Cross's first professionally trained social worker, Mrs. Moore.[25]

Newfield was a charter member of the Jefferson County Chapter in 1917 and from its beginning to 1934 acted as chairman of

Robert Jemison, Jr.,
a real estate developer, worked with Newfield
on the board of the Community Chest
in the 1920s and 1930s.
(Birmingham Public Library / Department of Archives)

the Home Service Committee whose responsibility was to assist returning veterans. In late 1919, he and the executive secretary of the committee, Miss Shields, were supervising more than 2,000 cases a month. By 1921, Newfield was taking a leading role in the chapter's work: he helped more than 10,000 men, including students and transients, secure treatment from the publicly assisted Veteran's Bureau; he investigated the free milk system in Birmingham and subsequently cooperated with the city nurses in organizing a well-managed program; and he was responsible for hiring Fanny M. Blynd, a professionally trained social worker, to manage the Civilian Relief Committee.[26]

After analyzing Morris Newfield's three relief efforts in Birmingham from 1909 to 1921, we can see that the relief agencies were financed primarily by private funds and were managed largely by "nonprofessionals" or humanitarians such as Newfield. Even in the six-year period 1916–1921, when the city halfheartedly accepted its responsibility to care for its needy citizens, the Department of Relief and Correction was run by a minister.

III The city's assumption of the care of its needy citizens in 1916 was supposed to augur a new era in Birmingham. Instead, after five years, social workers found public efforts clearly wanting. The conservative climate brought with it a reluctance to support public programs for the needy, and the Department of Relief faced continued management failures. As a result social workers and businessmen, believing that they had to develop another method of providing relief for indigent citizens, once again turned to private agencies. They developed a Community Chest in Jefferson County with the purpose of raising money for various individual agencies, thus eliminating their numerous drives, duplication of effort, and haphazard and ineffective management.[27]

By 1923, the relief situation in Birmingham was in a terrible state, as a number of public and private organizations worked desperately to solve relief problems with few resources at hand. Birmingham was in poor financial condition. The City Department of Relief and Corrections had no funds for food, fuel, or clothing. The private agencies tried to help. The Salvation Army looked after the occasional needs of a small number of poor families. The United Jewish Charities, founded in 1915, with Morris Newfield as its first president, helped poor Jewish families, while the Red Cross Civilian Relief Corps, under Fanny Blynd, handled the cases of poor Birmingham families.

One of the first responsibilities of the Community Chest in 1923 was to decide whether to take over the functions of the Department of Relief, to permit the city to abolish its department completely, and once again put the burden of relief on private donations. Although Morris Newfield did not speak directly to the issue at the Board of Directors' meeting of the Community Chest, he was irritated at the overlapping efforts of the Department of Relief and the Red Cross. As early as 1922, Newfield had complained that the city was not doing its fair share and was causing Fanny Blynd's Civilian Relief Committee to assume too much responsibility. He did, however, understand that the city's resources were extremely limited, and he suggested that the Red Cross find an alternative to reliance on the city for care of indigent citizens.[28]

By December 24, 1924, the Community Chest had agreed to undertake the burden of caring for Birmingham's poor. The city commissioners were even allowed to say in the *Birmingham News* that relief was not meant to be a public responsibility and that the Community Chest could now handle fund raising. Mary Echols, commissioner of Health and Education in Birmingham, claimed, "It has been our intention to relinquish welfare work at City Hall to the Community Chest. . . . The voluntary contributions have made it unnecessary to burden the taxpayer."[29]

As a result of the Community Chest's agreement with the city, the Department of Relief and Correction was officially taken from the city budget on January 1, 1925. Fanny Blynd, the secretary of the local chapter of the Red Cross, was appointed to organize the Family Relief Department to care for white and black needy citizens. Jewish families, however, were cared for by the newly organized Federation of Jewish Charities. As one of twenty-six members of the Board of Directors, Newfield agreed to organize relief activities on a private basis for five years, with the stipulation that in 1930 relief efforts would be transferred to the city and the county on joint public welfare basis.[30]

According to the record of the Jefferson County Red Cross, Fanny Blynd, Morris Newfield, and Henry Upson Sims agreed on January 30, 1925, to formulate the organization's policy concerning relief work. Within a week, they had proposed a budget of $34,600, $22,600 greater than the amount that the Red Cross had received in 1923 from the Community Chest. They agreed to help all families and single women, resident and transient, but the care of single men they left to the Salvation Army. A year later, Newfield was also granted permission to extend the Red Cross relief efforts by accepting tubercular patients who could not receive help from the Jefferson County Sanitarium because of crowded conditions.[31]

By September 1926 the rabbi was working closely with Roberta Morgan, another professional social worker who had been appointed secretary of the Red Cross when Fanny Blynd became ill. In the next two years industrial conditions worsened in Birmingham. On February 21, 1928, Newfield was elected chairman of the Advisory Case Committee, which was responsible for aiding the trained and untrained caseworkers in solving the most difficult relief case problems and for helping the community understand the problems in order to obtain more financial support. Newfield served as a liaison between the Community Chest and the Red Cross Family Service, informing businessmen of the caseworkers' needs.[32]

We might say that Newfield's personality assisted him in developing a significant role in the Red Cross relief work. Although Morris Newfield was not a professionally trained worker, his willingness to operate prudently probably won him the respect of those social workers like Blynd and Morgan, who had been educated in social work schools. Second, because he was a respected clergyman in Birmingham, he secured a good deal of money from businessmen for welfare projects.

By 1930, when the Red Cross Family Service was supposed to have transferred its caseload back to the city and county governments, the city was still unable to undertake its financial responsibilities, and the county refused to do so. Under a 1917 ordinance, the county did not have to subsidize private agencies and chose not to support the Red Cross.[33]

Since public money was not forthcoming, Morgan, Newfield,

and other Red Cross leaders had to work diligently to obtain further private support. Morgan continued to encourage businesses such as the Tennessee Coal, Iron, and Railroad Company not to lay off workers, and Newfield pleaded with the city for funding. Finally, by the winter of 1930–1931, the city commissioners had agreed to give the Red Cross Family Service $1,000 a month. The Red Cross hired six temporary untrained caseworkers to handle the relief load. Newfield, trying desperately to devise plans that would help poor citizens, supported the establishment of a placement bureau in the fall of 1931 that would find jobs for unemployed white-collar workers, and in June 1932 proposed spending $1,000 to plant vegetables on vacant lots so that families in Birmingham could eat.[34]

The Red Cross simply needed more public funds to provide adequate relief services. Although the Community Chest offered its $84,000 in normal relief money and collected an extra $200,000 in emergency relief drives for 1932, the caseload of the Red Cross Family Service had increased from 6,139 in December 1931 to 18,282 a year later, of which 16,626 were receiving relief. When the Emergency Fund of $200,000 was exhausted in March 1932, enabling legislation allowed the city and county to contribute $55,000 to the Red Cross Family Service. In August 1932, the Reconstruction Finance Corporation (RFC) also lent $75,000 a month to the city and the county for relief payments.[35]

That the Community Chest, a private group of responsible businessmen and religious leaders, and its relief agency, the Red Cross Family Service, were deemed the most stable agencies for dispatching relief payments, became clear in August 1932, when the Reconstruction Finance Corporation made Harry Early, as director of the Chest, the disbursing officer and administered the funds through the Red Cross. As Bessie Brooks argued in 1936, the Red Cross had become virtually a local government department because the city and the county had been largely unable to share in the assumption of relief efforts.[36]

More significantly, relief efforts became almost 95 percent publicly funded by 1933 only because the federal government was now willing to expand its services. The records of both the Community Chest and the Red Cross indicate that the city and county

Roberta Morgan was secretary
of the Birmingham Red Cross from 1926
to 1933 and later in the 1940s.
(Birmingham Public Library / Department of Archives)

Mervyn Sterne was head of the
Community Chest campaign in 1932 and was a
leader of the Birmingham Jewish community.
(Birmingham Public Library / Department of Archives)

governments were quite willing to have the Chest shoulder the relief load until it was clear that private sources had been exhausted. Even then, the state government was unsympathetic. On August 1, 1932, for example, Governor Benjamin M. Miller refused to borrow RFC funds for local relief in Birmingham against state highway revenues because he believed that local relief officials were exaggerating local needs.[37]

The Red Cross finally retired from the relief business after 1933 only because Harry Hopkins's Federal Emergency Relief Administration informed its state directors that public officials had to administer federal funds. As a consequence, Harry J. Early, as director of the Community Chest, submitted a proposal for a countywide Department of Public Welfare. This department, he indicated, would be governed by a commission of five who would be responsible for expenditures of both local public tax funds and the state and federal funds available under the Federal Emergency Relief Act of 1933. Because Roberta Morgan and her staff were so well acquainted with the relief problems, she became director of the countywide department, and the Red Cross Family Service, stripped of its name, furnished the personnel of the department. Most important, this smooth transition once again illustrated the effectiveness with which the Red Cross functioned as a quasi-public institution when there were no public models from which to draw.[38]

After the Red Cross had been released from its responsibility of supporting relief efforts in 1933, Rabbi Newfield was free to undertake a number of different jobs. From 1934 to 1936, he served as president of the Red Cross, discharging its traditional responsibilities. In this capacity, he raised funds for disaster relief and continued to look after the needs of former servicemen who were hurt when the Birmingham office of the Veterans' Administration closed. At this time, the Red Cross assumed responsibility for 350 cases.[39]

The rabbi did not choose to become a member of the five-man advisory board of the Department of Public Welfare because of his duties as president of the Central Conference of American Rabbis. As a result, Mervyn Sterne, one of his closest Jewish friends and co-workers on the Chest, was chosen. Sterne, an investment banker and a partner of former mayor George B. Ward, had been responsible in 1932 for raising the largest amount of money ever secured during a Community Chest drive.[40]

After 1933 the Community Chest also supported charities of a character-building nature, such as the Boy Scouts. Although its efforts were limited to these activities, Newfield believed that the Chest still had a responsibility as a privately funded federation to help needy citizens. From January to August 1936, as a close friend of Roberta Morgan, he not only supported her complaints against Governor Bibb Graves and Commissioner Jimmy Jones, who refused to allocate more state and local funds for relief, but also suggested in Chest meetings that the Chest operate as an advisory board to implement further private relief efforts. On three separate occasions, he criticized other Chest members because they did not want to take an interest in relief concerns, feeling that the Chest should wash its hands of the problem.[41]

Newfield also supported the ambitions of professional social workers to have more influence on the policymaking decisions of the Chest. In 1938 they asked for funds to organize a formal council as a functioning part of the Chest. The request was denied. In the face of obvious board hostility, the Birmingham Social Workers Club withdrew its proposal in 1938 and instead formed the Jefferson County Coordinating Council of Social Forces. Although Newfield was at this time ill and could not join the council, he supported the move as a member of the Social Workers Club. The council lacked staff, money, and a formal relationship to the Chest. It could therefore only recommend changes in programs to the Chest director and was virtually ignored when it did so.[42]

Since 1909 Newfield had pursued a role as a nonprofessional social worker, operating as a liaison between the professional social work community and the business elites who served on the Chest advisory boards. Newfield both respected professionally trained workers like Fanny Blynd and Roberta Morgan and also understood the businessmen's desires for decision-making power.

The rabbi's work indicates that some of the leaders of the Community Chest tried to bridge the gap between the business community and the professionals in order to develop successful privately funded relief efforts. As I have noted, he and Fanny Blynd worked together in 1921 to develop an adequate Civilian Relief Corps when the city Department of Relief and Correction proved unable to discharge its responsibilities. In 1925 he worked with Blynd and Roberta Morgan to develop a Family Service agency to provide relief when the city would not do so. In 1933 he helped Morgan, Early, and the Chest develop a countywide Department of Public Welfare to take advantage of federally sponsored relief monies for depression-ravaged Birmingham. In 1936 he supported Morgan when she left her job because of Governor Graves's and Commissioner Jones's refusals to pay for relief efforts, and he also reminded the Chest of its continuing responsibilities in the relief field. In 1938, too, he supported social workers when they suggested that they, as well as businessmen, should have some say in policy decisions regarding privately funded social programs in Birmingham.[43]

IV In addition to his work as liaison between the business and social work communities in relief activities, Newfield assumed a role in child care efforts that was more complex. On the one hand, he continued to act as a liaison between businessmen and social workers when he helped develop the Jefferson County and Alabama Children's Aid Societies. Both were privately funded agencies involved in finding homes for children. On the other hand, because the state of Alabama had made and honored a commitment to helping dependent and delinquent children, Newfield helped initiate two types of publicly funded programs. He assisted trained social workers in improving child labor laws in Alabama, and he helped establish ameliorative institutions such as the Juvenile Court in Birmingham in 1911 and the state Department of Child Welfare in 1919 to carry out the dictates of those laws.

As I have indicated, sometime after 1900, Newfield joined Edgar Gardner Murphy's Alabama Child Labor Committee. At the same time, he lectured his congregation on the evils of child labor. In a sermon, he concluded:

> For more than 30 years, there have been occasional warnings of the great increase in child labor, but . . . few people realized the extent of this evil. The figures of 1900 showed that there were 1,750,000 children or namely one to every six children. . . . This number did not include the thousands of children under ten years of age who are engaged. . . . The new industrial activity of the South had to contend with the short-sighted policy which claims that to meet modern industrial conditions, it is necessary to harness the child to the machine.

Newfield also told his congregation in 1904 about the history of child labor reform efforts. In 1887, Alabama's first Child Labor Act had been passed, restricting the activities of children under twelve, but it was repealed in 1895 by the state legislature, which acceded to the demands of a Massachusetts textile firm that wanted to relocate. Eight years later, Edgar Gardner Murphy, with the support of B. B. Comer, a Birmingham textile mill owner and gubernatorial aspirant, secured a second child labor law in 1903. It forbade children under ten from working and limited the number of hours for which children under twelve could do so. Newfield also claimed that in that fight the Alabama Child Labor Committee had to face not only the southern mill owners but also "the tremendous opposition of Northern capitalists whose funds were invested in the mills of our state." Similarly, the committee had to overcome the complaints of Alabama businessmen about interstate competition, for a law setting high standards for Alabama would have damaged the ability of Alabama mills to compete with mills in Georgia, where there was no state law.[44]

As a consequence of the stiff opposition to the Alabama Child Labor Law, Murphy organized the National Child Labor Committee in 1904. According to Newfield it had a twofold purpose. It sought not only to convince the American people that child labor was a "crime against the child and against society" and to interest legislatures in the passing of perfunctory laws against child labor but also to develop support for private agencies that would care for children. To what extent Newfield was actually involved in the efforts of the Alabama and National Child Labor Committees before 1914 is not known. In 1915, however, he was appointed by Governor Emmet O'Neal to be a delegate from Alabama to the meeting of the National Child Labor Committee in Washington.[45]

1911 was an important year in the development of child welfare efforts in Birmingham. In the week March 9–13, 1911, the seventh annual proceedings of the National Child Labor Committee were held in Birmingham. Leading figures in the movement, such as Jane Addams, Florence Kelley, Felix Adler, and Theodore Roosevelt, addressed the meetings about the necessity of developing further legislation to prevent child labor before the age of sixteen. Judge N. B. Feagin of the police court, a moving force behind the development of the juvenile court in Birmingham in 1911, was the opening speaker. Although Morris Newfield did not deliver a speech, he and most of the leading welfare workers of the Associated Charities and the Alabama Child Labor Committee were present.[46]

Five weeks later, on April 22, 1911, the first juvenile court in Birmingham was established by the state legislature. It was the result of efforts made by Birmingham social workers such as Rabbi Newfield, Nellie K. Murdock, Patty Ruffner Jacobs, and Mrs. James Weatherly, all of whom sat on the Advisory Board of Directors. Governor Emmet O'Neal appointed Samuel D. Murphy, a twenty-eight-year-old lawyer. Judge Murphy would remain in that position until his death in 1939.[47]

The development of the juvenile court was the culmination of fifteen years of effort both to understand and to ameliorate the lot of juvenile delinquents in Birmingham. In 1896, Judge Feagin of the Police Court, convinced that society should attempt to understand the problems of adolescents rather than just to penalize them for crimes, began remanding young offenders to the Boys' Club rather than committing them to the penitentiary. The Court of County Commissioners on May 1, 1896, also agreed to provide $500 toward building and repairing a reformatory for youthful offenders, but the plan was never carried out because the facility which was to be used as a reformatory was needed as a city jail. As a result, juvenile prisoners were confined in separate cells of the jail until the state Boys' Industrial School, supported by public money, was established.[48]

In the first decade of the twentieth century, efforts continued in the state legislature and through private agencies to help youthful offenders. The first juvenile court law was enacted in Alabama in 1907 but was repealed a short time later, for reasons which are not clear. The repealing act, however, was later declared unconstitutional by the state supreme court, so that the original statute remained in full force. Reflecting the view that the state is the ultimate parent, the law provided that when for any reason a child was not being properly cared for, protected, or disciplined, the court would have jurisdiction and the duty of offering such protection, care, and discipline. It served as the basis for the act of 1911, which established separate juvenile courts in all counties in Alabama of 200,000 or more, and provided that the probate court of other counties should act as the juvenile court for the separate hearing and detention of juvenile offenders.[49]

The support of social workers such as Newfield and Nellie K. Murdock was significant because they acted to secure private funding for the work of the juvenile court when it was clear that the city and county subsidies of $350 a month would not be enough money. On February 21, 1913, the incorporation articles of the Jefferson County Children's Aid Society stated that the first duties of the agency were to "relieve the Boys' Club and Juvenile Court of certain functions that have hitherto been assumed by these agencies." Newfield and the other directors raised funds to operate the detention home of the juvenile court, then called the Receiving Home of the Children's Aid Society and furnished volunteer probation officers as well as money to hire other salaried persons, including Ralph Barrow, who as superintendent of the Children's Aid Society also acted as chief probation officer of the juvenile court during these early years. Funds for this purpose were raised by "Tag Day" donations, which established one particular day a year when volunteers would raise money for the care of juvenile delinquents.[50]

In 1913, Newfield, Eaves, and Edmonds also revived the Alabama Sociological Congress to provide a forum for discussions of important issues such as where to develop child care services and how to secure further child labor legislation. From 1913 to 1921 Newfield served as the president of the Alabama Sociological Congress.[51]

The rabbi also participated in some of the meetings of the Southern Sociological Congress, which gave social workers trained and untrained, black and white, and of every religious background an opportunity to discuss social problems that they considered significant for the South, including child labor issues. The congress met every year from 1912 to 1921 in a southern city. Although Newfield never read a paper at the annual meetings, in 1918 he was elected vice-president of this congress when it met in Birmingham, and he helped develop a platform to help children and other groups.[52]

In 1917 Morris Newfield, as president of the Alabama Sociological Congress, helped develop the Alabama Children's Aid Society, whose object was to support local child welfare work in Alabama by assisting the probate courts in the smaller communities in placing homeless children in foster homes. Members of the Board of Directors of this society were selected from all over the state, on the basis of demonstrated ability to raise funds. They included Newfield, Edmonds, Nellie K. Murdock, Judge Murphy, and Frank P. Glass, publisher of the *Birmingham News,* like Newfield a member of Quid Pro Quo. In 1919 an article in the *Birmingham News* reported:

> An announcement of much interest has just been made to the effect that four very prominent Alabamians have pledged themselves to tour the state in the interest of Alabama's children. These men, Dr. Middleton S. Barnwell, Dr. Henry M. Edmonds, Judge Samuel D. Murphy, and Rabbi Morris Newfield, have donated their services to the people all over the state . . . in connection with the campaign undertaken by the [Alabama Children's Aid] Society to raise $30,000 to carry on its endeavors. . . . Dr. Newfield and Judge Murphy will cover the principal towns in Central and Southern Alabama. . . . The Society is supported entirely by voluntary contributions and . . . has helped hundreds of homeless babies to find permanent, happy homes. The work is not confined to infants alone, but dependent, despairing childhood of all ages.

The four men were dubbed the Flying Squadron. They spoke primarily to Kiwanis and Rotary Clubs to raise money for child care services.[53]

Newfield's efforts were not, however, limited to soliciting funds for the Jefferson County and Alabama children's aid societies. As a member of the Birmingham Social Workers Club and as president of the Alabama Sociological Congress, he lobbied in Montgomery to influence state legislators to pass the more restrictive Child Labor Law of 1915. It provided for the inspection and regulation of establishments employing children under eighteen and entrusted the enforcement of the law to the state prison inspector. The rabbi wanted the state to revise and extend the existing juvenile court legislation. In 1915, in part as a consequence of Newfield's activities, a new juvenile court law was passed, entitling not only delinquents but any child for "any other reason" to the care and protection of the state. As a companion law to this legislation, the state legislature enacted the Uniform Desertion and Non-Support Law of 1915, which gave probate courts in all counties, and the Juvenile Courts in Jefferson and Mobile counties, jurisdiction in desertion and nonsupport cases. Social workers fought for these two laws because they felt that these courts should deal with the problems of adults whose lives and actions affected children. As a result, the state legislature created a domestic relations court in Birmingham, which was made a part of the existing juvenile court system, and Newfield sat on its board. In 1923, the Jefferson County Juvenile and Domestic Relations Court was divided into two divisions with the same board, but with different judges. Murphy was the juvenile court judge and Virginia Mayfield served the court of domestic relations. The courts, however, were combined again in 1927, with Murphy serving both sections.[54]

By 1916 Newfield and other individuals interested in child welfare efforts were faced with the problem of developing a state-supported Children's Bureau to cooperate with the county juvenile and probate courts and their advisory boards, the state Education Department, the state Health Department, and the state factory inspectors in the enforcement of the newly established laws for neglected and dependent children. Judge Murphy and his advisory board of the juvenile court in Birmingham contacted Julia Lathrop of the Children's Bureau in Washington and asked her to recommend a trained social worker who could conduct a survey of the existing child welfare agencies in Alabama and could find local support for a state Department of Child Welfare. Evaline Belden, a special agent of the Children's Bureau, was commissioned to work with Murphy and his board and with other reformers throughout Alabama.[55]

As a consequence of Belden's work, the efforts of Newfield and other social workers in the Alabama Sociological Congress, and the willingness of the state legislature to develop programs to help children, the first state Child Welfare Department act was passed in 1919. It provided for a publicly funded Department of Child Welfare. The department's functions were to organize and supervise county child welfare boards, to train and license probation officers and county child welfare superintendents, to enforce the state Child Labor Law of 1915, to license and supervise maternity hospitals, boardinghouses, and child care institutions, and to provide guardianship for dependent children who needed foster homes. In addition, the Department of Child Welfare was to work jointly with the state Department of Education to enforce the first compulsory school attendance law, which was passed in 1919.[56]

Although he never served as one of the members of the state Child Welfare Commission, Newfield continued to act as a resourceful member of the Birmingham community to whom members of the commission, including Murphy and Nellie K. Murdock, could turn for help in developing programs to implement the laws. As president of the Alabama Sociological Congress from 1913 to 1927, and also as a member of the Alabama Children's Aid Society, he worked closely with Mrs. L. B. Bush, the director of the Child Welfare Department, to merge the Alabama Children's Aid Society and the Department of Child Welfare in 1922 when their home-finding services overlapped.[57]

Through the first three decades of the twentieth century, Newfield also helped social workers in Alabama define standards for their profession. Because he was the head of various social workers' conferences and was involved on a day-to-day basis in the Red Cross, the Anti-Tuberculosis League, and the Community

Chest in Birmingham, he was preoccupied with improving social welfare efforts. At the first meeting of the Alabama Conference of Social Work in 1921, President Newfield brought in Frank J. Bruno, a professor of sociology at Washington University in St. Louis and a leading figure in the National Conference of Social Work, to hold a three-day seminar in casework methods. At that same meeting, Julia Lathrop and Judge Ben Lindsay of Denver, the nation's leading juvenile court judge, also spoke on the organization of child welfare efforts. A year later, Newfield asked Jane Addams to speak on child care efforts.[58]

Newfield's work, however, indicates that this particular group of social workers was interested in institutional reform as well as in developing professional discipline. As a member of the Alabama Conference of Social Workers, Newfield wrote in 1923: "The main object of the meeting is to bring together the social workers of the State and those interested in the social welfare of the people between the two halves of our legislative session, in order that we may formulate and promote the progressive measures needed to improve the conditions of the people." Morris Newfield successfully marshaled support for the projects of trained social workers in his position not only as a well-regarded minister but also as an experienced untrained social worker. He helped develop both social reform legislation and the profession of social work in Alabama.[59]

V Morris Newfield's activities are significant because they help define the nature of social work in Alabama in the period 1909–1940. Newfield was interested in helping needy citizens as well as in developing both ameliorative and preventive solutions for the problems of children in Birmingham and in Alabama. He understood that politicians in the local and state governments viewed poor people and children differently. Because they refused in many instances to do more than provide minimal help to needy citizens, and as a result relied heavily on privately funded relief agencies, Rabbi Newfield raised money for relief agencies and promoted the improvement of casework methods in the agencies that he served.

Nevertheless, officials in state and local governments were willing to honor their commitments to Alabama's children through legislation and ameliorative efforts. Newfield's role therefore became more complex. He not only raised money for the Jefferson County and Alabama children's aid societies but also served on advisory boards of public institutions such as the juvenile court. As president of the Alabama Sociological Congress and the Alabama Conference of Social Work, Newfield worked for social reform and also served as an agent of transition in the development of the social work profession. In 1910, many of the child care and relief efforts were organized by ministers such as Edgar Gardner Murphy, George Eaves, and Newfield, but during the two following decades, Newfield worked with people who added professional training to his experience.

The rabbi brought to these efforts an altruistic concern for people who needed help from their communities before there were publicly funded programs of assistance. In doing so, he also extended his role as an ethnic leader. He believed that Jews could serve useful roles in this second helping profession. As a consequence, he became not only a Jewish leader in Birmingham but one of the leaders in the greater Alabama community.

SIX

A Moderate in Times of Reactive and Radical Change, 1920–1940

On a summer day in 1921, nearly three years after the armistice ending World War I had been signed, Morris Newfield met his friend Thomas D. Parke on a downtown street. The rabbi listened to Parke angrily denounce the increasingly violent atmosphere of Birmingham. Parke was concerned about the growing violence of labor and about the Ku Klux Klan. The month before, C. S. Cooley and Kate Alexander had been flogged for being too friendly to blacks. Only six months earlier, on January 27–28, 1921, the city had witnessed the first public initiation ceremony in the Klan's history, and Parke wondered whether Southerners could adjust to the demands of the twentieth-century industrial society.[1]

Parke and Newfield were members of a growing number of Birminghamians who were concerned about the nativist reaction against modernization and the growing enmity between capital and labor, tensions that were particularly virulent following World War I in Birmingham and in the South. They had witnessed the introduction of Fundamentalist influence in the political process after 1910, the rebirth of the Klan in Georgia in 1915 and in Alabama two years later, and violent strikes in the coalfields that were informed by economic and racial tensions.

These extreme tensions were intensified by the impressive

growth of Birmingham. The population swelled from 34,415 in 1900 to 178,806 two decades later. It had been a "pushy bragging busy little town with a northern and western flavor . . . completely alien to the quiet little hamlets that lay just over the mountain." By 1920, however, many of these "quiet" little hamlets were rapidly expanding suburbs of a metropolitan community. Moreover, the business of Birmingham in the 1920s was undeniably business. The intersection of First Avenue and Twentieth Street was billed as "the South's most developed downtown corner." It manifested the influence of a diverse, business-oriented middle class of small businessmen, industrialists, journalists, promoters, and professional men whose power went unquestioned. Through the Chamber of Commerce, the Business Men's League, the Merchants' and Manufacturers' Association, the Civitan Club, and a dozen other clubs and societies this business-minded class substantially determined the city's priorities for the decade.[2] The specters of the Klan, labor organizers, and the Chamber of Commerce vying for influence in this period, as George B. Tindall, Virginia V. Hamilton, Robert P. Ingalls, and Blaine A. Brownell have noted, suggest not only that Birmingham continued to be torn between past and future, between Old South and New, and between rural and urban values but also that none of these groups was totally effective in leading the city out of its period of transition.[3]

Rabbi Morris Newfield and other ministers offered a different kind of leadership in a time fraught with anxieties. He and they continued to stress the idea of noblesse oblige and promoted ameliorative change in various social, economic, and religious spheres, believing that men of every background could live together fruitfully and harmoniously. I have already discussed some of his feelings in the chapter on his social welfare activities. I shall now consider the range of his other social, economic, and religious activities in the decades between the wars.

As in the previous decades, Newfield recognized the need to distinguish between the issues which he could confront publicly and those that required him to be more circumspect. On the one hand, at a time when the prestige of the Klan was at its highest, Newfield, Edmonds, Father Eugene L. Sands, Reverend Charles

Monsignor Eugene L. Sands
worked with Morris Newfield to encourage
people of different faiths to respect
and cooperate with each other.
(Birmingham Public Library / Department of Archives)

Clingman, and other ministers spoke openly about their religious differences and their disagreements with the Klan to audiences throughout Alabama, hoping to combat the forces of prejudice that were causing people of different faiths to distrust rather than to rely on each other. In 1928 these men founded the Birmingham chapter of the National Conference of Christians and Jews.[4]

On the other hand, there were issues on which the rabbi felt compelled to move very carefully. In postwar Birmingham, strikes occurred in the coalfields in 1921, threatening the economic foundation of the city. Because many of the striking miners were black, racial tensions were intensified. This problem and the subsequent predicament of the Scottsboro Boys in the 1930s forced Newfield to develop solutions that would reiterate his commitment to social justice without threatening the achievements of Birmingham Jews or his mediating role as an ethnic leader in Birmingham.

I Family tradition holds that although Morris Newfield hated war, he served as a part-time chaplain in World War I at Camp McClellan in nearby Anniston, Alabama, because he loved the United States. In 1915 he fulminated against war to his congregation: "Jane Addams pointed out a decade ago that the greatest anti-militant speech ever made was that of Israel. We dare not forget that our acceptance of Israel as a prophet implies that we are one of the army of peace and irrevocably committed to the cause of international peace and justice." Although he believed that Jews should be men of peace, Newfield wanted to prove to Christians in Birmingham that Jews were patriotic, and so he agreed to serve at Camp McClellan. He served on a biweekly basis as the agent of the Jewish Welfare Board, giving support to Jewish servicemen preparing for war. He also raised money in Birmingham and in other parts of Alabama for the American Jewish Relief Committee, whose purpose was to aid the foreign Jewish victims of the war. The rabbi evidently worked diligently at his task, because he received a number of letters from Henry Morgenthau, chairman of the American Jewish Relief Committee, and from Harry Cutler, chairman of the Jewish Welfare Board, congratulating him on his efforts.[5]

During World War I
Morris Newfield served as part-time chaplain
at Camp McClellan in Anniston, Alabama.
(Birmingham Public Library / Department of Archives)

Despite his initial antipathy toward the idea of war, Newfield hoped that the peace conference at Versailles would create a peaceful federation of nations in postwar Europe. In 1918 he said, "The Congress of Peace now assembling is the first indication that the vision of Israel is to be fulfilled. . . . This Congress is different from any like body that ever met. . . . Something definite is to result from the League of Nations." Much to the rabbi's chagrin, his dream of a League of Nations turned to ashes when the U.S. Senate refused to ratify the Versailles Treaty in 1919 and the United States, as a result, did not take a more active role in the affairs of Europe.[6]

When World War I ended and Newfield had completed his stint as a part-time army chaplain, he found that his efforts had further improved his stature in his community. He began working hard in various relief and child care activities while also serving his flourishing temple. Chester G. Bandman had done an excellent job of substituting for Newfield when the rabbi was not in Birmingham. In 1919, Temple Emanu-El had 295 members and a total congregation of close to a thousand people. The income of the temple was $12,500 a year. Emanu-El's population represented approximately one-tenth of the 11,000 Jews in Birmingham.[7]

Some of Newfield's congregants had attained prominent positions in Birmingham. Two of the city's most successful lawyers were Jewish, Monte Ullman, the son of Samuel Ullman and Newfield's brother-in-law, and A. Leo Oberdorfer. Ullman, who had served as city attorney during the administration of Commissioner George B. Ward, developed an extensive private practice with Ben Leader, his partner, before his death in 1930. Oberdorfer, a Virginia native, began practicing law in Birmingham in 1901 and four years later wrote *Oberdorfer's Alabama Justice Practice,* which was used in the Alabama law schools as late as 1964. In 1928–1929, he served as president of the Birmingham Bar Association, and from 1933–1934 he was president of the Alabama Bar Association.[8]

Jews did very well in business, too. The department stores of Pizitz, Loveman, Joseph, and Loeb, and The Parisian Company, operated by the Hess and Holiner families, were successful enterprises. Joseph Loveman served as president of the Kiwanis Club and on the board of directors of the Birmingham Housing Authority, the Community Chest, and the Birmingham Symphony. Milton Fies, a cousin of Morris Newfield's by marriage, was a vice-president of the DeBardeleben Coal Company and was recognized as a leading engineer not only in Alabama but also throughout the South. Mervyn H. Sterne, as noted earlier, was another of Birmingham's influential civic leaders, as was Chester G. Bandman, the assistant superintendent of the Emanu-El Sunday school, who developed a very prestigious career in the Birmingham public schools.[9]

Morris Newfield remained firmly in control of his congregation, with his close friends Moses V. Joseph, Leo K. Steiner, and Elias Gusfield serving as officers of the Board of Directors. The rabbi's control increased with the various honors that he received from his temple. In January 1919, he was a member of the Temple Committee to change the constitution and by-laws of Emanu-El, a position that had not been open to him twenty years before. Six months later, on June 16, 1919, the rabbi was reelected for the eighth time, and for his fourth five-year period, at $6,000 a year. Nine months later, his salary was raised to $7,500 a year.[10]

On September 29, 1920, the rabbi was honored by his congregation and friends in celebration of the twenty-fifth anniversary of his ministry in Birmingham. It "proved one of the happiest social events ever given in our city . . . , in which the members of the Temple were joined by large numbers of non-members, and addresses were made by Moses V. Joseph, President of the Congregation; Simon Klotz, on behalf of the Board of 25 years ago; Ben Leader, representing the Board of 1920; and also by John Herbert Phillips, Henry M. Edmonds, and Rev. J. A. Bryan of the Third Presbyterian Church and the oldest clergyman in the city in length of service."[11]

Newfield received notes of congratulation as well from individuals who could not attend, including Rabbis Stephen S. Wise, David Marx, Max Heller, Emil W. Leipziger, David Philipson, Edward N. Calisch, Henry Englander, and Gotthard Deutsch and also from his Christian friends Middleton S. Barnwell, George H. Denny, president of the University of Alabama, J. E. Dillard, pastor of the Southside Baptist Church, Victor H. Hanson, publisher of the *Birmingham News,* and Judge Samuel D. Murphy of the Birmingham Juvenile Court.[12]

Both Hanson's and Murphy's letters indicated their personal and professional affection for Newfield. Hanson wrote, "Dr. Newfield is one of Birmingham's finest citizens. I have the greatest admiration for him as a man, for his breadth of view, his kindly, sympathetic attitude toward all things that look to the best interests of the community whether they are fostered by Jews or Gentiles." Murphy remarked:

> I wish to pay tribute to Dr. Newfield as the head of one of our great religious organizations; as a leader in all of the Civic and Philanthropic movements which are making for the betterment of the city—and of our entire state, and lastly as a man. I wish to thank him for the "beckoning on" to higher things which I have felt by reason of the warmth and loyalty of his friendship—which I shall ever prize.[13]

In 1924, Morris Newfield was awarded his highest honor from Temple Emanu-El when the Board of Directors elected him minister for life. This event was not an unusual occurrence in congregations throughout the country who wanted to make sure that their rabbi would remain with them. In 1899 the position was conferred on Emil G. Hirsch at Chicago Sinai Temple for this reason. The *Birmingham News* observed:

> In all probability, it had come to be a needless formality in the case of their beloved preacher. Perhaps some members of the congregation had come to regard that half-decade as a tie binding the minister to the congregation—a tie which might perchance be broken one of these days by the demands of some other congregation somewhere. . . . At any rate, after his conspicuous service of twenty-nine years for Temple Emanu-El, the congregation deemed it the part of love and wisdom and appreciation to "grapple him to their souls with hooks of steel."[14]

Two years later, the congregation published a humorous pamphlet commemorating the twenty-fifth anniversary of the marriage of Morris and Leah Newfield. Its editorial comments included the following: "Picture section left out after editor had looked over the old prints and recalled the fact that this was to be a happy occasion" and "Milton Fies, friend and relative, has been intimately associated with the couple of honor. . . . After two or three years, Milton, so he says, adopted the habit of congratulating Morris on the 'new arrival' every time he saw him. . . . Milton admits he has been wrong only three times in twenty years."[15]

There were other honors for the rabbi as well. Because of his participation in the campaigns of the United Jewish Relief Society from 1915 to 1922, Mervyn Sterne paid him homage at the beginning of their campaign in 1926.

> Those of you who have not worked with Dr. Newfield do not know what a many-sided man he is. You know him as a minister, perhaps as a teacher. . . . You don't know how readily he can solve a difficult problem in a simple matter. When the United Jewish Relief solicited me for State Chairman in Alabama, a totally inexperienced man, it was to Dr. Newfield that I looked for advice and assistance, and it was given and given readily, and with energy and ability, and when the campaign in Alabama shall have been written a success—as it will be—it will be to Dr. Newfield more than to any other man, that it owes success.[16]

Throughout the 1920s, Newfield developed a good working relationship with President George H. Denny of the University of Alabama. In 1921 the rabbi was awarded an honorary doctorate by the university. In 1929 he worked with Leo K. Steiner to secure funding for the University of Alabama from the Guggenheim Foundation for the organization of a department of aeronautical engineering (the university's request was not granted).[17]

Julian Morgenstern, president of Hebrew Union College and a close friend of Newfield's, asked him to spend the summer at the college advising young rabbis on the protocol problems of the rabbinate. Morgenstern wrote:

> May I suggest that what I believe would be most valuable would be if you base your lectures . . . upon the fact that your experience has fallen in a city of middle size, in which yours is the only Reform congregation, and is likewise recognized as the leading

> congregation of the State, so that your influence and that of your congregation has reached far beyond the confines of your city and given you a position somewhat similar to that of, shall I say, a Jewish bishop in that state.

A month later, in March 1931, Newfield helped other rabbis in Alabama, including Alfred Moses of Mobile, Albert Meyer of Selma, and Simon Wampold, president of Montgomery Beth Or, organize an Alabama state conference to promote cooperative efforts in Jewish activities in Alabama. Newfield led a symposium entitled "The University and the Jewish Student," in which his son, Mayer, then a law student at the University of Alabama, also spoke. After the meeting, the rabbi was approached by Harold Hirsch, chairman of the Southeastern Conference of the Union of American Hebrew Congregations, who wanted him to raise money to develop a Hillel Foundation with a separate rabbi at Tuscaloosa, the seat of the university. Despite Newfield's efforts, however, he could not raise enough money for a rabbi at the university.[18]

In 1932 Temple Emanu-El celebrated the fiftieth anniversary of its founding. The temple's membership consisted of 400 families. In the commemorative service that took place on October 20, 1932, rabbis from other parts of Alabama spoke, including Benjamin Goldstein of Montgomery as well as Newfield's old friends David Marx and Henry M. Edmonds. Seven years later, Marx and Edmonds were again present when Temple Emanu-El celebrated the twenty-fifth anniversary of the dedication of the new building in 1914.

The years following World War I, then, were happy and rewarding ones for Newfield because of the honors that he received from his congregation as well as from other Jewish and Christian organizations. By 1932 he had not only secured a lifetime position as leader of Temple Emanu-El but was also considered one of the most influential southern rabbis.

II Birmingham in the twenties continued to be a city in transition. On October 26, 1921, when the city celebrated its fiftieth birthday, President Warren G. Harding was the toastmaster.

Mayer U. Newfield, a spectator in the crowd, remembers that his father urged him to "come and meet a President of the United States." Harding praised the city for its economic progress but also observed that the future of the country lay in the ability of whites and blacks to live together in harmony. The blacks in the audience cheered; the whites were stonily silent.[19]

In postwar Birmingham many people reacted quite differently to the idea that they could adjust comfortably to social changes. Conditions were not conducive to feelings of security. First, the city's economic fortunes were not as promising as business promoters had hoped they would be. On the one hand, the bottom had fallen out of the cotton market in Alabama when prices slid from 41.75 cents in the New Orleans market in April 1920 to 13.5 cents in December 1920. The drop angered southern farmers, who, as Tindall explains, lost their first opportunity since the Civil War "to accumulate capital and break the chain of . . . debt to merchants and cotton factors." The decline in cotton prices also hurt Birmingham because it caused unemployment in the cottonseed industry, one of the city's most important businesses. On the other hand, the iron and steel industry advanced only slightly in some areas during the decade and actually declined in others. The percentage of rolled iron and steel increased only slightly, while the production of pig iron declined, primarily because the U.S. Steel Corporation, which had acquired the Tennessee Coal, Iron, and Railway Company in 1907, ensured that its southern subsidiary did not expand at the expense of its northern plants. The industry established prices on the basis of "Pittsburgh Plus," which was the price of steel at Pittsburgh *plus* the rail freight cost from Pittsburgh to Birmingham. This provision nullified Birmingham's natural advantages for most of the decade.[20]

Second, although the business boosters formed the core of the city's social and economic elites during these decades, the industrial workers were numerically predominant, exceeding 106,000 in 1924, and their lot "was none too good." Largely unskilled rural natives, primarily black, and a heavy influx of Jews and Italians from Europe migrated to the city in search of industrial employment, toiling long hours for low wages that made southern industries competitive with those in the North. Many lived in company towns in the dingy industrial suburbs on the city's fringe, where housing and social conditions were often at best barely adequate. The Tennessee Coal, Iron, and Railroad Company had begun in 1907 a number of planned workers' communities that by the 1920s had nine schools for whites and fourteen for blacks. Even so, the plight of the working men in Birmingham was often serious.[21]

The coal miners faced terrible conditions in the Birmingham region. Most of them lived in company towns in poorly constructed homes, had to buy expensive food at company stores, and worked twelve to sixteen hours a day for low wages. Moreover, from the mid-1870s onward they had failed to secure adequate representation. The first attempt to organize the coal and iron workers into the Amalgamated Association of Iron and Steel Workers in 1877 had failed because the miners who walked off their jobs in 1882 were not rehired. The first great strike of Alabama coal miners failed in 1894, and the miners as a result were prevented from engaging in any union activities in the mines operated by Truman Aldrich's TCI Company. In 1898 John Mitchell's United Mine Workers organized the coal miners in Alabama, but they failed to gain recognition in a 1904 coal strike because Governor B. B. Comer, who had been sympathetic to child labor reforms, threatened to force the strikers to leave the area of the mines. In 1908, a second great coal strike occurred when the United Mine Workers again attempted to organize the miners. The union was defeated, and conditions in the mines did not improve. Low wages and continuous arbitrary treatment of workers continued.[22]

During World War I, the greed of coal operators continued. In 1917, because of the shortage of coal, miners in Alabama were threatened with reprisals if they joined the United Mine Workers and tried to strike. Although the UMW never received official recognition, the coal miners did participate in the national coal strike of November 1919. As the strike continued into 1920, 12,600 of the 27,000 coal miners, three-quarters of whom were black, left their jobs. Violence erupted between coal operators and the striking miners. Although it stopped when the miners agreed to submit their complaints for arbitration, Governor

Thomas E. Kilby, as arbitrator, ruled in favor of the mine operators on every point. Most of the 12,600 lost their jobs, and the United Mine Workers lost not only members but also $3 million.[23]

The convict lease system was also a thorn in the side of organized labor. Used by coal operators to provide cheap employment, the convict lease system forced convicts to work for long periods of time to serve sentences for petty crimes such as gambling and drunkenness. Construction of municipal projects often used nonunion men. Labor was also hurt by outrageous rents. The voice of organized labor, the *Labor Advocate,* the weekly organ of the Birmingham Trades Council, claimed that rents and city utilities were often high because of private ownership.[24]

The problems of organized labor partially resulted from the fact that many workers were black. Race relations between blacks and whites in Birmingham remained poor in the 1920s. Blacks accounted for 39.3 percent of the city's total population in 1920, and many whites tried to enforce segregated living patterns. The heart of the black community lay along Eighteenth Street, two blocks from the city's main downtown thoroughfares. Black neighborhoods were often situated in the city's vacant spaces along creekbeds, railroad lines, or alleys—areas of undeveloped land bypassed by industry and white homeowners—and they lacked street lights, paved streets, sewers, and other city services. The houses usually resembled the tattered and loosely constructed sharecropper cabins of the rural districts from which almost all the Negro settlers had come. In short, Birmingham's residential patterns reflected the southern caste system, with the zoning laws designed "to keep the negroes to certain districts." In fact, the city commission considered the petitions of white citizens who protested the construction of Negro housing contiguous to white neighborhoods. On at least one occasion the Zoning Commission revoked the permits of several of the contractors involved.[25]

Patterns of racial segregation even won out over economic prerogatives in business-minded Birmingham. In 1923, the city enacted a streetcar segregation ordinance against the wishes of the Chamber of Commerce and the traction company, which vigorously opposed the new ordinance because of the expense of the "Jim Crow" operation. Nevertheless, as Blaine Brownell has commented, "apparently there was no widespread resistance to the new ordinance."[26]

Most Birminghamians were struggling with the need to confront a vast array of problems arising from rapid urbanization. The addition of 150,000 people in only twenty years had produced a crisis in city services of all kinds. Birmingham was remiss in the matters of paving, sewerage, lighting, and police protection. Even the park system was inadequate.

Efforts were made to deal with the problems; new business and future economic resources for the city depended on improvements in the environment. Per capita municipal expenditures almost doubled in seven years, rising from $12.82 in 1921 to $22.91 in 1928. Outdoor toilets were eliminated, and air pollution ordinances were passed. Birmingham clearly failed to allocate sufficient resources in the 1920s in critical areas such as welfare relief, public health, and recreation, but as Brownell comments, the city was not unique. Urban leaders simply had not anticipated the increase in their responsibilities.[27]

As Virginia Van der Veer Hamilton has noted in *Alabama: A Bicentennial History*, the basis for many of the problems lay in the failure of the business community in Birmingham to provide far-sighted leadership.

> [Harding's] presidential gesture [in 1921] could not obscure the fact that Birmingham had not achieved its vaunted potential. It was still "the great workshop town" rather than the cosmopolitan metropolis of the working class, sparsely-educated, economically insecure, and racially-divided. . . . efforts by middle-level merchants, real estate agents, professional and independent businessmen to institute improvements, which might prove costly to the dominant railroads and industries invariably failed.

The most obvious sources of economic power in the community, the iron and steel manufacturing firms, led by TCI and Republic Steel and also including the Sloss-Sheffield Steel and Iron Company, the Woodward Iron Company, and the Ingalls Iron Workers, were largely located outside the city limits in areas like Ensley and Fairfield and were beyond the city's taxing authority.[28]

Although it is beyond the scope of this study to investigate further the influence of large business interests on political and social decisions made by local government officials in the 1920s, the point can be made that large business interests, even with their participation in the Community Chest, did not contribute enough to make Birmingham a stable and secure economic community. The business community seemed to lack a strong sense of noblesse oblige.

Disaster came at the end of the decade as spending by consumers was curtailed and capital investments by Birmingham industry ceased. Pig iron and steel piled up; mills and mines were closed; furnaces ceased operations; and 123,000 people in Jefferson County lost their jobs. As in many other communities throughout the United States, neither the local government officials nor the businessmen developed an effective plan to relieve the distress. For one entire decade these groups had failed to provide adequate community leadership.[29]

A different solution to this difficult period of transition during the 1920s and early 1930s was found by many Birminghamians. After 1916 they chose to refound the Ku Klux Klan. The original Klan had formed in December 1865, in Pulaski, Tennessee, when six former Confederate officers banded together to uphold the honor of the South in the face of the threat perceived to come from freed blacks. Conceived as a vigilante group, the Klan roamed the countryside trying to drive out carpetbaggers and to put Negroes in their "proper place." Inevitably, the character of the group changed. The "upper class" dropped out, and the poor and ignorant whites, who had the most to fear from economic competition with free blacks, dominated the Klan. As a result, Klan units often committed violent acts against blacks—floggings, tar and featherings, mutilations, and murders. By 1869, conditions were so bad that the Klan leader Nathan Bedford Forrest ordered the Klan disbanded and all of its records burned. Three years later, the Klan ceased to function because Reconstruction was ending. Nevertheless, myths and legends about the night riders persisted in the minds of some southern youths.[30]

In 1915, one young man, William Joseph Simmons, formerly of Harpersville, Alabama, founded the second Klan on Thanksgiving Day, 1915, at Stone Mountain, Georgia. The revived Klan was inspired by D. W. Griffith's film *The Birth of a Nation* and by the exaggerated nationalism associated with World War I. Increased concern about "moral laxity" and depressed economic conditions also added impetus. The Klan gained money, power, membership, and notoriety as a result of the rituals and violence that gave meaning and "patriotic" purpose to men who, for the most part, were either powerless bigots or amoral zealots. They felt that the sheet and the whip placed them at the right hand of an Old Testament God. The deity, like their authority, was of their own creation.[31]

The first Alabama chapter of the revived Klan, the Robert E. Lee Klan Number 1, was organized in Birmingham in 1916. According to David Chalmers in *Hooded Americanism: The History of the Ku Klux Klan,* Alabama first appeared in the records of the revived Klan when an organizer, sent to recruit Confederate veterans, absconded with his collections. The resulting court case was handled by an efficient young county prosecutor named Hugo Black, whose name was loosely associated with Klan affairs for the next ten years. Having picked up a few recruits during the war, the Klan expanded its activities after 1918 when it demanded greater police action against criminal elements in Birmingham. More significantly, the Klan in Sylacauga, outside Birmingham, began attacking Catholics and Jews, while the Birmingham Klavern reportedly pressed employers to fire their Roman Catholic workers.[32]

In January 1921, the Klan staged its first publicly witnessed initiation ceremony. Two people were flogged for being too friendly to blacks, and another incident shocked Birminghamians as well. Rev. James E. Coyle, pastor of Birmingham's largest Roman Catholic church, was murdered in front of his parishioners by an itinerant Methodist minister and Klan member named E. R. Stephenson. Coyle's offense was that he had married Stephenson's daughter to Pedro Gussman, a Puerto Rican Catholic. Hugo Black had defended Stephenson, pleading irresistible impulse, and a Klan-dominated jury had declared him innocent. In 1922, more than twenty victims were flogged and abused by Klan members, including the Catholic city health officer, J. M. Dowling, who had tried to force various dairy farmers, many of whom were Klan members, to clean up their barns.[33]

Although a number of "better citizens" in Birmingham protested the actions of the Klan and pressed for an antimask ordinance, very little was done to combat the Klan in 1922. Thomas D. Parke, Newfield's friend, wrote of the Klan attempt to influence the city commission's decision about the antimask law on June 7, 1922. "Yesterday afternoon, the City Commission refused to pass the ordinance gotten up by the Bar Association in collaboration with the City Attorney penalizing masked men parading our streets. The KKK had a large number of men from outside districts jamming the meeting hall and yelling and hooting the speakers against masking." Although the city commission passed an antikidnapping law, it refused to outlaw gatherings of masked men in public places. As a result, in September 1923, the Robert E. Lee Klan Number 1 staged a monster rally to celebrate its seventh anniversary. A city park was leased, and invitations were sent out across the South. An audience of nearly 20,000 Klansmen and twice that number of spectators watched the initiation of 2,000 new members, including Hugo Black.[34]

By 1926 the Klan claimed 18,000 members in Birmingham and 15,000 of the city's 32,000 registered voters. Most local, county, and state officeholders recognized that Klan support was necessary to win elections, and as a result, ambitious politicians either became Klansmen or were sympathizers. Sheriff T. J. Shirley was well known as a Klansman, and "at least two judges and more than a score of county and city officials were claimed by the organization."[35]

Oscar W. Underwood, one of Alabama's senators, hated the Klan, however, and waged unceasing warfare against it. Since he was so well respected, the Klan hesitated to tangle openly with him, at least until he had failed to gain the Democratic presidential nomination in 1924. Thereafter the Klan openly attacked him, and as a result he refused to run for reelection in 1927. Hugo Black, who courted Klan support, won Underwood's senate seat. The Klan also helped elect Bibb Graves as governor.[36]

In the mid-1920s the Klan had great influence not only on the political affairs of Birmingham but on other matters as well. According to Mayer Newfield, only his uncle Monte Ullman and a few other Jewish lawyers such as A. Leo Oberdorfer and Ben Leader could practice their trade before the Birmingham bar, because Klan-influenced judges often ruled against Jewish attorneys. Two able lawyers—Isadore Shapiro, who had been an alderman from 1909 to 1914, and Irving Engel—could not get favorable judgments in Jefferson County and went to New York City to practice their trade. In March 1925, the *Birmingham Post,* which strongly opposed the Klan, "was quick to deplore the apparent effort of the Ku Klux Klan to secure the appointment of a new school board member."[37]

At the same time, the Woodlawn Klan, on the east side of Birmingham, managed to gain control of school affairs in this district by forcing Chester Bandman, the Jewish principal of Woodlawn High and a close associate of Morris Newfield's, to resign from his position. Although Bandman was a highly respected educator in Birmingham, the Klan's objection to his religious convictions caused him to leave.[38]

According to James A. Head, a Birmingham businessman and later a founder of the National Conference of Christians and Jews, the Klan produced "an atmosphere of fear on the part of a great many people who might not have tolerated them otherwise. . . . We don't know how many men were run out of a shop . . . , how many women were intimidated . . . , how many people suffered harm because of their religion. . . . Some were afraid to make a complaint." As a consequence, some people left town, and Catholic children left the church "because religious prejudice was a socially accepted ideal."[39]

The close relationship between the Klan and the Fundamentalist churches should not be underestimated. The Pastors Union, flexing its muscles with the prohibition of Sunday movies, refused to take a public stand against the Klan, and a number of Christian ministers allowed the Klan to recruit in their churches. The Klan members, masked and robed in white, marched silently down the church aisles, presented ministers with money, and asked the congregants to join their organization. Some ministers, such as

Henry Edmonds, tried to forestall such activities by publicly announcing that they would not tolerate the Klan in their churches.[40]

The Klan reached the pinnacle of its success in Birmingham during 1925–1926. Within the next year, it began to lose its power for a number of reasons. Bibb Graves refused to support Grand Dragon James Easdale's appointment as an assistant attorney general in Alabama, while a number of courageous newspaper editors such as Victor Hanson of the *Birmingham Post* and Grover Cleveland Hall of the *Montgomery Advertiser* exposed the malicious deeds of the Klan. For his work Hall won a Pulitzer Prize. The flogging of a white youth from Blount County precipitated public outcries against the Klan.[41] Afterward Edmonds publicly challenged his parishioners to fight the Klan and "to do it in the open as Jesus did."[42]

In the spring of 1927, the state legislature passed a law making masked violence a felony, while judges became less reluctant to call grand juries and victims were willing to testify against the Klan. In 1928, Hugo Black deserted the Klan and supported Al Smith, the Catholic Democratic candidate, for president. By 1930, Benjamin M. Miller, the anti-Klan candidate for governor, was able to defeat his opponent, an event which marked the end of the Klan decade in Jefferson County and in Alabama.[43]

The Ku Klux Klan had succeeded for two reasons. It ostensibly protected Americanism, the Caucasian race, and the moral and religious tenets of Protestantism and continued the activities of the vociferous anti-Catholic, antiblack, antiunion "true Americans" who were politically successful during World War I in Birmingham. At the same time, however, the Klan activities represented a reaction to modernization in Birmingham. The preoccupations with purity and "true American" values suggested an inability to cope with the changing realities and cosmopolitan possibilities confronting Birmingham after 1920.

Doubts about the efficiency of moderate change were also expressed during the 1920s by the Communists. As Robert P. Ingalls has noted, the hard times that came after 1929 were accompanied by challenges to the status quo. Communist party organizers used Birmingham as a staging area for drives among local residents and sharecroppers farther south. In 1930 Communists started a newspaper called the *Southern Worker* in Birmingham, and affiliated groups, such as the International Labor Defense, established offices in the city. Despite its lack of political success, the Communist party made some headway both among the jobless and among workers in the mining and metal industries. By the mid-1930s it had several hundred members, mostly blacks, in the Birmingham area. The party's activities led the Ku Klux Klan to charge that "destroyers of American civilization" had turned Birmingham into "the hub of alien radicalism in Southeastern United States."[44]

When police action after 1934 failed to stop radical activities such as union organization, vigilantes resorted to physical attacks. As late as 1934, the Robert E. Lee Klan was still active, and Birmingham Klansmen attending a statewide convention were told, "The Klan will either run Communism out of the country or will itself be run out." The specter of blacks joining the Communists in an uprising against Southern folkways persuaded the vigilantes to foment attacks against both blacks and leftist sympathizers in the 1930s.[45]

Two manifestations of these attitudes occurred in the hysteria surrounding the trials of the Scottsboro Boys and the beatings of a Newfield family friend, the notorious union organizer Joseph S. Gelders. In 1931, nine black youths aged twelve to eighteen were accused of raping two white girls on a train near Scottsboro, Alabama, 100 miles from Birmingham. After their conviction in 1931, Judge James Edwin Horton, Jr., overturned the verdict in a second trial, suggesting that the original trial had been clearly prejudiced against the defendants. As a consequence of Horton's decision, he was defeated in his reelection attempt. The cause of the Scottsboro Boys was taken up by the International Labor Defense, and they were defended by Samuel Leibowitz, a New York Jewish lawyer. The combination of radicalism with black rights only further angered the reactionary groups, which were satisfied only when the nine youths went to prison. To some Alabamians justice was a secondary consideration.[46]

Gelders provided the vigilantes with yet another indication that "damned reds" and "nigger lovers" were to be feared and their ideas stamped out. Gelders, the southern representative of the National Committee for the Defense of Political Prisoners, an outspoken advocate of black equality and union activities, and a close friend of the Newfield family, was beaten on a number of occasions.[47]

Rabbi Newfield had known Joseph Gelders from his birth because the Newfields and Louis and Blanche Gelders, Joseph's parents, were best friends. When Gelders was young, the rabbi delighted in taking him to the Birmingham Barons' baseball games, especially when his family was vacationing during the summer. Gelders eventually earned a master's degree in physics from the University of Alabama and later joined the physics faculty. He married Esther Frank, who was related by marriage to Mervyn H. Sterne, another of Newfield's closest friends.

An idealistic young man, Gelders quickly became disgusted with the nativist activities of the Klan in Alabama. Whether or not he was a member of the Communist party is uncertain, but he had definite Marxist leanings. Despite the beatings, Gelders refused to stop working on behalf of black enfranchisement and labor organization. Hugo Black later called Joseph Gelders "the bravest man he had ever known."[48]

III In the period between the world wars, a time of continuing transition in Birmingham, Rabbi Morris Newfield's solutions were different from those of the Klan, labor organizers, and the Chamber of Commerce because of his highly developed sense of noblesse oblige. On the one hand, as I shall note later, Newfield's leadership, in its humanitarian impulse, departed from the views of many Birmingham businessmen, who had hoped that prosperity could "trickle down" to the masses, farmers and laborers all, without admitting that workers, farmers, and businessmen represented separate but equally legitimate economic interest groups whose needs had to be served. On the other hand, Newfield's leadership stance also reflected greater confidence in Birmingham's future than the Klan or the Communists could muster. A number of scholars claim that the Klan declined because many citizens tired of the fear and violence that the Klan's activities engendered in Birmingham. Morris Newfield may thus be seen as having countered the Klan's efforts when he elected to promote interfaith programs and to accentuate what the historian John Higham has called the "cosmopolitan ideals" of America.

Newfield's cosmopolitan stance was a shrewd position. The rabbi understood that he, as a member of a religious group that was one of the secondary targets of the Klan, could not publicly attack the Klan as his friend Henry M. Edmonds had done. Rather he could attack the psychological fears stemming from this period of transition by reaffirming his faith in a common humanity among religious groups in Birmingham. In the mid-1920s Morris Newfield joined with Eugene L. Sands, a Catholic priest and later monsignor, and Henry M. Edmonds to develop a program of interfaith forums to educate citizens of Birmingham and of Alabama regarding religious brotherhood. In doing so, Newfield and his friends, as James A. Head suggests, "tried to set an example as deeply devoted individuals who sensibly realized that there was a great deal more that we as Protestants, Catholics, and Jews all agreed on. Living in the same community, we needed to know about each other."[49]

This idea of an interfaith colloquium to combat the Klan in the 1920s was an outgrowth of the early cooperative efforts by Emanu-El's Jews and their Christian neighbors in Birmingham. As I have noted, Newfield was already working closely with ministers such as Edmonds, Barnwell, A. J. Dickinson, and E. C. McVoy of the Methodist Episcopal Church South, by speaking at their churches as well as by having them address Jewish services at his temple. McVoy, as early as March 5, 1914, had announced to his congregation that he had received a warm reception when Newfield's new temple opened.

> It was a peculiar pleasure to the Pastor to be present at the Fellowship Service of Temple Emanu-El last Sunday afternoon, and to bear to our Jewish friends a message of love and congratulation from the people of this church and congregation. . . . The Fellowship Service was delightful—Jews and Gentiles mingled together as brethren, which is as it should be. The Pastor shall not soon forget the cordial reception accorded him by Rabbi Newfield and the splendid people of his congregation. Let brotherly love continue. We are brethren.[50]

In 1920, in an editorial that he penned in the *Birmingham Age-Herald* entitled "The Claims of Religion," Newfield underscored his belief that religious institutions "have ever been social centers, places that make for brotherhood. They are the great hope of democracy, the most inclusive institutions found in society today whose aim is to break down barriers of caste, class, and conditions." Although he did not directly confront those individuals in Birmingham who, he sensed, were undermining his efforts to promote brotherhood, Newfield's message was clear: ministers had a responsibility to develop a society "for human betterment, to a desirable consummation." Moreover, Newfield's idea of a "desirable consummation" was not to restore Jewish or Christian group exclusivity, but to continue to work with Christian ministers so that each religious group in Birmingham could see worth in the others.[51]

In the 1920s and later, Temple Emanu-El continued to host brotherhood nights attended by Protestants, Catholics, and Jews. During one such meeting in 1930, at which Arthur Moore, pastor of the First Methodist Church, W. J. Pritchard, a Roman Catholic, Newfield, and other men were present, various resolutions were adopted: men had the inalienable right to practice their religion and to hold firmly to the tenets of their own faith; differences in faith were a matter of conscience between individuals and God, and therefore individual religions were entitled to universal respect; disagreements over fundamentals of respective faiths should not interfere with active cooperation in matters concerning the welfare of the community; and discrimination based on religious prejudice and intolerance not only violated the Constitution but also caused great peril to the country.[52]

Beginning in the late 1920s, Newfield, Sands, and Edmonds went on "barnstorming tours of the state to show that religions could get together." They lectured mostly on college campuses, but "they'd take invitations to any place." According to Henry M. Edmonds, "We talked about points of tension among the three great American faiths."[53]

Each of the interfaith forums followed a standard format. The three ministers delivered introductory talks and then asked each other questions to clarify issues for their audiences. Edmonds might ask Sands, "Is it true that Catholics regard marriages performed by Protestant and Jewish ministers and state authorities as null and void?" For his part, Newfield might ask Sands, "How do Catholics look upon intermarriage between Catholics and people of other faiths?" Sands would say to Edmonds, "What about the statement that this is a Protestant country and we ought to keep it so?" Edmonds would ask Newfield, "Is the charge true that all Jews are radicals and Communists?" or "What would you answer to the charge that Jews are clannish?" or "Why do Jews call themselves the Chosen People?" In discussing doctrinal and social matters, the three ministers sought to explode the stereotypes to which the heavily Protestant population of Birmingham and of Alabama often clung. Significantly, few explicit references were made to political and racial matters.[54]

The three men also noted the contributions made by each faith. "As a Protestant," Edmonds remarked, "I owe my faith to the churches of these two men." Newfield also acknowledged that his faith had a debt: "We are grateful to the Protestants for giving world circulation to our religion—we never would have done it. . . . We also thank them for founding a very great asylum for the Jew—we found our first freedom from oppression in America." Sands added, "The Catholics owe the Protestants many things. They also owe the man who stands here beside me a debt of gratitude for speaking out on their behalf when anti-Catholic feeling was running high in this community." Eating and speaking together, and discussing interfaith issues before college, Rotary, and Kiwanis audiences, the ministers demonstrated to Alabama that men of all faiths could be friends.[55]

Immediately following the elections of 1928, when the Catholic Al Smith lost the presidential election to the Protestant Herbert Hoover, the three clergymen led a colloquium at Mary Beard's Tea Room on Twentieth Street in Birmingham. Although Smith had narrowly carried Alabama in the election, Newfield and the other ministers felt that they had to contend with the nativist influences of the Fundamentalist preachers and the Klan. James A. Head later recalled, "This was almost like . . . enough is enough. We've got to find an answer in this community." From this meeting, under the leadership of the three ministers, the

Birmingham chapter of the National Conference of Christians and Jews was founded to develop a common ground between people of different faiths. A few months later Harry M. Ayers, an influential Anniston newspaper publisher, joined the group. Ayers, who had managed Thomas E. Kilby's successful gubernatorial campaign in 1918, had been a lieutenant colonel in the Alabama National Guard on Kilby's staff from 1919 to 1923 and was widely known throughout Alabama for his progressive activities. He was a member of the executive committee of the Alabama Citizens Advisory Educational Council and state School Board, a member of the National Conference of Editorial Writers, and president of the Alabama Press Association. Ayers was "deeply concerned with what was going on," according to Head. His career of service in the National Conference of Christians and Jews continued until his death in 1962.[56]

In 1931, Newfield and Edmonds asked Everett R. Clinchy, president of the National Conference of Christians and Jews, to come to Birmingham to organize their Birmingham chapter formally. Clinchy came on March 6 and gave at Emanu-El a speech entitled "Some Problems in Human Relations." At Edmonds's Independent Presbyterian Church he delivered the address "Jews and Christians in the American Democracy." On June 24, 1931, Clinchy returned to complete the formal organization of the chapter.[57]

In the 1930s, Newfield and other liberal clergymen and educators also founded the Alabama Conference of Human Relations, which was affiliated with the National Conference of Christians and Jews. Its stated purpose was "to promote justice, amity, understanding, and cooperation among Jews, Christians, and Protestants in America." The 1937 meeting involved not only Newfield, Edmonds, and Sands but also Guy E. Snavely, president of Birmingham-Southern College, a Methodist institution; J. M. Broady, pastor of the Sixth Avenue Presbyterian Church; James G. Heller, rabbi of Isaac M. Wise Temple of Cincinnati and the son of Newfield's friend Maximillian Heller; C. B. Glenn, superintendent of the Birmingham Public Schools; and Glenn's assistant, L. Frazier Banks.[58]

IV Morris Newfield's religious background allowed him gradually to support the notion that all economic classes should be represented fairly, a position that made him more liberal than many of the businessmen who were his associates in Birmingham during the period between the wars. Nevertheless, his accustomed role of mediator, reflecting his sense of noblesse oblige, was made difficult to maintain by the labor and racial unrest unleashed by the economic hardships of the time. In responding to the Klan, Newfield knew that he had the support of a responsible and rational majority against a truculent and intolerant minority of disaffected whites. Because the opponents of labor unions and equal rights for blacks were often conservative and well-regarded leaders of Birmingham, it was difficult for Newfield to act without bringing disfavor on Birmingham's Jews, his primary constituency.

Initially the rabbi was more conservative: before World War I, he did not support labor organization efforts in the coal mines or steel foundries of Birmingham. In 1914 he criticized workers who complained about their wealthy employers:

> There is bitter complaint by agitators against the rich. It is true there is much poverty. . . . Some of it, no doubt, is due to that fertile source of all poverty, idleness, intemperance, improvidence, or disease, against which not even the richest land, nor the highest wages are a remedy. But it is not true that every employer is an enemy of labor. Nor is it true that the laborer is worse off today than he has ever been. Never before has the laborer's working hours been so few, or his working conditions so good. Never has his independence been so great.

In this sermon, Newfield either showed his ignorance of the problems that industrial laborers faced in the Birmingham area or acted as an apologist for business interests. The rabbi was not sympathetic to the coal miners, who had completely failed to secure adequate representation.[59]

In formulating his attitude toward controversial questions relating to the business world, Newfield proceeded under certain restraints. First, he was the rabbi of a 400-family congregation.

Many of its members were enterprising businessmen. The pleas for social justice and stewardship which he made quite often in his early years at Emanu-El would not have alienated them, but more radical pleas for labor organization might have done so. As a result, Newfield may have initially agreed with the paternalistic schemes of congregants like Milton Fies. As a leading engineer, vice-president first of the DeBardeleben Coal Company, and later of the Alabama Power Company, Fies believed in a system of "company welfare." In company towns such as Westfield and Fairfield, both suburbs of Birmingham, DeBardeleben Coal Company built for white and black miners and steel workers separate communities complete with schools, health departments, and company cooperatives, thereby making laborers totally dependent on the beneficence of the companies for which they worked. Fies believed that company policies should be dictated, not by trade unions, but "from above." In 1922, in a speech before the Alabama Mining Institute, Fies bluntly acknowledged that his company's welfare program was a reward for "the Negro [coal miners'] contribution to non-union Alabama."[60]

Second, Newfield may have been influenced by the ideas of some Christian businessmen such as George Gordon Crawford and William Farrington Aldrich, who were his friends. Crawford, president of the Tennessee Coal, Iron, and Railroad Company, believed in a strong company welfare policy, as did Aldrich, who was the son of Truman Aldrich, a TCI official (Newfield named his sixth child John Aldrich Newfield).[61]

Third, Newfield was a social reformer who, as Robert Buroker has ably shown, was willing to change the existing laws to protect women and children in order to "restore" the dignity of the family in America, but he did not involve himself in efforts to help working men attain more secure employment positions. In 1914 Newfield did not work with reformers such as Isaac Max Rubinow and Louis Brandeis, who wanted to develop a system of social insurance and labor organization that would protect working men from the irrational fluctuations of the business cycle.[62]

Fourth, Newfield's initial conservatism may have stemmed from his idea that social justice implied moderate solutions. Although the rabbi recognized that class divisions existed in America, he rejected labor unions because he felt that they promoted class conflict. In another speech in April 1914, Newfield remarked, "Those who agitate and arouse enmity between the classes do not serve the interest of humanity. What is needed is a better understanding and a truer appreciation of each other's work." At this time, he believed that employers generally treated their workers well and that company towns were just solutions.[63]

The greed of coal operators during World War I changed the rabbi's mind. Convinced that businessmen had tried to take advantage of World War I to reap quick profits, Newfield for the first time viewed employers and employees as separate interest groups. No longer did he believe that businessmen would necessarily honor the interests of their workers. As a result, by the end of 1917, Newfield was arguing that capitalists, laborers, and consumers were three potentially antagonistic forces that had to be reconciled. Two years later, he wrote that laborers as well as employees had a right to organize: "If capital has the right to be and is today under the necessity of combination, labor has the same right while it is under greater necessity to combine. Trusts of money were met by trust of men. Money proclaiming with Cain's insolence 'As I may,' will always provoke men to responsive defenses."[64]

By acknowledging in 1919 that the two interest groups were separate, Newfield conceded that many of his former ideas were antiquated. "We do not claim that all Jews have been friendly to those demands for social justice and common progress. There have been among us, too, many who have been conservative if not reactionary. If a majority believe in the cause of labor, it is certain that a minority refuse to give assent to these reforms. . . . We cannot tread old paths." Nevertheless, the rabbi refused to accept the notion that class conflict was inevitable in America. Because he believed that America was a "land of opportunity" for all ethnic groups, he further criticized people who perpetuated conflicts by scurrilously calling all Jews "Communists" because some of the leading Bolsheviks in Russia, such as Trotsky and Litvinov, were Jewish.

> And this labeling or libeling is especially exasperating in the instance of industrial groups. We all are prejudiced by self-interest,

> by our attitude of suspicion and antagonism which is largely traditional. Such sharp divisions are only exacerbated by irritating names—by labels, such as socialist and communist and Bolshevik and capitalist. This labeling is especially an evil thing in a country where the wheel of fortune turns so freely and swiftly; where our social classes are so fluid that men readily pass from one unto another.[65]

Newfield's uncertainty regarding labor organization may be similar to the dilemma that he felt confronted him in his defense of blacks in Birmingham. The rabbi may have been caught between his belief that blacks deserved fair and equal treatment under the law and his awareness that Jews, as one of the less influential subcultures in Birmingham, could not afford to oppose the traditional southern belief that blacks were inferior.

The rabbi's support of labor organization in the coal fields in 1921 suggests that he supported equal legal treatment for blacks because approximately 75 percent of the 12,000 striking miners were black. Newfield also helped Ed Jackson, a black janitor of Temple Emanu-El, in the 1920s when he was accused of murder. Because some Jews in his congregation were afraid of negative publicity, they asked Newfield to fire Jackson before he had been tried. Newfield refused to do so and continued to employ Jackson after he had been acquitted. More important, the rabbi developed a working relationship, according to his son Mayer, with Booker T. Washington. Not only was Newfield invited to speak at Tuskegee Institute and to dine at Washington's home, but he also visited Washington as a personal emissary of Julius Rosenwald, the Chicago philanthropist, who donated great sums of money to various black causes.[66]

There is evidence that Newfield, despite his activities on behalf of blacks, offered little public support for the Scottsboro Boys because he understood that leading Gentiles would not accept him as an ethnic leader unless his public conduct accorded with that of other Jews, whatever their private opinions. Two years later, when the Scottsboro Boys were incarcerated in Birmingham, Newfield, serving as president of the Central Conference of American Rabbis (CCAR), investigated the dismissal of his friend Rabbi Benjamin Goldstein of Temple Beth Or in

Montgomery. Goldstein had complained that Ernest Mayer, president of the congregation, had fired him because of his strong public support of both the Scottsboro Boys and black sharecroppers in Alabama. After Newfield had talked with Goldstein and with a few members of the board of Beth Or, he concluded in a letter to Edward L. Israel of Baltimore, president of the Social Justice Commission of the CCAR:

> Dissatisfaction and friction have existed in that congregation almost since the first month of Goldstein's occupancy of that pulpit. His radical ideas on matters of religion [Goldstein claimed to be an atheist] did not suit the vast majority. . . . The racial issue alone was not the cause of friction, but it added fuel to the fire of dissatisfaction.[67]

Simon Wampold, a former president of Temple Beth Or and a supporter of the dismissed rabbi, indicated in a letter to Israel, however, that Newfield had not conducted a full and impartial investigation of the facts. Wampold complained about Newfield:

> I made a strenuous effort to see him [Newfield] but was unable to do so. But I am informed that he obtained most of his information from Mr. Ernest Mayer, Mr. Charles Moritz, and Dr. Djalma Hausman, and that these men are trying to excuse the real situation by injecting the religious point of view at the time. I am sending Dr. Newfield a copy of this letter.

Wampold was convinced that Newfield and many Montgomery Jews did not want to help Goldstein because of his support of the Scottsboro Boys. He did not, however, suggest why this was so.[68]

Rabbi Newfield also refused to serve on a special commission established by the CCAR to investigate the situation further. On July 21, 1933, he wrote to Samuel Goldenson, president of CCAR:

> Have had some unpleasant correspondence with Rabbi Benjamin Goldstein. He charges me with the endeavor of inducing his former congregation and his friends to shift the cause of his disagreement to religious grounds. . . . I am inclined to believe that it would be unwise for me to act on the Special Committee. . . . After all, my judgment is formed. I have formed it honestly on the basis of a thorough investigation. . . . I hope you see my point of

view. I don't want to give Goldstein the opportunity of saying that the Conference appointed someone whose judgment was already formed.

Despite the rabbi's words and in the absence of other evidence, we might speculate about the factors that informed Newfield's decision. Perhaps Newfield was being candid and was simply not willing to support Goldstein's case against the board of the latter's congregation. On the other hand, his motives could have been mixed. He may have chosen to support Mayer's case against Goldstein because the president of the board was a friend. Or Newfield may have feared the repercussions that were involved in supporting Goldstein, an outspoken advocate of black rights. The rabbi may not have wanted to jeopardize his standing among white Protestants by taking an equally outspoken position on behalf of the Scottsboro Boys.[69]

Newfield's membership on the Independent Scottsboro Committee further suggests that the rabbi was straddling a difficult line on the issue of black rights in the South. Ostensibly this was a committee, formed on June 10, 1936, with the purpose of obtaining justice for the nine black youths. Although the committee was not convinced of the boys' innocence, it felt that Samuel Leibowitz as a New York Jewish lawyer could not win in Alabama because he was employed by the International Labor Defense, a Marxist organization. The committee wanted to dismiss him in favor of an Alabama lawyer. On the committee were Morris Newfield, the sole Jew, and some of his closest friends and professional associates, including Harry M. Ayers, Henry M. Edmonds, Guy E. Snavely, and Roderick Beddow, at that time the leading criminal lawyer in Alabama. The efforts of the committee amounted to very little, however. Dan Carter in *Scottsboro* suggests a number of reasons, arguing that nothing came of the efforts because the committee had little money and because its activities conflicted with those of other individuals who were involved in the affair.[70]

Little information exists about Newfield's actions as a member of the committee, and his role is difficult to understand. It seems probable, however, that the rabbi was not nearly as outspoken on behalf of blacks as he was on behalf of children and needy people. Perhaps Newfield's position as a Jew in a community that feared and resented blacks as well as Jews can explain this stance. As Leonard Dinnerstein and John Shelton Reed observe, the marginality of southern Jews made them eager to conform to regional mores inasmuch as Jewish acceptance by Gentiles often depended on continuous public manifestations of accommodation by Jews, whatever their private opinions. Although there is evidence that Morris Newfield was far more sensitive to black needs than were many of his white Protestant neighbors, the rabbi may have felt that he could not afford to offer much public opposition to the mores of the dominant white Protestant subculture in Birmingham. As a consequence, he did not involve himself in union organization beyond acknowledging his sympathies to his congregation, nor did he work as tirelessly for the Scottsboro Boys as his friend Edmonds did.[71]

In his decision to act cautiously when confronted by both racial and labor tensions, the rabbi might be contrasted with Joseph Gelders, the outspoken advocate of racial equality and union activities. Because of his political sympathies, Gelders fell out of step with leading Jews in Birmingham, and with the white Protestant power structure as well, although there is no record of Newfield's own feelings about Gelders's conduct. Gelders simply did not have the responsibilities of leadership that Newfield exercised among Birmingham Jews, and Gelders could be much less circumspect in his political activities.

V In the period after World War I, then, Rabbi Morris Newfield did not despair over the failure of his hopes for World War I, as did many reformers and intellectuals across the country, because both Jews and non-Jews in Birmingham needed his constructive leadership. His stance was determined by two different variables. The first was his convictions regarding noblesse oblige. Not only did he participate in Community Chest activities, but he also promoted brotherhood among Alabamians, believing that all men could share ideals of progress and prosperity. Justice, proclaimed Newfield, suggested that men cared for their brothers: the priorities advocated by businessmen, emphasizing profits at the expense of jobs, the radical solutions offered by the Klan, which accentuated reaction and racism, and the Communists' dismantling of the system of private enterprise held little appeal for him. He simply believed in moderate and ameliorative change.

Second, having spent the first twenty years of his ministry at Emanu-El building a base for his role as a leader of many groups, Newfield was concerned that Birmingham Jews might lose their hard-won stature in their community. Because the Klan and some Fundamentalist churches represented forces of reaction that sought to override the cosmopolitan ideals to which Newfield adhered, the rabbi decided to find a way to combat them. He understood that he could not respond directly to the Klan, because this reactionary force was particularly appealing to some Christians in this largely evangelical Protestant area. He continued to espouse accommodationist goals for Jews, believing that Christians of goodwill in Birmingham would work with Jews through interfaith workshops and in the National Conference of Christians and Jews to offset the forces of division and hatred.

The rabbi clung to his belief that Jews could coexist happily with Christians. He chose in some cases not to act on his newfound awareness that society was represented by a number of interest groups with often conflicting but legitimate demands. By working openly and fearlessly on behalf of blacks and labor, the rabbi probably felt he might compromise some of his other interests and might jeopardize the position of his congregants in Birmingham. As a result, he chose rather to aid children and needy people—groups that he felt could help without engendering further conflict.

SEVEN

Altered Attitudes toward Zionism, 1895–1938

In June 1931, Morris Newfield both achieved his greatest honor and confronted his most formidable challenge when he was elected president of the Central Conference of American Rabbis, the Reform Jewish rabbinical governing body, for the customary two-year term. In this capacity, the rabbi became one of the leaders of Reform Jewry in the United States. He was forced then to reassess his theological precepts because he wanted to help European Jews find a place of refuge from the anti-Semitic outbursts of the 1920s and the Nazi atrocities that occurred after January 1933.

It was doubly difficult for Newfield to work on behalf of the European Jewry. He had grown up in Hungary and was acutely aware of Jewish difficulties both from his own experiences and from the letters of his relatives in Hungary. At the same time, the Birmingham rabbi had refrained for thirty-five years from supporting Zionism or the establishment of a Jewish state in Palestine, since he felt that an American Jew's allegiance belonged first to the United States. As a Jewish clergyman in a city where conformity to American ideals was expected, he perhaps believed that Jews had constantly to prove their commitment to those ideals.

By 1931, when he became president of the Central Conference

of American Rabbis, Newfield came to see that support for Jewish cultural and economic development in Palestine was necessary. He could not, however, endorse the idea of a Jewish political state there. His position allowed him to maintain his belief that Jews should be loyal Americans but also permitted him to offer generous support for the development of an outpost for European Jewish refugees. As a result, he may be called a "non-Zionist" rather than an "anti-Zionist." By 1938, less than two years before his death, however, the rabbi had become a Zionist. Together with a group of Christian ministers in Birmingham, Newfield urged President Franklin D. Roosevelt to help make Palestine a Jewish homeland.[1]

I In his early involvement with the Central Conference of American Rabbis, Morris Newfield was primarily concerned with improving his position in that august body of Reform rabbis. Such accomplishments pleased his congregation and also satisfied the rabbi's urge for stature among his peers. On July 10, 1897, Newfield wrote to Leah Ullman from the Montreal convention, "Had more than my share of honors showed me by Dr. Wise when it came to opportunities on committees. He put me on the Committee to which was referred in his annual message, the most important one." In 1903 Newfield was to discuss "The Place of Ritual and Ceremony in the Modern Synagogue" by Henry Berkowitz, but the discussion was canceled when Berkowitz could not give the paper. In 1906 Newfield told his wife that his work as parliamentarian at the CCAR meetings had drawn praise from Joseph Stolz, the former Emanu-El rabbi and later president of CCAR.

> My mind isn't clear from the work of the Conference. For the first time I took quite an active part in the deliberations, and my voice was heard in all important matters. Somehow I also got the reputation of being a good parliamentarian, and Stolz . . . consulted me throughout his rulings, going even to the extent of requesting me to take a seat beside him in making decisions.

A year later, Newfield disputed Max Heller's "Zionism and Reform Judaism," claiming that Reform Jews could not be Zionists and good Americans at the same time. In 1908 he was asked to criticize a paper entitled "The Reform Movement Post Geiger." In 1915 the Birmingham rabbi was assigned to read the evening service at the first session of the CCAR meeting, and in 1919, he gave the opening prayer.[2]

Although his responsibilities were not especially significant ones, he clearly enjoyed more opportunities than some other rabbis, such as his friend and former classmate George Solomon of Savannah, Georgia. In 1919 the rabbi of Mikvah Israel wrote Louis Wolsey, then corresponding secretary of CCAR:

> Replying to yours of the 29th, wishing me to prepare resolution in memory of the late Rabbi Joseph Bogen. I regret to say first that my knowledge of the man is too small, and the relations that existed between us too strained to admit of my undertaking of the task. . . . For twenty-three years, I faintly nourished the hope that the conference might really consider that I was living, but this, the first faint recognition of my existence, convinces me that they put me in the class of "dead ones."

Wolsey wryly answered:

> Dear George,
>
> I heartily agree with you that the Conference has been anything but just to you. . . . You must remember, however, that your complaint is the complaint of many of us. I have been honored with the conference sermon this year and that is the first time in my twenty year membership in the conference that I have ever been on the program. . . . I had all along come to the conferences with the belief that my colleagues did not think I had any brains. Why do you kick then? The Conference is completely just in its injustices. It doesn't discriminate when it comes to doling out its injustices.[3]

Newfield either did his lesser jobs well, however, or was more fortunate than his 1895 Hebrew Union College classmate, because he was elected treasurer of the CCAR in 1923, an office that put him in line for even higher offices such as vice-president and president. Newfield attained this high office no doubt in recognition of his continuous service on CCAR projects.[4]

The Birmingham rabbi served six years as the treasurer of the Central Conference, working very closely with his friends Abraham Simon of Washington, D.C., Louis Wolsey of Philadelphia, and Hyman G. Enelow of New York City, who were presidents for successive two-year terms. The investment reports of the CCAR indicate that Newfield also bought a number of bonds in projects in Jefferson County and in Alabama with CCAR money. In 1929, after six years of service, Newfield was elected vice-president of the CCAR under David Lefkowitz, an office that he held until June 1931.[5]

While serving as vice-president and as a member of the Relief Committee of CCAR, Newfield became aware of the financial problems of Samuel Krauss, the head of the Jewish Theological Seminary of Vienna, and Ludwig Blau, the leader of the Budapest Jewish Theological Seminary. Krauss, a former classmate, and Blau, a former teacher of Newfield's at the Budapest Jewish Theological Seminary from 1883 to 1887, were Jewish scholars with outstanding reputations but were having difficulties raising money for their school at a time of worldwide depression. They wrote Newfield to ask for help. In a letter dated February 27, 1930, Newfield expressed his hope that Krauss remembered him and also said that he wanted very much to help the rabbi:

> Glad as I was to hear from you, I regretted to learn of the poor economic condition in which you find yourself and which condition is a latter after-effect of the Great War. But pray, do not be discouraged! A scholar of your type and achievements will not be forgotten or permitted to suffer financial distress. I shall bring your situation to the attention of the Governing Board of the Central Conference of American Rabbis and am confident of favorable action. . . . I often think of those happy years when we combined earnest study and great aspirations with partial starvation because of our limited allowance. Still, they were happy years when we had the inspiration of a Bacher, a Kaufmann, a Bonoczy. . . . You always stood out with distinction among your classmates. I followed your career with interest and with admiration. . . . Do not hesitate to speak quite frankly about your circumstances. I am interested in you personally, both for the sake of old friendship and because of your eminent contributions to Jewish scholarship.

Newfield was glad to help the scholar and was probably also thankful that he had left Hungary many years before and had come to the United States to pursue his rabbinical career. Krauss was the greater scholar, but he needed help from his American colleague after World War I.[6]

By May 1930 Newfield was able to assure Krauss that his salary of $125 a month would be paid by the Committee of Subvention of the Central Conference. Blau, too, received aid from Newfield and the Central Conference, and also a note on March 10, 1930, from his former student "assuring you of my continued interest in the welfare of the Seminary, of yourself as my old teacher and of my former classmates and colleagues."[7]

On June 21, 1931, Rabbi Newfield was elected president of the Central Conference of American Rabbis, with Samuel H. Goldenson of Pittsburgh's Morewood Avenue Temple as his vice-president. His election was recognized as a significant honor for all of Birmingham Jewry by long-standing friends such as Bert Jacobs, Milton Fies, and by the Beth El rabbi, Abraham Bengis. Fies wrote: "To the members of your congregation, sir, and I may truthfully add, to the citizenship of Birmingham generally, you are something more than a learned rabbi, an eminent teacher, and a champion of social justice among all people. You are to us primarily a cultured man . . . capable of choosing values, assaying accurately the dross and gold of life." Bengis wired his colleague, "Congratulations. Honor Merited and Shared by All Birmingham Jewry." Newfield's rabbinical compatriots Abraham Simon of Washington, D.C., Nathan Krass of New York City, David Marx of Atlanta, Henry Cohen of Galveston, Texas, Joseph S. Kornfeld of Toledo, and William Rosenau of Baltimore sent felicitations. Rosenau wrote: "Please accept my hearty congratulations and sincere wishes. Having sat in back of Presidents for so many years, and having helped them to decide knotty parliamentary problems, you are eminently fitted for that position from every point of view, not to mention that of rabbinical representation."[8]

II One of the most significant questions that confronted Newfield and the other members of the Central Conference in the first three decades of the twentieth century was how to view the Zionist call for a Jewish state in Palestine. Theodore Herzl, a Viennese Jewish journalist, had written *Der Judenstaat* in 1896 and a year later had called the First Zionist Congress at Basel, Switzerland. Influenced by the fervor that nationalistic movements throughout nineteenth-century Europe had produced, Herzl believed that Jews could never attain full and equal civil rights in Europe, and as a result he advocated separation and statehood.[9]

As I have suggested, Morris Newfield learned as a rabbinical student at Hebrew Union College from 1892 to 1895 that Reform Jews, and especially Isaac Mayer Wise, the president of HUC, had forsaken the idea of a return by Jews to Zion or Palestine. Instead Reform Jews had taken the concept of the Dispersion as Exile, or as a punishment for sins, and converted it into the ideal of Mission, with Israel chosen to spread the knowledge of God among the nations. The loss of a homeland was viewed not as a calamity but as an opportunity that allowed Jews to break out spiritually from the confines of a nation-state. This view made prayers for a return to Zion incongruous within Reform theology, and in 1845 at the Frankfort Rabbinical Congress, and subsequently in 1885 at the Pittsburgh Conference, it was decided that all petitions for the return to Palestine, and for the restoration of a Jewish state, were to be eliminated from prayers.[10]

Morris Newfield also found out from Wise at HUC, and from other Reform theologians at the meetings of the CCAR that he began attending after 1895, that Reform Jews had no use for a Jewish nation because they intended to take full advantage of the social and economic opportunities that they believed existed in the United States. Melvin I. Urofsky in his *From Herzl to Holocaust—American Zionism* describes the thoughts of many Reform rabbis at the turn of the century. "The lack of an anti-Semitic tradition in this country, the economic opportunities available, made many of the newcomers [German and Eastern European Jewish immigrants] look on the United States as their new Zion, and those with brains and skills and ambitions soon reaped the reward of their labor." But in the minds of the framers of the Pittsburgh Platform, although America offered Jews freedom and opportunity in a land built by immigrants, it also demanded their full loyalties. As a consequence, many Reform rabbis in 1900 viewed Zionist aspirations as contrary to their hopes of succeeding in the American promised land.[11]

In his early sermons at Temple Emanu-El in Birmingham, Newfield did not deviate from Reform principles as he emphasized the new reliance on religiosity at the expense of political identity. In 1898, one year after Herzl's Congress, he explained to his congregation:

> Israel is not a political entity; it is a people that has long ago discovered its real being in the form of the synagogue and hopes to become the universal church. . . . Reform Judaism is optimistic; it declares that humanity, in spite of temporary aberration, will not retrograde; but that the ideals of Truth, Justice, and Freedom will prevail. . . . Reform Judaism utters the hope for the time when all men will worship God in Truth and Justice.

In an undated speech entitled "Zionist Movement," the Birmingham rabbi also spoke of the Reform insistence that Jews who had nationalistic aspirations would alienate American Christians and would make all Jews appear disloyal to their adopted country:

> There has been much discussion of the Zionist movement. We Jews find that most Christians can, without stopping to analyze the proposition, take it for granted that every Jew in the world is looking forward with intense hope to the time when he would immigrate to Palestine, and abandoning his present citizenship, would become a member of a restored Jewish nation there. . . . The famous Shylock pronouncement of Jewish sensibilities might well be paraphrased to describe the status of the Jew today in whatever land he is a citizen, "Hath not the Jew loyalty? Hath not a Jew patriotism, sense of duty, love of his country, pride in his citizenship, appreciation of his rights? . . . Fed with the same propaganda of national righteousness . . . warmed by the same political arguments as a Christian is?" . . . The American Jew is as American as any of his native or nationalized neighbors of other creeds. . . . He has proven this in a thousand ways—in civic life, in his industrial and commercial activities, as well as in war. . . . He is a lover of country.

In his ministry in Birmingham, Newfield continued to proclaim to his congregation that, because Jews aspire to prestigious positions in Birmingham, they had to be prepared to practice a religion that would allow them to be 100 percent Americans. According to the rabbi, there was no room for dual loyalties to America and to Palestine, because Christians in Birmingham could neither understand nor tolerate this position. As a consequence, Newfield rationalized for them, "We are convinced that He wants us . . . to show our appreciation of the blessings it [the United States] gives us by being Americans now and forever." Exactly what Newfield meant by the word "He" is questionable: ostensibly, he meant God, but if the term "white Protestants" is substituted for "He," Newfield's statement explains his perceptions of the anomalous Jewish position in Birmingham.[12]

Newfield's attitudes toward Zionism were not changed by Louis D. Brandeis's attempt to fashion a different theoretical position for American Zionists in 1914. At this time, Brandeis accepted the chairmanship of the Provisional Executive Committee of the Federation of American Zionists and agreed to raise money for Zionist causes because he believed that a Jewish state could be established following the ethical tenets of Judaism, principles he viewed as closely akin to American ideas. Addressing the 1915 American Zionist convention, Brandeis said, "The highest Jewish ideals are essentially American in a very important particular. It is Democracy that Zionism represents. It is Social Justice which Zionism represents, and every bit of that is the American ideal of the twentieth century."[13]

Brandeis's justification of Zionism as a means of spreading the American dream outward was in keeping, the Boston lawyer thought, with American reform ideals of self-determination and with American ideals generally. As a Reform Jewish rabbi, Newfield was not inclined to think positively about the possibility of a Jewish state in Palestine, which the English government officially favored in the Balfour Declaration of November 2, 1917; he was more concerned that Jews throughout the world live peacefully with their Christian neighbors.[14]

In September 1918, he wrote a sermon for Rosh Hashana Eve: "We need not be Zionist—I am not—to appreciate the difference in the attitude of the world. . . . What care we about the diplomatic implications of a new buffer state? Israel has been chosen for an illustration of the right of the people to self-determination." Three months later the rabbi castigated the Zionists more strongly, arguing that attempts to establish a homeland for Jews ran counter to Woodrow Wilson's principles of self-determination because they would cause problems for Jews who wanted equal rights in their adopted countries. In a December 1918 speech entitled "Jews and the Peace Conference," he announced:

> The Jews must insist on obtaining absolute equality of citizenship in every land at the hand of the Peace Conference. . . . But the force of our demand for equal rights for Jews everywhere is bound to be weakened if the Zionists ask the Peace Conference to establish a nationalistic state for Jews in Palestine. . . . If it be admitted that the Jews are to have a national homeland of their own, then their persecutors can argue that there is no need to give them equality of citizenship in other lands. . . . the tremendous majority of Jews will always remain outside of Palestine. . . . Do not cast upon them the suspicion of being strangers.

In this speech, Newfield reiterated his most significant concern—that American Jews needed the right to coexist happily with Christians. Because he believed that idealistic aspirations for a Jewish homeland sometimes threatened Birminghamians who were inclined to question the loyalties of Jews, Newfield rejected these notions.[15]

Although many southern Reform rabbis, including Edward N. Calisch of Richmond, David Marx of Atlanta, Henry Cohen of Galveston, and Emil W. Leipziger of New Orleans, were not Zionists at this time, some Reform rabbis in the South felt differently. Two New Orleans rabbis, Max Heller of Temple Sinai and Mendel Silber of Gates of Prayer, in the period between 1896 and 1936 wrote many editorials in the weekly *New Orleans Jewish Ledger,* strongly proclaiming that Jews had both the right and the responsibility to support a Jewish state in Palestine. These men were perhaps not as troubled with fears of "backlash" by non-Jews against their expressions of dual loyalties as some non-Zionists or anti-Zionists were.[16]

III In the aftermath of World War I, Newfield not only faced the Ku Klux Klan in Birmingham but also recognized that European Jews felt anti-Semitic pressures for a number of reasons. First, Jews were often seen by national groups in countries such as

Romania, Hungary, and Russia as either cosmopolitan or Communist and therefore part of a foreign interest group. Second, Jews were sometimes identified as a parasite economic group which frustrated the ambitions of native middle- or lower-class groups in the societies of these countries. Third, anti-Semitic reactions often resulted from the traditional Christian hatred of Jews as "Christ-killers." Fourth, most Europeans, including Jews, suffered economically in the aftermath of World War I and in the economic crises of the early 1930s, and many blamed Jews for these conditions.[17]

As has been suggested, Rabbi Newfield, in response to the vociferous activities of the Klan, continued to espouse an accommodationist position in Birmingham because he believed that most Christians could accept Jews when they understood both the similarities and differences between Christians and Jews. Newfield and his associates in the Central Conference of American Rabbis, however, faced a more difficult task when he was confronted by the problems of European Jewry because various anti-Semitic groups in Europe threatened the very existence of Jews in their midst. Continued advocacy of an accommodationist position for European Jews was not a solution.

The problem that Eastern European Jews faced was twofold. On the one hand, as victims of anti-Semitic obsessions, these people could not come to the United States because the National Origins Act of 1924 effectively limited immigration from Eastern Europe. On the other hand, Jews who chose to remain in their native lands or were emigrating to Palestine needed help from their American coreligionists.

Responding to these dilemmas, Morris Newfield and many of his colleagues in the Central Conference endorsed a plan by Louis Marshall and the American Jewish Committee and supported Jewish development of Palestine through the Jewish Agency without accepting the idea of a political Jewish state in Palestine. Many Reform rabbis, while refusing to sanction Zionist plans officially, ultimately contributed to the development of a Jewish nation by supporting financial efforts to colonize Palestine with European Jewish refugees.[18]

As early as 1915, Newfield worked diligently on behalf of the

American Joint Distribution Committee, established by the following groups to aid European Jewry: the Central Relief Committee, an Orthodox aggregate; the People's Relief Committee of Labor Zionists; and the American Jewish Committee. As I have suggested, Newfield was probably more responsible than any other leader in Alabama for raising the $50,000 annually that Alabama Jews contributed to these efforts.[19]

In the 1920s, Newfield acknowledged the need to use Palestine as a place of refuge for oppressed European Jews. On April 1, 1928, the three Birmingham temples, Emanu-El, K'nesseth Israel, and Beth El, honored Newfield's friend Rabbi Maximillian Heller of New Orleans on his return from Palestine. Although Heller was a Reform rabbi of German background, he was also an avowed Zionist who had strongly criticized the official non-Zionist position of the Central Conference for thirty years, viewing it as "weak-kneed." In the *Birmingham News* of April 2, 1928, an article appeared, probably with Newfield's blessing, that stated:

> The purpose of the Palestine movement, obscured for years by lack of understanding, is now clear. It might be added that this purpose . . . is intended to revive ancient Judea, not as a national entity that might awaken in Jews of other countries, a sense of divided and doubtful allegiance, but only as a haven to which may repair Jews oppressed in other lands, particularly in certain European ones.

Later that year, on November 11, 1928, the same newspaper announced that Morris Newfield was a member of a committee in Birmingham to raise funds for Palestine.[20]

When Morris Newfield was elected president of the CCAR in Wawasee, Indiana, in June 1931, the atmosphere was thick with conflict between pro-Zionist rabbis and those who either continued to support the traditional Reform position against a Jewish state or were at best supporters of Jewish settlement in Palestine. In his acceptance speech, Newfield indicated that he did not favor the Zionist faction. He praised those older rabbis like Isaac M. Wise, David Philipson, Joseph Stolz, Moses J. Gries of Cleveland, and Leo M. Franklin of Detroit, none of whom favored a Jewish political state in Palestine.[21]

ATTITUDES TOWARD ZIONISM

Newfield spent a large part of his incumbency dealing with the conflicts surrounding the issue of Zionism. At times, all of his powers of persuasion were needed to keep the CCAR from exploding into open warfare. The Zionist supporters plainly resented his continued refusal to endorse their position. In March 1932 Newfield received an angry letter from Stephen S. Wise, one of the most influential pro-Zionist Reform rabbis in America. Wise was disturbed because Newfield had appointed his friend Jacob D. Schwarz rather than Rabbi Goldstein, one of Wise's associates at the Jewish Institute of Religion, as director of the Bureau of Synagogue Activity. Newfield subsequently appointed Wise's associate.[22]

A month later, however, Newfield indicated in a letter to his vice-president, Samuel Goldenson, that Wise's aggressive stance on the Goldstein matter would surely mean further difficulties for Jews who, like himself, were not committed Zionists. He told Goldenson that he wanted to postpone the conference which had been scheduled for June 1932 because he was afraid of Zionist power. Furthermore, he said he was

> very apprehensive regarding the attendance of the Conference. Am afraid due to economic conditions, very few congregations will agree to pay the expenses of their rabbis. . . .
>
> As things look to me, the attendance will consist mainly of rabbis located in the East. If the attendance is small, as I fear it will be, certain *new* elements in the Conference membership will have a predominant influence. They may be in a position to commit the Conference to new policies subversive to some of our cherished traditions and initiate policies to which the large majority would object but which they being absent could not prevent. . . . What do you think of the possibility of postponing the Conference to late fall? Perhaps, by that time, conditions will be better. . . . I fear the Conference will consist largely of graduates of Wise's institution [Zionists]. No telling what may happen.[23]

Since the executive board of the CCAR had the power to postpone the meeting, the Birmingham rabbi depended on its members to help him keep control of the proceedings away from Wise and other Zionists. Non-Zionists on the board, who included Calisch of Richmond, Hyman G. Enelow of New York City, Samuel M. Gup of Providence, David Lefkowitz of Dallas, Julian Morgenstern of Cincinnati, Irving F. Reichert of San Francisco, and Louis Wolsey of Philadelphia, helped him accomplish his goal.[24]

Newfield probably found the strain of keeping harmony while at the same time promoting his own position very taxing. In a letter that he wrote to the executive board as a whole, Newfield tried to soothe the feelings of Zionists such as Abba Hillel Silver of Cleveland and Abraham J. Feldman of Hartford. By October 11, 1932, however, he wrote Goldenson of the trepidation that he felt regarding the upcoming meeting in Cincinnati in November:

> I do not like to anticipate or forecast developments. However, I am seriously thinking of requesting the nominating committee not to propose my name for re-election. Usually, of course, the President is re-elected for a second term. I have been honored by the Conference beyond my merits and will be satisfied to become again a private in the ranks. . . . Have not discussed this matter with anyone. It is just a thought that has been brooding within me. Of course, you will treat this in absolute confidence.

Goldenson talked him out of it, and the rabbi went to the November meeting in Cincinnati determined to reaffirm the official non-Zionist position of the CCAR.[25]

Newfield's presidential message of 1932 is filled with various remarks that show the difficulties of World Jewry, indications of the internal conflicts over the Zionist issue in the CCAR, and Newfield's solutions to both these sets of problems. The rabbi began his speech by identifying the terrible conditions faced by European Jews.

> The first year has been a critical one. . . . Mankind the world over has been distraught on a bed of illness. . . . the Jew is made the unhappy victim of all unpleasant conditions. . . . In the land of Lessing and Heine, the atmosphere is charged with passion that harks back to the spirit of medieval fanaticism and persecution. . . . Nor is the Jewish situation a happy one in Hungary. . . . Conditions in Russia are unchanged. . . . The danger lies in the ruthless suppression of Jewish religious life.

Newfield's solution to the problems of European Jewry, once again a compromising stance, was to find a middle ground that would help Jews but also to refrain from committing the CCAR and American Reform Jewry to the support of a Jewish state in Palestine. As he had done in 1928 he supported the development of Palestine by the Joint Distribution Committee and the Jewish Agency and further remarked:

> More hopeful and favorable is the situation in Palestine, which has suffered less than other lands from the general economic depression. . . . There is promise of peaceful settlements of differences which is a hopeful token for the rehabilitation of the land and for an increased immigration so surely needed both in the interests of our oppressed brethren and for the upholding of Palestine.[26]

But the rabbi refused to encourage further pro-Zionist expressions. When Jacob R. Marcus, a professor of history at Hebrew Union College and chairman of the Committee of Contemporaneous History and Literature of the CCAR, moved to establish a world congress, consisting of the CCAR, the Joint Foreign Committee of England, the Alliance Israelite Universelle of France, the World Zionist Organization, and other groups, Newfield voted against it. He supported the views of non-Zionists who felt that Christians would see this as a Jewish worldwide conspiracy and stalled Marcus by recommending in his presidential report that the CCAR keep the matter under consideration for another year.[27]

After the convention, Newfield and Goldenson again found themselves at odds with Stephen S. Wise, who continued to complain that Zionist rabbis were being ignored by individuals who favored a non-Zionist position. Goldenson wrote a reply to one of Newfield's letters:

> I am sorry indeed to learn that he [Stephen Wise] feels hurt because of the omissions made in the committee appointments. . . . I have just looked over the constitution of the Congress committee to refresh my mind and it seems to me that it fairly represents the Conference as a whole. . . . This surely is significant evidence that we meant to be fair to the other side.[28]

Newfield's 1933 presidential message at the June meeting in Milwaukee, Wisconsin, indicated that the problems of European Jewry were continuing to wreak havoc for the Central Conference:

> We meet this year with saddened hearts. The deplorable events in Germany cast a pall of gloom and sorrow over our deliberations, as they do over America and World Israel. What is transpiring in the land of Kultur has shocked the moral sense of the civilized world. . . . The whole truth concerning the terrible incidents of last spring in Nazi-controlled Germany has yet not been made known to the world.

Nevertheless, the Birmingham rabbi continued to maintain his previous stance. On the one hand, he called for the further development of Palestine. On the other hand, as the outgoing president of the CCAR, Newfield tried to ensure that his close friend David Marx, a non-Zionist like himself, would be elected vice-president and would thus be in a position to succeed Samuel Goldenson, another non-Zionist, after his term expired in 1935.

According to Jacob R. Marcus, who took part in the meetings, however, Newfield failed to put Marx into office because many rabbis felt that Marx had not paid his dues as a hard-working member of the CCAR in lesser activities and, as a result, probably could not be elected. This point cannot be substantiated because the CCAR yearbook of 1933 mysteriously states that David Marx, "despite the unanimous nomination, gratefully declined the honor." Treasurer Felix A. Levy, a Zionist sympathizer, was elected vice-president, and the Zionists gained control of the Central Conference.[29]

Samuel Goldenson, Newfield's faithful lieutenant in the attempt to maintain the non-Zionists' control of the CCAR, paid tribute to his friend Rabbi Newfield:

> I wish I could express sufficiently to the Past President my appreciation of his training of me. . . . I am not an organizer. . . . During the last two years, I have watched this man very carefully. I have studied his methods . . . , but I have learned more from his nature than I have his methods. His gentleness, his thoughtfulness, his

ability to foresee consequences and to enter into the subtle situations—of personal and collective life—have been of great help and inspiration to me, and I am glad that I have had such a teacher immediately before me, or behind me.[30]

ATTITUDES TOWARD ZIONISM

After he stepped down as president of the Central Conference, Newfield continued to lobby against its official pronouncements on behalf of Zionism. In a letter to Rabbi Edward L. Israel dated December 13, 1934, he objected to a resolution that referred to Palestine as "the Jewish homeland." Instead, he suggested to Israel the words "a Jewish homeland." He also continued to lobby against the Zionist attempts to control the conference.[31]

In 1937, however, because the Zionist rabbis had taken control of the Conference two years earlier, the CCAR adopted an official pro-Zionist stance. It resulted, as Cyrus L. Arfa suggests, from the fact that many of the younger rabbis were more self-assured than the older German Jews such as Newfield and could more easily accept notions of cultural pluralism, or more specifically ideas of "dual" loyalties, without fearing adverse Christian responses.[32]

Although we do not know how Newfield voted on the Columbus Platform of 1937, or the pro-Zionist position adopted by the CCAR, the Birmingham rabbi was clearly distressed by the actions of the British government in Palestine. That year Britain's Peel Commission recommended a partition of Palestine between Arabs and Jews, once again thwarting Zionist aspirations for a Jewish state. Ever since the San Remo Conference of 1920, when the British had agreed to support the creation of a Jewish state, they had wavered constantly when asked to implement their original promise to Jews. In the late 1920s, the British had done very little to stop Arab attacks on Jewish settlements in Palestine. They had temporarily stopped Jewish immigration to Palestine in 1936 because strained Arab-Jewish relations threatened British interests in the oil-rich Middle East. The 1937 decision by the Peel Commission only exacerbated the problems of European Jews who needed a place to live.

The Anschluss of March 1938, by which Germany took over neighboring Austria, further complicated matters for European Jews who were in danger from Nazi atrocities. Because the U.S.

State Department and Secretary of State Cordell Hull refused to allow increased Jewish immigration into America, American Jewish leaders of every stripe were convinced that Palestine represented the only haven for Jewish refugees.[33]

Six months later, on October 10, 1938, Harry Schneiderman of the American Jewish Committee cabled Morris Newfield, informing him that Britain was considering the abandonment of its mandate providing for a Jewish state and asking the rabbi for his support in this political matter. In his customary way, Newfield agreed to help Schneiderman. There were probably a number of reasons for the rabbi's decision to champion the establishment of a Jewish state in Palestine at this time. First, his support for Jewish colonization in Palestine in the late 1920s and early 1930s indicates that his non-Zionist position was never very far from a Zionist stance. Second, as I have suggested, in Birmingham Newfield had always associated himself closely with Christians. When Schneiderman asked for help, Newfield asked his Christian friends who were ministers to help him lobby for a Jewish homeland, and he received their support.

On the same afternoon that he received the cable from Schneiderman, he did two things. He and a "number of influential Jews," whose names are not available, traveled to Jasper, Alabama, to the office of William B. Bankhead, the Speaker of the U.S. House of Representatives, and met with him and his brother, John Bankhead, one of the two senators from Alabama. Newfield and his friends urged the Bankheads to ask Cordell Hull and the State Department not to let the British government abandon its commitment to a Jewish state in Palestine.[34]

The Birmingham rabbi also called upon his Christian associates that night in Birmingham. He asked the Synod of the Presbyterian Church of Alabama, and the Baptist Association, both of which were meeting that week in Birmingham, to pass sympathetic resolutions to be sent to President Franklin D. Roosevelt. He also contacted Ewart H. Wyle, president of the Pastors Union, Henry M. Edmonds, Eugene L. Sands, T. V. Neal, president of Howard College, and other pastors from the Highlands Methodist Church, the Sixth Avenue Presbyterian Church, and the Episcopal Bishop of Alabama, asking them to send strongly worded messages to the White House. Newfield explained to Solomon Goldman, president of the Zionist Organization of America, his reason for calling on these people in particular. "Of course, many telegrams were sent by Jewish organizations and individuals," he observed. "But I am inclined to believe that the messages from non-Jewish organizations and representative leaders will do most good."

Newfield's responses on behalf of a Jewish state in Palestine represented his last important act. Five months later, in February 1939, he suffered a heart attack, which largely curtailed his activities.[35]

IV Morris Newfield decided to support a Jewish state in Israel because he understood that it represented the only solution to the problems faced by European Jewry at the hands of Adolf Hitler and the Nazis. Newfield's last important act of mustering support for that state was consistent with his lifelong view of his position as an American Jew. Because he lived in the midst of an overwhelmingly non-Jewish area in the United States, he was always concerned with the relations between Jews and their Christian neighbors: many of his thoughts and deeds were considered with Christian reactions in mind.

Newfield's opposition to Zionism throughout much of his life largely reflected his belief that American Jews should be integrated into American society in every area except the religious. He had little time for Brandeis's equations of Zionism with the fulfillment of American ideals because he was so aware of the dominant influence of his Birmingham environment. As a consequence, Newfield's responses to the problems of world Jewry were similar to many of his other ideas: they were designed to create positive solutions without jeopardizing the status that both he and his congregants had achieved in Birmingham.

Still, the rabbi also exhibited a flexible mind. His solutions to the problems that world Jewry faced in the 1930s were different from his responses to the Ku Klux Klan in the 1920s. To answer the charges of the nativists in Birmingham that Jews were no longer welcome, Newfield worked with other Christians to prove that cosmopolitan influences still operated in his city. He knew, however, that he could not issue this same response to the Germans; it was apparent in 1938 that cosmopolitan influences no longer operated in the Reich. As a result, after clinging steadfastly to the belief that men of different backgrounds could live together, he supported a Jewish state in Israel because he knew that European Jews had to live apart.

Conclusion

On May 7, 1940, Morris Newfield died at his home in Birmingham, Alabama. Within a week, Henry M. Edmonds and Father Eugene L. Sands, two of his closest Gentile friends, conceived the idea of a Newfield Memorial Lectureship on interracial and interreligious tolerance and goodwill as a tribute to Newfield's work in Birmingham. Under the terms of this memorial, an outstanding speaker would be brought to Birmingham to give an annual address dedicated to these causes. The thought was appropriate to Newfield's career; unfortunately the lectures never materialized, probably because Edmonds left Birmingham shortly after the rabbi's death.[1]

The present biography of Morris Newfield, a twentieth-century rabbi, reformer, and social worker, has been written, not as a tribute, but as a case study in the nature of ethnic leadership in America. In it I have tried to account for Newfield's success with both Jews and Christians in Birmingham as well as to explore the personal motivations that informed his decisions as a rabbi and social leader. Morris Newfield's life and work shed much light on the development of Birmingham in a transitional period, in the years 1895–1940, on the southern rabbinate and Judaism, and on the nature of liberal reform in the South in the first part of the twentieth century.

Newfield was a humane, intelligent man who sought to resolve the conflicts that beset his early life and succeeded because he was not only sensitive to the needs of his entire community but also able to show men with different viewpoints how to communicate with each other.

Morris Newfield's Hungarian background gave him the confidence to lead as well as the realization of the heavy responsibilities of leadership. His love for his father, his early deprivations, his awareness of his father's pain, his comprehension of the gaps between traditional and Neolog Jews in Budapest, and his understanding of how Jews might productively contribute to the emergence of a multiethnic society in Hungary, and perhaps in any society, brought him to America, to Hebrew Union College in Cincinnati, and then to Birmingham, Alabama, to find a meaningful outlet for his dreams and ambitions. His outlook also enabled him to lay a foundation from which he could develop his own styles and goals of leadership.

The rabbi became a leader of Birmingham Jews and a Jewish leader in Birmingham for at least three reasons. First, as Nathan Glazer has suggested, Reform rabbis wielded influence because they helped American Jews, in a new and often threatening environment, to maintain a link with their tradition. Second, Newfield became an effective Jewish leader in Birmingham because Christians for the most part respected religious leaders. Gentiles helped the rabbi attain influential positions because they did not fear his authority. Third, Newfield was chosen as a Jewish leader in Birmingham because Emanu-El's Jews wanted someone who was popular with Christians as well as a "defender of the faith." The rabbi not only mediated between tradition and new ideas for his congregants but also between Jewish and Christian needs as he perceived them. He was, then, a leader who coped successfully with the needs of a number of different groups in Birmingham.

Nevertheless, to determine how the rabbi maintained his leadership in particularly stressful times it is necessary to appreciate the complexity of the rabbi's goals and the methods that he chose to achieve his objectives. I have characterized Newfield's father-in-law, Samuel Ullman, as an outspoken man given to often direct methods which succeeded for him because he was respected as one of the charter members of the Birmingham community and also because his leadership goals were probably less ambitious than Newfield's. The younger man's style varied. He was very outspoken when he believed that explanations and actions had to be straightforward and direct; at other times Newfield was circumspect and accommodating because he understood that quiet but effective presentation could influence the groups that he led. He knew that Jewish group survival depended on the careful efforts of a leader who knew how to work with Christians on behalf of Jews. Nevertheless, because he knew that Jews were often idealized as a forthright "people of the book," he chose to speak bluntly when resolute defenses of Jewish interests were needed. Given the often conflicting nature of his goals as a leader of Jews and a Jewish leader of both Jews and Christians in Birmingham, Newfield's diverse methods had to reflect his varied interests.

The rabbi was concerned about the needs of a number of different groups in the Birmingham community. Faced with reinforcing a consensus of moderation against what he perceived as a reactionary but easily combatable influence in the Ku Klux Klan in the 1920s, he quietly organized interfaith workshops to combat the fear and anxiety unleashed by the economic pressures facing Birmingham after World War I. In other instances, Newfield was even more reticent. I have suggested that Newfield did not strongly defend black rights in Alabama, nor did he speak out publicly in favor of labor organization, even when it was clear that his sympathies, as expressed to his congregation, were on the side of these oppressed groups; Newfield worried that Jews would suffer if their leader supported unpopular causes. At other times, however, he supported activities such as unpopular social welfare projects when less controversial and significant stands might have caused him less frustration not only with Christians but with Jews as well. His different objectives, attended by varied styles of leadership, indicate that Newfield was not only a flexible leader but also a man of diverse interests who recognized the need for different means of expression.

In analyzing Newfield's leadership as a function of his ethnic imperatives, we must focus on a number of different issues in the field of American historical writing. Because scholars have begun to view America as a land of many ethnic groups whose interaction strongly affected the course of America's history, we must consider the ways in which Newfield's leadership in Birmingham, in Alabama, and throughout the country reflected his concern with the interaction of a number of different ethnic groups. In addition, because ethnic historians have recently underscored not only the common virtues of various ethnic groups but also their conflicts, we need to understand the means by which Newfield successfully coped with conflict.[2]

The present book differs from many biographies of other American Jewish leaders, then, because it does not simply chronicle Newfield's deeds and thoughts. It describes the efforts of a Jewish leader in Birmingham to grapple with problems that Jews everywhere were facing. More important, however, it argues that conflict existed between Jews and Christians in Birmingham because each group maintained ambivalent feelings toward the other, and it shows how Newfield and Christians influenced each other as the different ethnic groups, with sometimes competing needs, offered leadership in the Birmingham community.

I have suggested that Newfield not only operated as an "ethnic broker," or a leader who mediated between tradition and change within his own ethnic group, but also understood the needs of a number of ethnic groups. He operated as a representative of a number of ethnic groups in Birmingham and in Alabama; helped Birmingham Jews develop a strong sense of Jewishness without threatening the sometimes prickly dominant white Protestant subculture in Birmingham; showed white Protestants that religious leaders of every stripe could be trusted to provide leadership in Birmingham; and defended the interests of poorer and younger members of the Birmingham and Alabama communities without directly attacking other constituencies.[3]

In his role as ethnic broker, Newfield's career may be compared favorably with those of other southern rabbis, such as David Marx of Atlanta, the rabbi of the Hebrew Benevolent Congregation, or "The Temple." Marx was not only a close friend of Morris Newfield but also his predecessor at Temple Emanu-El in

Birmingham in 1894. Both were heavily involved in many community activities, such as social welfare projects, and both operated as leaders of Jews and as Jewish leaders in their respective communities. Reform rabbis had to mediate effectively in order to be successful in their jobs.[4]

CONCLUSION

Morris Newfield's life and work, then, manifest a number of different ideas. Newfield, and probably Jewish leaders in other communities as well, sought followers among Christians as well as Jews, deeming it necessary to do so in order to advance Jewish interests. Like other important leaders, too, he identified the common as well as competing needs of the various ethnic communities and was able to base authority on his perceptions. Contrary to the belief of some historians that the immigrants' adjustment to American culture was a one-way process, Newfield's work suggests that Jews and Christians learned to accommodate each other, identifying with leaders who helped them develop fruitful relationships. Finally, it is particularly important to note that liberalism continues to be present in Birmingham, and elsewhere in the South, thanks to the efforts of men such as Morris Newfield. He, and others like him, chose to accentuate the common interests that unite men and women rather than the differences, and anxieties about differences, that keep them apart.

NOTES

Preface

1. The quoted words appear in Anita Lebeson, *Pilgrim People* (New York: Harper, 1950), xi. Cf. Lee M. Friedman, "An Introduction to American Jewish History," *Publication of the American Jewish Historical Society* 38 (September 1948):21; also see Salo W. Baron, "American Jewish History: Problems and Methods," *Publication of the American Jewish Historical Society* 39 (September 1949):207–66.

ONE. The Early Years: From Hungary through Hebrew Union College

1. Elsa Schreiber [niece of Morris Newfield], telephone conversation, November 1980; Morenu Diploma of Rabbi Seymon Shabsi Neufeld, trans. Rabbi Isaiah Levy (New York, 1842), pamphlet in author's files. According to *The Jewish Encyclopedia* (1st ed., 1903), *morenu* means literally "our teacher" and is a term that has been used since the middle of the fourteenth century as a title for rabbis and Talmudists. Every ordained rabbi has the power to grant it, and it is occasionally conferred as an honorary title in recognition of services rendered to a community. The German reformer Leopold Zunz thought that the title was intended to add to rabbinical dignity, for the title of rabbi had lost its significance as "scholar" or "master," since it had become customary to bestow it upon every Jewish rabbi, whether or not he was a scholar.

2. Elsa Schreiber, telephone conversation, November 1980.

3. Elsa Schreiber, telephone conversation, November 1980; and Albert Markovits of Budapest to Morris Newfield, November 18, 1892, pp. 1–2, in the Morris Newfield Papers, American Jewish Archives, Hebrew Union College, Cincinnati.

4. Erno Márton, "Family Tree of Hungarian Jewry," in Randolph Braham, ed., *Hungarian Jewish Studies*, vol. 1 (New York: World Federation of Hungarian Jews, 1966), pp. 1–94.

5. Nathaniel Katzburg, "Hungarian Jewry in Modern Times," in Braham, ed., *Hungarian Jewish Studies*, 1:137–42.

6. Ibid., 1:140.

7. Ibid., 1:142, and see Morris Newfield Collection, Alabama State Department of Archives and History, Montgomery.

8. Various writers on Hungarian Jewry have noted the trade-off between Jews and Magyars in the period of the Dual Monarchy, 1867–1914. See William McCagg, *Jewish Geniuses and Nobles in Modern Hungary* (New York: Columbia University Press, 1972); McCagg, "Jews in Revolution: The Hungarian Experiment," *Journal of Social History* (1972–73):78–105; István Deák, "The Jewish Dilemma in the Multinational Empire of Francis Joseph" (lecture presented at the Leo Baeck Institute, January 22, 1975), pp. 1–14; and István Végházi, "The Role of Jewry in the Economic Life of Hungary," in Braham, ed., *Hungarian Jewish Studies,* vol. 2 (New York: World Federation of Hungarian Jews, 1969), p. 59.

9. For statistics on the role of Jews in the professions in the Dual Monarchy period, see the *Universal Jewish Encyclopedia* (1943 ed.), s.v. "Hungary."

10. Végházi, "The Role of Jewry," p. 169; and Végházi, "The Jewish Congress of Hungary, 1868–1869," in Braham ed., *Hungarian Jewish Studies,* vol. 2.

11. "Certificate of the National Rabbinical Training Institute of Budapest or Jewish Theological Seminary, Lower School or Bizonyitvány a Budapesti Országos Rabbi-képző-Intézet, Alsó Tanfolymában Végzett Tanulmányokról, 1884–1885," in the author's files. Also see the *Jahresbericht der Landes-Rabbinerschule in Budapest für das Schuljahr 1884–5, 1885–6, 1888–9,* Budapest, Buchdruckerei des Atheneum, 1885–89, Hebrew Union College (copy in the author's files). Also see Samuel Lowinger, ed., *Seventy Years: A Tribute to the Seventieth Anniversary of the Jewish Theological Seminary, 1877–1947* (Budapest: Jewish Theological Seminary, 1948). This book lists the doctorates awarded and rabbis graduated at the seminary. Newfield's name is not among them. There is some question as to whether Newfield received the B.D. degree from this seminary, because written documentation cannot be found. In various autobiographical sketches that Newfield wrote, for example those on file at the Alabama State Department of Archives and History, Montgomery, the rabbi suggested that he had received a degree in 1889 from the Royal Rabbinical Seminary in Budapest.

12. Articles on David Kaufmann, Wilhelm Bacher, and Josef Bonoczy appear in the *Universal Jewish Encyclopedia* (1943 ed.), pp. 21–22, 67, and 342–43. Also see Lowinger, ed., *Seventy Years.* David Kaufmann, 1852–99, a graduate of the Jewish Theological Seminary in Breslau, taught history, Jewish philosophy, and homiletics at the seminary in Budapest from 1877 to 1899 and published twenty-six books and more than 550 essays and reviews. One of his classic achievements in the field

of Jewish philosophy in the Middle Ages was his *Geschichte der Attributenlehre in der Judischen Religionsphilosophie von Saadia bis Maimuni* (1877). He also published a number of writings on the history of Jewish families and scholars, mainly in the seventeenth and eighteenth centuries, and was a chief promoter of the Society for the Preservation of Jewish History in Vienna in 1896. Bacher's scholarship also brought renown to the seminary in Budapest. His special fields of research were biblical exegesis, Hebrew philology, the Talmud, the Haggadah, and Judaeo-Persian literature. His writings were the first to present the material systematically and critically. Bacher's chief contributions to Jewish studies were his six volumes dealing with Haggadic material in the Talmud. He also served in 1907 as a director of the seminary. Bacher and Bonoczy, a teacher of philosophy at the seminary in Budapest until 1893, founded the *Hungarian Jewish Review* (*Magyar zsidó szeml*) and edited it from 1884 to 1890. Bonoczy also translated important philosophical works into Hungarian, notably Kant's *Kritik der reinen Vernunft* and Lewe's *History of Philosophy.*

13. "Minutes of the Fortieth Anniversary of the Graduating Class of the Royal Catholic Grand-Gymnasium, Budapest, 2nd District," pp. 1–3, in author's files. Mór Neufeld is listed as one of the graduates of the Class of 1889.

14. Elsa Schreiber, telephone conversation, November 1980; and Markovits to Neufeld, November 18, 1892.

15. Elsa Schreiber, telephone conversation, November 1980; and "Declaration of Intention for Naturalization of Morris Newfield" (September 22, 1894), in Morris Newfield Papers, American Jewish Archives, Cincinnati.

16. Michael Meyer, "A Centennial History," in Samuel E. Karff, ed., *Hebrew Union College–Jewish Institute of Religion: At One Hundred Years* (Cincinnati: Hebrew Union College Press, 1976), p. xvi.

17. Ibid., p. 26.

18. Mayer U. Newfield, personal interview, Birmingham, September 1979; see also "They Are Three," the *Cincinnati Enquirer,* June 1895; and *Yearbook of the 1895 Graduating Class of the University of Cincinnati,* p. 5, in Special Collections, University of Cincinnati. Morris Newfield, while a student at the college, lived in a boardinghouse at 458 West Eighth Street, a block from his friend and classmate George Solomon. Michael Meyer, in "A Centennial History," comments on the experiences of rabbinical students at this time: "Life in a boardinghouse was hardly luxurious. Students lived four in a room, slept together in trundle beds, and sometimes had to study in overcoats for want of proper heat. The food was cheap and poorly cooked. Explicit rules and regulations governed the life of the student in his boardinghouse. He was required to rise at 6:15 A.M. in the winter months and at 5:45 A.M. during the

summer (in Samuel E. Karff, ed., *Hebrew Union College–Jewish Institute of Religion at One Hundred Years* (Cincinnati: Hebrew Union College, 1976), p. 27.

19. Markovits to Newfield, November 18, 1892.

20. Grade Books of the Hebrew Union College, 1895–1900, American Jewish Archives, Cincinnati, p. 1; Newfield's grades from the University of Cincinnati are not available.

21. "Fifty Years of Service to God and Man," in the David Marx File, Temple Emanu-El Collection, American Jewish Archives, Cincinnati.

22. *Universal Jewish Encyclopedia* (1943 ed.), s.v. "Joseph S. Kornfeld."

23. Ibid., s.v. "Emil W. Leipziger."

24. *Who's Who in American Jewry* (1942 ed.), s.v. "Henry Englander."

25. *Universal Jewish Encyclopedia* (1943 ed.), s.v. "Abraham J. Messing."

26. M. Mohr to Morris Newfield, May 11, 1897, Morris Newfield Papers, American Jewish Archives.

27. Newfield to Hausman, May 12, 1897, Morris Newfield Papers, American Jewish Archives.

28. Carl Herman Voss, *Rabbi and Minister: The Friendship of Stephen S. Wise and John Haynes Holmes* (Cleveland: World Publishing, 1964), p. 114.

29. Rev. Washington Gladden, "Baccalaureate Address," in the *Seventeenth Annual Commencement Exercises of the University of Cincinnati* (June 5, 1895), p. 13, in Special Collections, University of Cincinnati.

TWO. A Leader of Birmingham Jews, 1895–1914

1. Jere C. King, Jr., "The Formation of Greater Birmingham" (M.A. thesis, University of Alabama, 1935).

2. Ibid.

3. Malcolm C. McMillan, *Yesterday's Birmingham* (Coral Gables: E. A. Seeman, 1975), pp. 10–20; C. Vann Woodward, *Origins of the New South* (Baton Rouge: Louisiana State University Press, 1971), pp. 8–10, 126–27; Jonathan M. Weiner, *Social Origins of the New South: Alabama, 1860–1885* (Baton Rouge: Louisiana State University Press, 1978); and Leah Rawls Atkins, *The Valley and the Hills: An Illustrated History of Birmingham and Jefferson County* (Woodhills, Calif.: Windsor Publishing, 1981), pp. 49–50.

4. Atkins, *The Valley and the Hills,* pp. 53–54.

5. Ibid., p. 56; McMillan, *Yesterday's Birmingham,* pp. 32–34; and

Martha Bigelow Mitchell, "History of Birmingham, 1870–1910" (Ph.D. diss., University of Chicago, 1946), p. 2 (copy in the Tutwiler Collection of Southern History, Birmingham Public Library).

6. Weiner, *Social Origins,* p. 162; and Atkins, *The Valley and the Hills,* pp. 60–61.

7. The quoted passages appear in Carl V. Harris, *Political Power in Birmingham, 1871–1921* (Knoxville: University of Tennessee Press, 1977), p. 17, and Bigelow, "History of Birmingham," p. 23, respectively; also see Woodward, *Origins of the New South,* pp. 126–29.

8. Ethel Armes, "The Spirit of the Founders," in *Survey,* January 6, 1913, 1455–56 (reprint in Tutwiler Collection, Birmingham Public Library); Weiner, *Social Origins;* and Bigelow, "History of Birmingham," p. 126.

9. Harris, *Political Power,* p. 21.

10. McMillan, *Yesterday's Birmingham,* p. 38.

11. Ethel Armes, "The Spirit of the Founders," *Survey Magazine,* January 6, 1913, p. 1456; and Virginia Van der Veer Hamilton, *Alabama: A Bicentennial History* (New York: W. W. Norton, 1977).

12. Hamilton, *Alabama,* p. 135; and Ann McCorquodale Burkhardt, "Town within a City: The Five Points South Neighborhood, 1880–1920," *Journal of the Birmingham Historical Society* 7, nos. 3 and 4 (November 1982):ii–90.

13. Atkins, *The Valley and the Hills,* pp. 84–86.

14. Mark H. Elovitz, *A Century of Jewish Life in Dixie: The Birmingham Experience* (University: University of Alabama Press, 1974), pp. 30–32; also see James Bowron, Autobiography, typescript, 3 vols., William Stanley Hoole Special Collections Library, University of Alabama Library, Tuscaloosa.

15. Hamilton, *Alabama,* p. 136.

16. Ibid.

17. King, Jr., "Formation of Greater Birmingham"; and Carl V. Harris, "Annexation Struggles and Political Power in Birmingham, Alabama, 1890–1910," *Alabama Review* 27 (July 1974):163–84.

18. Harris, "Annexation Struggles."

19. Isaac Mayer Wise to Adolph S. Ochs, September 13, 1892, Morris Newfield Papers, American Jewish Archives.

20. Robert G. Corley, *Paying Civic Rent: The Jews of Emanu-El and the Birmingham Community* (Birmingham: A. H. Cather Publishing, 1982), unpaginated.

21. Morris Newfield, "A History of the Birmingham Jewish Community," in *Reform Advocate,* November 4, 1911, pp. 6–33. Rabbi Hirsch of Temple Sinai in Chicago, a friend of Newfield's, was writing the histories of various Jewish communities throughout the country and asked Newfield to do a piece on Birmingham Jews. Also see Elovitz, *A Century of Jewish Life,* pp. 7–9 and 23.

22. Newfield, "A History," pp. 17, 19, 21; and Elovitz, *A Century of Jewish Life,* pp. 24–25.

23. Newfield, "A History," pp. 15, 17; and Elovitz, *A Century of Jewish Life,* pp. 27, 62–63.

24. Newfield, "A History," pp. 17, 19; and Elovitz, *A Century of Jewish Life,* pp. 30–32.

25. Corley, *Paying Civic Rent;* and Newfield, "A History," pp. 15, 17, 21.

26. Corley, *Paying Civic Rent.*

27. Newfield, "A History," p. 7.

28. Ibid., pp. 7, 9.

29. Ibid., p. 9.

30. Ibid., p. 11; and Samuel Ullman to Max Samfield, May 21, 1890, and Samfield to Ullman, June 1, 1890, in Temple Emanu-El, Birmingham.

31. Minute Books of Temple Emanu-El (December 7, 1890), in Temple Emanu-El, Birmingham.

32. For a discussion of Ullman's and Steiner's contributions to Emanu-El, and Marx's year in Birmingham, see Minute Books of Temple Emanu-El (1887–1905).

33. Burghardt Steiner to Isaac Mayer Wise, March 13, 1895, in author's files.

34. Samuel Ullman to Richard Fries, 1920, in author's files.

35. "Minutes of the Birmingham Board of Education," (1884–1902), Board of Education, Birmingham.

36. Ibid.; and Mayer U. Newfield, personal interview, Birmingham, September 1979.

37. Corley, *Paying Civic Rent* (unpaginated).

38. For information about Ullman and the various members of the Board of Aldermen and Board of Education, see scrapbooks in the George B. Ward Collection (December 6, 14, 1900), Department of Archives and Manuscripts, Birmingham Public Library.

39. Samuel Ullman was sixty years old when he was removed from the Board of Education. Samuel Ullman's legacy is even more far-reaching, however. Ironically, in 1952 the Birmingham Board of Education asked Ullman's grandson and Newfield's son, Mayer Ullman Newfield, whether the family would have any objection if the school became a high school for black students. In the period between 1902 and 1952, the population in the school's neighborhood had changed from predominantly white to predominantly black. In a letter to Josephine Lowman dated November 30, 1972 (in the files at Mark Elovitz), Mayer Newfield commented, "I told the superintendent . . . , we would be delighted, and I recalled to the superintendent that as a youngster I had been deeply impressed by the statements made by my grandfather in which he referred to his continuing struggle on the Board of Education to obtain a fair share of money for

the education of black pupils. He emphasized that . . . the dual school system was indeed separate but shockingly unequal." In 1971 the Samuel Ullman School became an administrative building (the Ullman Building) for the University of Alabama at Birmingham, which has a student body in excess of 6,000, including black students. Thus the school ultimately helped combat injustice toward black children, as Samuel Ullman would have wished. Samuel Ullman's granddaughter, Marie Ullman, the daughter of Ullman's fourth son, Moses Montefiore Ullman (Monte), not only attended the school but also taught second grade there from 1928 to 1932 at the request of Charles B. Glenn, the superintendent of the Birmingham public schools. Samuel Ullman, *From a Summit of Years—Four Score* (Birmingham: privately published, 1920), copy in author's files. Also see George E. Sokolsky, "From a Summit of Years—Four Score," *New York Journal American,* March 10, 1955, and "Second Front Page," *Birmingham News,* April 7, 1964.

40. Morris Newfield to Leah Newfield, July 29, 1898, in author's files. Emma Newfield Minisman, personal interview, Birmingham, November 1980.

41. Burghardt Steiner to Officers and Members of Congregation Emanu-El, "Report of the President" (August 12, 1898), p. 1, in author's files. See also Newfield, "A History," p. 13.

42. Morris Newfield to President and Members of Congregation Emanu-El, "Rabbi's Report," August 29, 1897; and Burghardt Steiner to Morris Newfield, January 13, 1897, in author's files. For a discussion of the battles that Kaufmann Kohler and Emil Hirsch fought with the Boards of Directors of Temple Sinai, Chicago, c. 1874–1900, see Records of Temple Sinai, American Jewish Archives.

43. Minute Books of Temple Emanu-El (April 6, 1899).

44. Ben Blumenthal to Emil Neufeld, July 12, 1896; Morris Newfield to David Weil, March 8, 1897; and S. Haas, president of Shaarai Shomayim, Mobile, to Morris Newfield, March 13, 1898, all in author's files.

45. Samuel Katz to Morris Newfield, January 6, 1899; Newfield to Katz, January 12, 1899; Alex Sanger to Newfield, March 2, 1900; Newfield to Sanger, April 3, 1900; Sanger to Newfield, June 12, 1901; and Newfield to Sanger, June 18, 1901, in Morris Newfield Papers, American Jewish Archives.

46. Newfield to Sanger, April 3, 1900, in Morris Newfield Papers, American Jewish Archives.

47. Ibid.

48. Newfield, "A History," p. 25; Elovitz, *A Century of Jewish Life,* p. 69; and Morris Newfield to Leah Newfield, September 3, 1905, in author's files.

49. Elovitz, *A Century of Jewish Life,* p. 69; also see Morris Newfield to Leah Newfield, 1896–1914, in author's files.

50. Minute Books of Emanu-El, 1904–1905; Newfield, "A History," p. 23; and Elovitz, *A Century of Jewish Life,* p. 70. Also see Mayer U. Newfield, personal interview, Birmingham, October 1980.

51. Morris Newfield to Leah Newfield, October 2, 1902, and September 18, 1904, in author's files.

52. Mayer U. Newfield, telephone conversation, October 1984.

53. The quoted phrases appear in Sylvia Blascoer Kohn, *By Reason of Strength: The Story of Temple Emanu-El's Seventy Years, 1882–1952* (Birmingham: Temple Emanu-El, 1952), pp. 17–18; and Elovitz, *A Century of Jewish Life,* pp. 71–75.

54. Dedication Service of Temple Emanu-El (March 6–8, 1914), pp. 1–16, in author's files; and Thomas D. Parke, Diaries, 1895–1923 (entry for March 15, 1914), Department of Archives and Manuscripts, Birmingham Public Library.

55. Kaufmann Kohler to Newfield, March 5, 1914; Solomon to Newfield, March 7, 1914; Deutsch to Newfield, March 6, 1914; Stolz to Newfield, March 7, 1914; Stephen Wise to Newfield, February 26, 1914; Max Heller to Newfield, March 2, 1914, all in author's files.

56. Burghardt Steiner to Morris Newfield, March 6, 1914, in author's files.

57. Elovitz, *A Century of Jewish Life,* pp. 54–59; also see Ande Manners, *Poor Cousins* (New York: Coward, McCann, and Geoghegan, 1972); and Oscar Handlin, *Adventures in Freedom: 300 Years of Jewish Life in America* (New York: McGraw-Hill, 1954).

58. Morris Newfield to Leah Newfield, September 8, 1905, in author's files.

59. Morris Newfield, Yom Kippur Eve Address (October 1911), sermon delivered at Temple Emanu-El, American Jewish Archives; and Morris Newfield to Leah Newfield, July 26, 1911, and August 2, 1911, in author's files.

60. Minutes of the Young Men's Hebrew Association (June 27, August 4, October 27, November 24, 1909, and March 28, 1910), Jewish Community Center, Birmingham.

61. Morris Newfield, "Immigration," sermon delivered to Birmingham Women's Club (1913), pp. 1–5, Morris Newfield Papers, American Jewish Archives.

62. Morris Newfield to Leah Newfield, November 15, 1909, in author's files.

THREE. Newfield the Man

1. Mayer U. Newfield, personal interviews, Birmingham, September 1979, March 1983.

2. Ibid.

3. Ibid.

4. Emma Newfield Minisman, personal interview, Birmingham, October 1980; and Mayer U. Newfield, personal interview, March 1983.

5. Newfield, personal interview, March 1983.

6. Ibid.

7. Ibid.

8. Ibid.; and "Rabbi Had Special Seat," *Birmingham Age-Herald,* May 17, 1940.

9. Mayer U. Newfield, personal interview, Birmingham, March 1983.

10. Ibid.

11. *Birmingham Age-Herald,* May 27, 1919.

12. Mayer U. Newfield, personal interview, March 1983; and Emma N. Minisman, personal interview, October 1980.

13. Morris Newfield to Leah Newfield, August 31, 1914, in author's files.

14. Morris Newfield to Leah Newfield, January 15, 1901, August 5, 1902, July 1 and July 4, 1906, in author's files.

15. Morris Newfield to Leah Newfield, April 3, 1909, in author's files.

16. Mayer U. Newfield, personal interview, March 1983.

17. Ibid., September 1979, and October 1980; and Emma N. Minisman, October 1980.

18. Mayer U. Newfield, personal interview, March 1983.

19. Morris Newfield to Leah Newfield, April 3, 1909, in author's files.

20. Mayer U. Newfield, personal interview, March 1983.

21. See Morris Newfield Collection and Thomas M. Owen, *History of Alabama and Dictionary of Alabama Biography* (1921; reprint, Spartenburg, Reprint Company, 1978), copy in Alabama State Department of Archives and History, Montgomery. Also see interviews with Newfield family.

22. Interviews with Newfield family.

23. Ibid.

24. Ibid.

FOUR. A Leader in Birmingham, 1895–1920

1. Corley, *Paying Civic Rent* (unpaginated).

2. Ibid.

3. Ibid.; and Atkins, *The Valley and the Hills,* p. 121.

4. Atkins, *The Valley and the Hills,* p. 121; and Harris, *Political Power in Birmingham.*

5. Atkins, *The Valley and the Hills,* p. 121.

6. Edwin Scott Gaustad, *Historical Atlas of Religion in America* (New

York: Harper and Row, 1976); Bureau of the Census, U.S. Department of Commerce and Labor, *Religious Bodies* (Washington, D.C., 1910); and Woodward, *Origins of the New South,* pp. 449–50. Also see *American Jewish Yearbook* (1919–20 ed.), s.v. "Characteristics of Jewish Population in the United States." To speak of the approximate strength of the 170,000 Christians may be misleading; approximately 50 percent of the Protestants were black. Jews were far more interested in what the white Protestants were thinking, because they held the most powerful political, social, and cultural positions in the city. Black Protestants, on the other hand, like all blacks in Alabama, were disenfranchised in 1901, and segregation laws were in force by the end of the first decade of the twentieth century. As a result, blacks held no prestigious positions in Birmingham. Nevertheless, the figure does attest to the strength of Protestantism in the South. The various sects attracted many blacks and whites. In addition it is clear that Newfield's congregants represented a much larger percentage of the white population in the business and professional classes of Birmingham, although absolute figures are not available. This generation of Jews consisted primarily of businessmen and lawyers, while its sons and daughters became doctors and other professionals.

7. For a more extensive discussion of the idea of Reform rabbis as "ambassadors to the Gentiles," see David Bernstein and Adele Bernstein, "Slow Revolution in Richmond, Virginia: A New Pattern in the Making," in Leonard Dinnerstein and Mary Palsson, eds., *Jews in the South* (Baton Rouge: Louisiana State University Press, 1973), pp. 251–64. Also consult Eli Evans, *The Provincials: A Personal History of Jews in the South* (New York: Atheneum, 1973); and W. Gunther Plaut, *The Growth of Reform Judaism: American and European Sources until 1948,* vol. 2 (New York: World Union for Progressive Judaism, 1965), pp. 3–17.

8. Plaut, *The Growth of Reform Judaism,* p. 14; and Morris Newfield, "Isaac Mayer Wise," sermon delivered at Temple Emanu-El (1900), in Morris Newfield Papers, American Jewish Archives.

9. Benny Kraut, *From Reform Judaism to Ethical Culture* (Cincinnati: Hebrew Union College Press, 1979); and Plaut, *The Growth of Reform Judaism,* pp. 29–31.

10. Plaut, *The Growth of Reform Judaism,* pp. 26–28.

11. Ibid., pp. 32–36.

12. Morris Newfield, "The History of the Jew" (n.d.) and "Address on Shavuoth" (1896), sermons delivered at Temple Emanu-El, American Jewish Archives.

13. Nathan Glazer, *American Judaism* (Chicago: University of Chicago Press, 1972), p. 53; Kraut, *From Reform Judaism*; and Newfield, "High Holidays" (1894), p. 8, and "Pesach" (1899), p. 10, sermons delivered at Temple Emanu-El, American Jewish Archives.

14. For a full discussion of the reasons why Jews and Christians did not develop a universal religion in 1900, see Egal Feldman, "The Social Gospel and the Jews," *American Jewish Historical Quarterly* 58, no. 3 (March 1969):308–34; Glazer, *The Growth of Reform Judaism;* and Kraut, *From Reform Judaism.* Feldman claims that Reform Jewish rabbis and progressive Christian ministers shared a number of ideas about the development of a universal religion but that Christian ministers rejected Jewish participation in a religion of humanity. Glazer and Kraut, while they do not speak directly to this issue, suggest that Reform rabbis were unwilling to join with Christians in a religion of humanity because doing so might cost Jews their distinctive group identity.

15. Newfield, "Doctrine of Evolution and Its Effect on Modern Religious Thought" (n.d.), pp. 4–5; "The Ghetto Jew" (April 28, 1913), p. 1; "Why We Are and Remain Jews" (February 12, 1909), p. 1; and "Orthodoxy and Changing Beliefs" (1910), p. 1, all sermons delivered at Temple Emanu-El, American Jewish Archives.

16. Newfield, "Yom Kippur Eve" (1899), p. 10; and "The Religion of Greed versus that of Deed" (January 8, 1915), pp. 1–2, sermons delivered at Temple Emanu-El, American Jewish Archives.

17. Newfield, "Religion of Dogmatism" (March 1914), p. 1; and Yom Kippur Eve Address (1898), pp. 4–5, sermons delivered at Temple Emanu-El, American Jewish Archives.

18. Newfield, "Yom Kippur Eve" (1899), p. 11, sermon delivered at Temple Emanu-El, American Jewish Archives.

19. Newfield, Yom Kippur Eve Address (1895), p. 5; Yom Kippur Address (1898), p. 6; Rosh Hashana Address (1896), p. 8, sermons delivered at Temple Emanu-El, American Jewish Archives.

20. Newfield, "True Greatness" (February 1906), p. 5; "New Year's Eve" (1913), p. 1; "New Year's Thoughts" (1920), p. 1, sermons delivered at Temple Emanu-El, American Jewish Archives.

21. Newfield, "Festival of Conclusion" (October 1907), pp. 2–3, sermon delivered at Temple Emanu-El, American Jewish Archives.

22. Newfield, "Doctrine of Evolution and Its Effect on Modern Religion" (n.d.), p. 4, and "The Bible in the Light of Scientific Study" (n.d.), pp. 1–2, sermons delivered at Temple Emanu-El, American Jewish Archives.

23. Newfield, "Pesach" (1900), p. 6; and "True Aristocrats" (February 1906), p. 4, sermons delivered at Temple Emanu-El, American Jewish Archives.

24. Historians of southern religion disagree about the nature of religion in the South, especially in Birmingham. Samuel S. Hill of the University of Florida, who has written and edited a number of books and articles, claims that southern Protestantism is inherently conservative and very little interested in any type of social reform. Not only is the southern church simply interested in the regeneration of human hearts,

according to Hill, but dissonant doctrines, approaches, or emphases are rarely heard. See Samuel S. Hill, ed., *On Jordan's Stormy Banks: Religion in the South, A Southern Exposure Profile* (Macon: Mercer University Press, 1983); and Hill, ed., *Religion in the Southern States: Essays on the History of Religion in the Southern United States* (Macon: Mercer University Press, 1983). Rufus Spain, in his unpublished doctoral dissertation, "Attitudes and Reactions of Southern Baptists to Certain Problems of Society, 1865–1900," suggests, too, that southern Baptists were very conservative and that the reason why they failed to develop a greater degree of social consciousness was the logical consequence of certain characteristics of the denomination and of the region in which the denomination flourished. He argues that the congregational structure of Baptist church life made it possible for lower- and middle-class members to determine policy, thus perpetuating customary ways of thinking and acting. Since the emphasis of social Christianity was on innovation, Baptists responded to it with suspicion. Baptist ministers also contributed to the conservatism of the denomination. They were for the most part poorly trained and readily conformed to the conservative tendencies of the laity and actively defended many of the traditional views and practices of the denomination which better-educated and more sophisticated ministers would have sought to change. Finally, Spain argues that conditions in the South were not conducive to the development of social Christianity. Industrialization, immigration, urbanization, and other problems which gave rise to social Christianity in the North, he argues, were largely absent from the South. Consequently Baptists saw little immediate need for a change in emphasis. The old-time gospel was still adequate for the rural South. Kenneth K. Bailey, in his *Southern White Protestantism in the Twentieth Century* (New York: Harper and Row, 1964), suggests that C. Vann Woodward in his *Origins of the New South* overstates the influence of evangelical Christians in southern Protestant churches. "Between the turn of the century and World War I," he writes, "the three major Southern white Protestant groups underwent significant changes in program and outlook. Absorbed at the turn of the century in evangelism and little mindful of social needs beyond blue laws and prohibition, they emerged during the next fifteen years as advocates of social justice proclaiming the Christian obligation to fashion Christ's kingdom on earth" (pp. 41–42). Bailey carefully refrains, however, from suggesting that southern Protestant churches emphasized social concerns: "To resolve, to proclaim, and to pronounce was not to strive or emphasize. Except for prohibition, few social problems received much attention below the level of the conference, the association, or the presbytery" (p. 43). Wayne Flynt, in his "Religion in the Urban South: The Divided Mind of Birmingham, 1900–1930," *Alabama Review* 30, no. 2 (April 1977):108–35, although admitting that evangelical Protestant churches were a potent force in Birmingham at this time, observes,

"Birmingham, as a city of the 'New South,' could not escape the industrial and urban stresses that were transforming American life in the late nineteenth century . . . , forcing pietistic Protestantism to begin dealing with the city's critical social problems" (pp. 109–10). He makes a persuasive argument for his assertion that Birmingham churches were more liberal and charted a "new course that led them further and further from the other-worldly salvation gospel of the nineteenth century . . . which resulted in 'Social Gospel' reform."

25. Many churches in Birmingham were characterized by Protestant traditionalism. Their congregants, generally called evangelical Christians, wholeheartedly accepted a supernatural religion expressed by their beliefs in the centrality of Scripture, in the personality of Jesus or in God's immanence more than God's transcendence, and in being "born again," or the choice of adult baptism. Furthermore, the task of spreading the gospel, or the word of God—"evangelizing" in churches and schools of Birmingham—was very important. There was, it must be noted, no typical evangelical Christian, nor was there a consensus as to what constituted evangelical beliefs. We can, however, distinguish between more moderate and Fundamentalist evangelical types. The term "Fundamentalist" was reserved for the more conservative, right-wing members of the evangelical community. The major theological issue that divided moderate from conservative evangelicals was whether Scripture was inerrant and infallible. Conservatives insisted that the Bible was without error historically or scientifically. Fundamentalist Christians after World War I were noted, especially in Birmingham and throughout the South, for their extremist, anticultural, and hostile expressions to the developing modern America. Theologically these very conservative Protestants feared those individuals who attempted to reconcile Christianity with scientific advances. They rejected theories of evolution, eschewed biblical criticism, and spent little time applying Christian teaching to the social milieu. Birmingham's three traditional southern denominations, Baptists, Methodists, and Presbyterians, were involved in activities that emphasized saving of souls. Furthermore, two denominational newspapers of the period that were published in Birmingham, the *Alabama Baptist* and the *Alabama Christian Advocate,* the official organ of Methodists, also indicate that these two groups spent a great deal of time saving souls and molding the conduct of people. The *Alabama Baptist* in 1906, for example, kept weekly counts of Baptist missions and published articles arguing that children might benefit from a just labor law but that they could be better reached by the spreading of the Gospel.

26. Wayne Flynt, as I have noted, has written extensively and persuasively on the notion that southern Protestants, and more particularly Birmingham Protestants, were concerned with social issues and the development of a Social Gospel theology. See Wayne Flynt, "Religion in the Urban South"; Flynt, "Dissent in Zion: Alabama Baptists and Social

Issues, 1900–1914," *Alabama Review* (November 1969):523–42; and Wallace M. Alston, Jr., and Wayne Flynt, "Religion in the Land of Cotton," in H. Brandt Ayers and Thomas H. Naylor, eds., *You Can't Eat Magnolias* (New York: McGraw-Hill, 1972), pp. 99–112.

27. Wayne Flynt, "Religion in the Urban South."

28. Dinnerstein and Palsson, eds., *Jews in the South;* and Alfred O. Hero, Jr., *The Southerner and World Affairs* (Baton Rouge: Louisiana State University Press, 1955).

29. Newfield, "Succoth" (1896), pp. 2–3; and "Succoth" (1897), p. 5, sermons delivered at Temple Emanu-El, American Jewish Archives.

30. Dinnerstein and Palsson, eds., *Jews in the South,* introduction.

31. Ibid.; also see Newfield, "Alexander the Great" (n.d.), and "Confirmation" (1897), p. 1, sermons delivered at Temple Emanu-El, American Jewish Archives.

32. Newfield, "A Jewish View of Jesus: Declares He Can Accept Jesus as Great and Good Teacher" (n.d.), in author's files.

33. Newfield, "Pesach" (1898), p. 15; and "Jews: Religion, Nation, and Race" (n.d.), p. 2, sermons delivered at Temple Emanu-El, American Jewish Archives.

34. Newfield, "Rosh Hashana Morning" (September 9, 1907), p. 2; and "New Year's Morning" (1903), p. 3, sermons delivered at Temple Emanu-El, American Jewish Archives.

35. Newfield, "Dream of Temple" (n.d.), p. 5, sermon delivered at Temple Emanu-El, American Jewish Archives.

36. Newfield, "Pesach" (1911), p. 1, "Rosh Hashana Morning" (1896), p. 8; "Revelations in Judaism" (1900), p. 4, sermons delivered at Temple Emanu-El, American Jewish Archives.

37. Newfield, "Atonement Morning" (1898), p. 5, sermon delivered at Temple Emanu-El, American Jewish Archives.

38. Newfield, "Atonement Eve" (October 4, 1908), p. 2, sermon delivered at Temple Emanu-El, American Jewish Archives.

39. Harris, *Political Power,* pp. 196–98.

40. Ibid.

41. Newfield to P. B. Wells, April 20, 1918, and P. B. Wells to Newfield, April 25, 1918, in author's files.

42. Anonymous to Newfield, May 7, 1918, in author's files.

43. Alfred J. Dickinson to Newfield, n.d., and Robert Simpson to Newfield, April 22, 1918, in author's files.

44. Harris, *Political Power,* p. 198; and Minute Books of the Pastors Union, 1911–1917, in the possession of Dr. D. R. Price, Birmingham.

45. Until recently, American religious historians argued that only Christian ministers articulated a Social Gospel theology at the turn of the century. The most significant contribution to the idea of a Christian social gospel is Charles Hopkins, *The Rise of the Social Gospel in American Protestantism, 1865–1915* (New Haven: Yale University Press,

1940), which treated the ideas of progressive Christian ministers such as Gladden, George Herron, and Walter Rauschenbusch in concise and responsible fashion. The first edition of the *Encyclopedia of the Social Sciences* (1933) discussed the concept of the social gospel under the subject "Social Christianity." Other contributions that have dealt with a Christian social gospel include Aaron I. Abell, *The Urban Impact on American Protestantism, 1865–1900* (Cambridge, Mass.: Harvard University Press, 1943); Paul Carter, *The Decline and the Revival of the Social Gospel* (Ithaca: Cornell University Press, 1954); Robert D. Cross, ed., *The Church and the City, 1865–1910* (New York: Bobbs-Merrill, 1967); Robert T. Handy, ed., *The Social Gospel in America* (New York: Oxford University Press, 1966); and Cushing Strout, *The New Heavens and New Earth: Political Religion in America* (New York: Harper and Row, 1974). More recently, however, historians have begun to notice the efforts of Jews and Catholics in the Social Gospel movement. Hopkins and Ronald White edited *The Social Gospel: Religion and Reform in Changing America* (Philadelphia: Temple University Press, 1976) and included chapters on Jews and Catholics. Their discussion of Jews, however, is not comprehensive, and they do not compare Jews and other religious groups. Egal Feldman's "The Social Gospel and the Jews," mentioned above, discusses the Christian unwillingness to promote a religion of humanity. As a result, it does not consider why Jews were also unwilling to promote a religion of humanity. Benny Kraut's *From Reform Judaism to Ethical Culture* (Cincinnati: Hebrew Union College Press, 1979) grapples with the desires of Jews to maintain their separate religious status, although this is not the main thrust of the book. See also Mittie Owen McDavid, *A History of the Church of the Advent* (Birmingham: Church of the Advent, 1943), pp. 63–67; Henry M. Edmonds, *A Parson's Notebook* (Birmingham: Independent Presbyterian Church, 1960); and Washington Gladden, *Applied Christianity: Moral Aspects or Social Questions*, ed. Gerald N. Grob (reprint; New York: Arno Press, 1976).

46. For a discussion of the parallels between Newfield's teaching and that of Protestant theologians of the era, see Mark Cowett, "Rabbi Morris Newfield and the Social Gospel: Theology and Societal Reform in the South," *American Jewish Archives* 34, no. 1 (April 1982), pp. 52–74. Theologians of national stature such as Walter Rauschenbusch, Washington Gladden, and Theodore Munger, like Newfield, rejected selfish, acquisitive values, suggesting that churches could not forget the ideas of social justice and Christian fraternity.

47. Jenkin Lloyd Jones to Morris Newfield, March 2, 1898, and Thomas D. Parke, Diaries, 1895–1923 (entry for March 15, 1914), Department of Archives and Manuscripts, Birmingham Public Library. Also see *National Cyclopedia of American Biography* (1918 ed.), s.v. "Jenkin Lloyd Jones."

48. Parke, Diaries (entries for April 15, 1917, September 30, 1920, and March 26, 1917).

49. Flynt, "Religion in the Urban South," p. 112; and see John Howard Burrows, "The Great Disturber: The Social Philosophy and Theology of Alfred James Dickinson" (M.A. thesis, Samford University, 1970).

50. A. J. Dickinson to Morris Newfield, n.d., a personal letter commenting on "The Jewish Christian Sabbath," in author's files.

51. Frank Wills Barnett, "Men, Women, and Things," in *Birmingham Age-Herald,* October 1, 1920, copy in author's files.

52. Newfield, "A Jewish View of Jesus," n.p.

53. Mayer U. Newfield, personal interview, Birmingham, October 1980.

54. For a fuller discussion of the controversy, see Presbytery of North Alabama, *A Review and an Exposition of the Case of Dr. H. M. Edmonds and the Presbytery of North Alabama* (n.p.: privately published, 1915), pp. 3–20, Tutwiler Collection of Southern History, Birmingham Public Library. Also see Henry M. Edmonds and the Officers of the Independent Presbyterian Church, *The Other Side of the Recent Case of Dr. Henry M. Edmonds and the North Alabama Presbytery* (n.p.: privately published, 1915), pp. 1–12, Tutwiler Collection.

55. Edmonds and the Officers of the Independent Presbyterian Church, *The Other Side,* pp. 1–12.

56. Ibid., pp. 12–13.

57. Sydney J. Bowie to Morris Newfield, October 22, 1915, in author's files; and Edmonds, *A Parson's Notebook,* pp. 194–96.

58. Newfield, Edmonds, et al., "A Thanksgiving Message to the People of Birmingham" (November 25, 1915), sermon delivered at civic Thanksgiving service, Lyric Theatre, Birmingham, American Jewish Archives.

59. Edmonds, *A Parson's Notebook,* p. 195.

60. Ibid.

61. Ibid.

62. Ibid.

63. McDavid, *A History of the Church of the Advent,* pp. 63–64.

64. Middleton S. Barnwell to Morris Newfield, May 18, 1922, pp. 1–2, in author's files; and McDavid, *A History of the Church of the Advent,* p. 65.

FIVE. A Leading Social Worker in Alabama, 1909–1940

1. Social historians have written hundreds of volumes about the period 1900–1930, including many about the Social Justice movement

among the Progressives. Some of the more significant works on the Progressives, the 1920s, and the New Deal include: Robert Wiebe, *The Search for Order* (New York: Hill and Wang, 1967); Wiebe, *Businessmen and Reform* (Cambridge, Mass.: Harvard University Press, 1962); Richard Hofstadter, *The Age of Reform* (New York: Alfred A. Knopf, 1955); Eric F. Goldman, *Rendezvous with Destiny* (New York: Alfred A. Knopf, 1952); Allen F. Davis, *Spearheads for Reform* (New York: Oxford University Press, 1967); Robert Buroker, "From Voluntary Association to Welfare State: The Illinois Immigrants' Protective League, 1908–1926" (M.A. thesis, University of Chicago, 1971); and James Weinstein, *The Corporate Ideal in a Welfare State* (New York: Beacon Press, 1969). On the 1920s see William Leuchtenberg, *The Perils of Prosperity* (Chicago: University of Chicago Press, 1958); Arthur Link, "What Happened to the Progressive Movement in the 20's?" in Arthur Mann, ed., *The Progressive Era* (1963; reprint, Chicago: University of Chicago Press, 1975); and Clarke Chambers, *Seedtime for Reform* (Minneapolis: University of Minnesota Press, 1963). For the 1930s and the New Deal, see Otis L. Graham, *An Encore for Reform* (New York: Oxford University Press, 1967); and Leuchtenberg, *Franklin D. Roosevelt and the New Deal, 1932–1940* (New York: Harper and Row, 1963). These are only a few of the monographs that deal with the development of social reform in the twentieth century. More significantly, for the purposes of this study, four writers have written on social reform efforts in the South in this period. C. Van Woodward, *Origins of the New South* (Baton Rouge: Louisiana State University Press, 1971), sees southern Progressivism as a movement led by middle-class businessmen and farmers who fought plutocrats from the northeastern section of the United States. He also argues that it was a movement for "whites only." The biggest weakness with his work is that he concentrates on reform activities in the sphere of business and says very little about humanitarian reform. George Tindall in *The Emergence of the New South, 1913–45* (Baton Rouge: Louisiana State University Press, 1967) also sees it primarily as an economic revolt, but he does mention the work of some of the social reformers. Unfortunately, his discussion is limited to a comment on the Southern Sociological Congress, 1912–18. Although his observation that reformers' efforts carried religious overtones is apt, he does not delve deeply into some of the issues with which social reformers were concerned, such as child care, relief problems, and so forth. Dewey Grantham's *Hoke Smith and the Politics of the New South* (Baton Rouge: Louisiana State University Press, 1958), is an adequate biography of one of the Progressive governors, but it is largely limited to Georgia's political and economic affairs. Finally, Arthur Link's "The Progressive Movement in the South, 1879–1914" (*North Carolina Historical Review* 23:2 [April 1946]:172–95) does little more than quibble with Robert La Follette's idea that there was no southern Progressive movement. One other recent study, F.

Sheldon Hackney's *Populism and Progressivism in Alabama* (Princeton: Princeton University Press, 1969) is a far more comprehensive effort that tries to define the nature of Progressivism in Alabama. Hackney, however, seems to do little more than restate Wiebe's idea that the proponents of Progressivism consisted of businessmen who were trying to rationalize their environment in a search for order. Nevertheless, it is a good place to start for a discussion of the key issues with which social reformers were concerned. In order to understand the relationship between the Progressive movement and the Social Gospel contributions, see the notes for chapter 4. The relationship is especially significant because the influence of ministers was so strong in this heavily Protestant area. Also see Washington Gladden, "Baccalaureate Address," pp. 1–13.

2. Bessie Brooks, *A Half Century of Family Welfare in Jefferson County* (Birmingham: Roberts and Sons, 1936); and Anita Van DeVoort, "Public Welfare Administration in Jefferson County" (M.A. thesis, Tulane University, 1935).

3. Edward S. LaMonte, "Politics and Welfare in Birmingham, Alabama, 1900–1975" (Ph.D. diss., University of Chicago, 1978), pp. 5–6.

4. LaMonte, "Politics and Welfare," pp. 177–80.

5. Thus far, historians have disagreed about the goals of professional social workers in the period 1910–30. Some, like Roy Lubove (*The Professional Altruist* [Cambridge, Mass.: Harvard University Press, 1965]), have emphasized the development of a casework method and have suggested that professional social workers turned away from social reform. Other writers, including Robert Bremner (*American Philanthropy* [Chicago: University of Chicago Press, 1960] and *From the Depths: The Discovery of Poverty in the United States* [New York: New York University Press, 1956]), Walter I. Trattner (*From Poor Law to Welfare State* [New York: Free Press, 1974]), and Clarke Chambers (*Seedtime for Reform*), stress the idea that social workers not only developed a professional discipline but also continued to push for social reform. A good starting point for a discussion of social work in the South would be Elizabeth Wisner, *Social Welfare in the South* (Baton Rouge: Louisiana State University Press, 1938). Two primary sources that are useful to read to understand the developments of the discipline include Mary Richmond, *Social Diagnosis* (New York: Russell Sage Foundation, 1917), and Frank J. Bruno, *Trends in Social Work as Reflected in the Proceedings of the National Conference of Social Work, 1874–1946* (New York: Columbia University Press, 1948). To understand why there were few trained workers in the South, the reader can also go to the *Encyclopedia of Social Work*, vol. 1, A–N (1929), and the *International Directory of Schools of Social Work* (1954). Of the twenty-eight professional schools of social work in 1929, only four were in the South: Tulane, Atlanta University, University of North Carolina at Chapel Hill, and William and Mary.

Although students could go to northern schools and then return to work in the South, professional training seems to have been less important in the South; trained workers were lacking in the various welfare agencies, and there was a dearth of schools in the immediate vicinity.

6. Ibid.

7. Leonard Mervis, "The Social Justice Movement and the American Reform Rabbinate," *American Jewish Archives* (Fall 1955):172.

8. Ibid., p. 176.

9. Daniel Levine, "Edgar Gardner Murphy: Conservative Reformer," *Alabama Review* 15 (April 1962):100–15; and Hugh C. Bailey, *Edgar Gardner Murphy, Gentle Progressive* (Coral Gables: University of Miami Press, 1968).

10. Morris Newfield to Leah Newfield, September 26, 1907, in author's files.

11. Van DeVoort, "Public Welfare Administration," pp. 5–23.

12. Brooks, *A Half Century*, pp. 2–4.

13. Morris Newfield to Leah Newfield, March 21, 23, 24, 1909, in author's files; Brooks, *A Half Century*, p. 4; and LaMonte, "Politics and Welfare," pp. 112–20.

14. Van DeVoort, "Public Welfare Administration," pp. 36–38.

15. LaMonte, "Politics and Welfare," p. 114.

16. Ibid., pp. 114–20.

17. Ibid., pp. 114–15.

18. Van DeVoort, "Public Welfare Administration," pp. 38–39.

19. Ibid., pp. 43–49; and LaMonte, "Politics and Welfare," pp. 125–26.

20. Van DeVoort, "Public Welfare Administration," pp. 53–57.

21. LaMonte, "Politics and Welfare," pp. 108–109; and Minutes of the Jefferson County Tuberculosis Society (May 31, 1910), Jefferson County Lung Association, Birmingham. Newfield's interest in combating tuberculosis was shared by many Jews across the country as well. Two special hospitals for consumptives were established in Denver, one founded by German Jews, the other by Eastern European Jews. Newfield corresponded with their staffs from time to time.

22. Alabama Lung Association, *Lung Health News, 1914–1974* (n.p.: privately published, 1974), Jefferson County Lung Association, Birmingham. Alabama Lung Association, "History of the Alabama Tuberculosis Association" (n.d.), Jefferson County Lung Association, Birmingham.

23. Alabama Lung Association, *Lung Health News*.

24. Jefferson County Red Cross, "History of the Jefferson County Red Cross" (n.d.), pp. 1–4, Jefferson County Red Cross, Birmingham.

25. Minutes of the Jefferson County Red Cross (July–August 1921, October 14, 1921, April 18, 1922), Jefferson County Red Cross, Birmingham.

26. Ibid.

27. Brooks, *A Half Century,* p. 27; and Van DeVoort, "Public Welfare Administration," p. 47.

28. Minutes of the Jefferson County Red Cross (April 18, 1922).

29. Brooks, *A Half Century,* p. 27.

30. Ibid., pp. 28, 46–50; and Minutes of Jefferson County Community Chest (1923–25), United Appeal, Birmingham.

31. Minutes of Jefferson County Red Cross (June 15, 1926).

32. Ibid. (February 21, May 21, July 10, 1928).

33. Minutes of Jefferson County Community Chest (January 14, December 22, 1932).

34. Minutes of Jefferson County Red Cross (January 13, 1932); and Minutes of Jefferson County Community Chest (December 16, 1931).

35. Minutes of Jefferson County Red Cross (August 16, 1932); and Minutes of Jefferson County Community Chest (August 24, 1932).

36. Brooks, *A Half Century,* pp. 57–74; and Van DeVoort, "Public Welfare Administration," pp. 60–73.

37. Minutes of Jefferson County Red Cross (1930–32); Minutes of Jefferson County Community Chest (1930–32); and LaMonte, "Politics and Welfare," pp. 213–15 and 224–26.

38. LaMonte, "Politics and Welfare," pp. 217–20.

39. See n. 25.

40. Minutes of Jefferson County Community Chest (June 23, 1933); and Mayer U. Newfield, personal interview, Birmingham, September 1980.

41. Minutes of Jefferson County Community Chest (January 29, March 25, April 29, June 16, 1936). Susan Ackridge, "Roberta Morgan" (term paper, University of Alabama, 1973), Department of Archives and Manuscripts, Birmingham Public Library. Also see Morris Newfield to Roberta Morgan, April 23, 1936, Department of Archives and Manuscripts, Birmingham Public Library.

42. LaMonte, "Politics and Welfare," pp. 186–87.

43. See Minutes of Jefferson County Red Cross and Minutes of Jefferson County Community Chest (1923–36).

44. Morris Newfield, "Child Labor" (1904), pp. 1–2, sermon delivered at Temple Emanu-El, in author's files.

45. Governor Emmet O'Neal to Morris Newfield, December 23, 1914, in author's files.

46. *Birmingham News,* March 9, 11, 13, 1914.

47. Ethel M. Gorman, "History of the Juvenile Court and Domestic Relations Court (n.d.), pp. 1–5, family court, Birmingham.

48. "Summary of Major Efforts in Alabama to Deal with Juvenile Delinquency" (September 1957), family court, Birmingham.

49. Gorman, "History of the Juvenile Court."

50. "Milestones of the Children's Aid Society" (n.d.), Children's Aid Society, Birmingham.

51. "Proceedings of the Alabama Sociological Congress" (1913–15), in author's files.

52. *Proceedings of the Southern Sociological Congress: The Coming Democracy* 5 (1918):3–176, Tutwiler Collection of Southern History, Birmingham Public Library.

53. "Alabama's Charity for Alabama's Own," *Birmingham News* (1919), copy in the Children's Aid Society, Birmingham; Scrapbooks of the Alabama Children's Aid Society (January 14, 1919), Children's Aid Society, Birmingham.

54. See nn. 45 and 47.

55. See U.S. Children's Bureau Collection, Department of Archives and Manuscripts, Birmingham Public Library.

56. See Child Welfare Department, Reports, 1919–28, Alabama State Department of Archives and History, Manuscript Department, Montgomery.

57. See nn. 45 and 47.

58. See *Reports of the Alabama Conference of Social Work,* Alabama State Department of Archives and History, Manuscript Department, Montgomery, and at the Office of the Alabama Conference of Social Work, Montgomery. Also see "Proceedings of the Alabama Sociological Congress (1913–1915)," in author's files.

59. *Reports of the Alabama Conference of Social Work* (1923), located at the Office of the Alabama Conference of Social Work, Montgomery.

SIX. A Moderate in Times of Reactive and Radical Change, 1920–1940

1. Thomas D. Parke, Diaries (entry dated July 1921). For a historical discussion of these issues, see, for example, Woodward, *Origins of the New South;* Tindall, *The Emergence of the New South;* and George Mowry, *Another Look at the Twentieth Century South* (Baton Rouge: Louisiana State University Press, 1972).

2. Blaine A. Brownell, "Birmingham: New South City in the 1920's," *Journal of Southern History* 38 (February 1972):22–26.

3. Ibid.; Hamilton, *Alabama: A Bicentennial History,* pp. 137–39; and Tindall, *The Emergence of the New South.*

4. I have described Newfield's position here as accommodationist because it does not imply a total loss of cultural identity. Newfield hoped to lead Birmingham Jews into an accepted position in the larger Birmingham and Alabama communities by helping Jews acquire certain attitudes and sentiments that were held dear by white Protestants in Birmingham. Still, the rabbi never wanted Jews to lose their identity as a separate religious group in this largely Protestant community. Rather he hoped that Jews could develop personal friendships, professional rela-

tionships, and a spirit of brotherhood with Protestants without giving up their religious traditions.

5. Newfield, "In the Twilight of the Year—The Twilight of Peace" (September 8, 1915), sermon delivered at Temple Emanu-El, American Jewish Archives. Also see Henry Morgenthau to Morris Newfield, December 3, 11, 1917; and "Certificate of Service to Morris Newfield" (December 21, 1918), in author's files.

6. Newfield, "Jews and the Peace Conference" (1919), sermon delivered at Temple Emanu-El, American Jewish Archives.

7. *American Jewish Yearbook* (1919 and 1920), s.v. "Birmingham."

8. Elovitz, *A Century of Jewish Life,* p. 78.

9. Ibid., pp. 77, 118–19; and Minute Books of the Community Chest (1932); also see Mayer U. Newfield, personal interview, Birmingham, September 1979.

10. Minute Books of Temple Emanu-El (January 19, June 16, 1919, and March 8, 1920), Temple Emanu-El, Birmingham.

11. *Emanu-El Bulletin* (October 1920), in author's files.

12. Wise to Newfield, September 23, 1920; Marx to Newfield, September 27, 1920; Deutsch to Newfield, October 15, 1920; Englander to Newfield, September 30, 1920; Calisch to Newfield, September 29, 1920; Dillard to Newfield, October 1, 1920; Barnwell to Newfield, September 28, 1920; Denny to Newfield, September 23, 1920; Leipziger to Newfield, n.d., all in author's files.

13. Victor Hanson to Sidney, September 7, 1920; and Murphy to Newfield, September, pp. 2–3, in author's files.

14. *Birmingham News,* June 10, 1924.

15. Temple Emanu-El, "Birmingham Jews" (unexpected edition, January 28, 1926), in author's files.

16. Mervyn H. Sterne in the "Proceedings of the Pre-Drive Meeting Campaign of United Jewish Relief at Birmingham, Alabama" (April 18, 1926), pp. 40–41, in author's files.

17. George H. Denny to Morris Newfield, May 28, 1921, and November 4, 1929, in author's files.

18. Julian Morgenstern to Newfield, February 3, and 12, 1930; "Tentative Program of the Alabama State Conference" (March 15, 1931); and Harold Hirsch to Newfield, April 20, 1931, in author's files.

19. Atkins, *The Valley and the Hills,* p. 132.

20. Tindall, *The Emergence of the New South,* pp. 111–12; Wayne Flynt, "Organized Labor, Reform, and Alabama Politics, 1920," *Alabama Review* 23 (July 1970):163–81; Philip Taft, "Labor Organization in Coal Fields" (incomplete manuscript), Department of Archives and Manuscripts, Birmingham Public Library; and McMillan, *Yesterday's Birmingham,* pp. 38 and 147.

21. Brownell, "Birmingham: New South City," pp. 26–28.

22. Flynt, "Organized Labor," pp. 163–81; Taft, "Labor Organiza-

tion"; and Robert D. Ward and William W. Rogers, *Labor Revolt in Alabama: The Great Strike of 1894* (University: University of Alabama Press, 1975).

23. Ibid.

24. Brownell, "Birmingham: A New South City," pp. 25–27.

25. Ibid., pp. 28–30.

26. Ibid.

27. Ibid., pp. 30–33.

28. Ibid.; and Hamilton, *Alabama: A Bicentennial History,* p. 134.

29. Hamilton, *Alabama: A Bicentennial History,* p. 134.

30. David Lowe, *Ku Klux Klan: The Invisible Empire* (New York: W. W. Norton, 1967), pp. 10–12; and David Chalmers, *Hooded Americanism: The History of the Ku Klux Klan* (New York: Franklin Watts, 1981), pp. 8–21.

31. William R. Snell, "The Klan in Jefferson County" (M.A. thesis, Samford University, 1967), p. 8; and "Twice City Met, Beat Klan Down," *Birmingham News,* December 19, 1971. Also see Kenneth Jackson, *The Ku Klux Klan in the City* (New York: Oxford University Press, 1967).

32. Chalmers, *Hooded Americanism,* pp. 78–79.

33. "Twice City Met."

34. Chalmers, *Hooded Americanism,* p. 79; and Parke, Diaries (entry for June 7, 1922).

35. Snell, "The Klan in Jefferson County," pp. 62–64.

36. Chalmers, *Hooded Americanism,* pp. 79–81.

37. Snell, "The Klan in Jefferson County," pp. 95–99.

38. Mayer U. Newfield, personal interview, Birmingham, September 1980.

39. James A. Head, Sr., personal interview, Birmingham, September 1979.

40. Chalmers, *Hooded Americanism,* pp. 34–35; and Henry M. Edmonds, "Good Morning," *Birmingham Post-Herald,* June 29, 1957, p. 2, copy in Henry M. Edmonds Collection, Department of Archives and Manuscripts, Birmingham Public Library.

41. Chalmers, *Hooded Americanism,* pp. 81–84.

42. Snell, "The Klan in Jefferson County," p. 159.

43. Chalmers, *Hooded Americanism,* pp. 82–84; and Snell, "The Klan in Jefferson County."

44. Robert P. Ingalls, "Antiradical Violence in Birmingham during the 1930's," *Journal of Southern History* 47, no. 4 (November 1981):521–25.

45. Ibid.

46. Ingalls, "Antiradical Violence," pp. 526–43. Mayer U. Newfield, personal interview, Birmingham, September 1979; Dorah Sterne, personal interview, Birmingham, November 1980; and Buddy Cooper, personal interview, Birmingham, September 1979. Also see Dan T. Carter, *Scottsboro: A Tragedy of the American South* (New York: Oxford Uni-

versity Press, 1969), pp. 355–63; and Esther Frank Gelders, "Professor, How Could You?" *New Republic* 94 (1938):96–97.

47. Ingalls, "Antiradical Violence," pp. 526–43.

48. Buddy Cooper, personal interview, September 1979; Buddy Cooper, after his graduation from Harvard Law School in 1936, was Justice Hugo L. Black's first law clerk when the latter was appointed to the U.S. Supreme Court.

49. James A. Head, Sr., personal interview, September 1979.

50. *Methodist Episcopal Church South Publications* (March 15, 1914), p. 3, in author's files; and Rev. E. C. McVoy to Newfield, February 17, 1914, in author's files.

51. Newfield, "The Claims of Religion," *Birmingham Age-Herald,* March 28, 1920.

52. "A Matter of Conscience," *Birmingham Age-Herald,* undated clipping [probably 1930], in author's files.

53. Henry M. Edmonds, "Good Morning," *Birmingham Post Herald,* May 13, 1960 (copy in Edmonds Collection, Department of Archives and Manuscripts, Birmingham Public Library); also see Edmonds, *A Parson's Notebook.*

54. "Religious Forum: Talk of Newfield, Edmonds, and Father Sands" (n.d.), in author's files.

55. Lorine Alexander, "Second of Tolerant Trio Goes to Reward," *Birmingham News,* undated clipping in author's files.

56. James A. Head, Sr., personal interview, September 1979; "Harry Mell Ayers" (autobiographical sketch) in Harry M. Ayers Collection, William Stanley Hoole Special Collections Library, University of Alabama Library, Tuscaloosa.

57. "The National Conference of Christians and Jews: Twentieth Century Dinner" (November 16, 1948), in author's files. Also see Everett R. Clinchy to Newfield, February 14, November 20, 1930, February 21, June 11, 1931, in author's files.

58. "Program of the Alabama Conference of Human Relations" (February 26–28, 1937), pp. 1–4, in author's files.

59. Newfield, "Exaltation of the Spirit" (January 2, 1914), p. 2, sermon delivered at Temple Emanu-El, American Jewish Archives.

60. Tindall, *The Emergence of the New South,* p. 330. This paternalism is sometimes called "welfare capitalism." Also see Irving Bernstein, *The Lean Years* (Boston: Houghton Mifflin, 1960).

61. Mayer U. Newfield, personal interview, Birmingham, September 1979.

62. Robert L. Buroker, "From Voluntary Association to Welfare State: The Illinois Immigrants Protective Association" (M.A. thesis, University of Chicago, 1971).

63. Newfield, "Social Justice" (n.d.), sermon delivered at Temple Emanu-El, American Jewish Archives.

64. Newfield, "Industrial Relations" (n.d.), sermon delivered at Temple Emanu-El, American Jewish Archives.

65. Newfield, "Federation of Nations" (January 1919), and "Labels and Libels" (November 5, 1925), sermons delivered at Temple Emanu-El, American Jewish Archives.

66. Mayer U. Newfield, personal interview, September 1979; and Henry M. Edmonds, "Beau Geste," *Birmingham Post Herald* (n.d.), Edmonds Collection, Department of Archives and Manuscripts, Birmingham Public Library.

67. Newfield to Edward L. Israel, April 1933, CCAR Collection, American Jewish Archives. Also see Jacob R. Marcus, personal interview, July 1981.

68. Simon Wampold to Edward L. Israel, April 27, 1933, CCAR Collection, American Jewish Archives.

69. Newfield to Samuel H. Goldenson, July 21, 1933, CCAR Collection, American Jewish Archives.

70. Carter, *Scottsboro.*

71. Dinnerstein and Palsson, eds., *Jews in the South,* pp. 9–11; and John Shelton Reed, "Ethnicity in the South: Some Observations on the Acculturation of Southern Jews," *Ethnicity* 6 (1979), pp. 97–106.

SEVEN. Altered Attitudes toward Zionism, 1895–1938

1. Recently, historians of American Jewry have suggested that, within the Central Conference of American Rabbis, there were three and not two positions regarding Zionism. Heretofore historians identified a conflict between those rabbis who supported a Jewish state, or "Zionists," and those who refused to ratify a Jewish state, or "anti-Zionists." Historians such as Stuart E. Knee (*The Concept of Zionist Dissent in the American Mind, 1917–1941* [New York: Robert Speller, 1979], pp. 88–116), and Cyrus L. Arfa ("Attitudes of the American Reform Rabbinate toward Zionism, 1885–1948" [Ph.D. diss., New York University, 1978]) have argued that some rabbis were "non-Zionists," or men who were not supporters of a Jewish political state in Palestine but advocates of economic and cultural development for Jews in Palestine. Following the lead of Louis Marshall, they recognized that oppressed European Jews needed a place to go in order to survive. In 1929, the Jewish Agency was asked to funnel "non-Zionist" money to Palestine. There was not, however—according to Jacob R. Marcus, professor of history at Hebrew Union College—a great deal of money given by "non-Zionist" Jews until after Adolf Hitler rose to power. Also see Morton Rosenstock, *Louis Marshall, Defender of Jewish Rights* (Detroit: Wayne State University Press, 1965).

2. William Rosenau to Morris Newfield, January 11, 1903, in CCAR Collection, American Jewish Archives; Morris Newfield to Leah Newfield, July 5, 1906, July 3, 7, 1907, in author's files; Julian Morgenstern to Morris Newfield, June 17, 1908, in CCAR Collection, American Jewish Archives; Joseph S. Kornfeld to Newfield, June 22, 1915, in CCAR Collection, American Jewish Archives; Louis Wolsey to Newfield, February 28, 1919, in CCAR Collection, American Jewish Archives.

3. George Solomon to Louis Wolsey, February 4, 1919; Wolsey to Solomon, February 10, 1919, in CCAR Collection, American Jewish Archives.

4. Jacob R. Marcus, personal interview, April 1981.

5. Isaac E. Marcuson, ed., *Yearbook of the CCAR* 44 (1934).

6. Newfield to Samuel Kraus, February 27, 1930; Kraus to Newfield, March 18, 1930; Newfield to Ludwig Blau, March 10, 1930; Kraus to Newfield, June 19, 1930, in author's files.

7. Newfield to Kraus, July 17, 1930, in author's files.

8. Milton Fies to Newfield, July 1, 1931, p. 1; Fies, *A Tribute to Dr. Morris Newfield* (n.p.: privately published, June 30, 1931); Abram Simon to Newfield, June 25, 1931; Nathan Krass to Newfield, June 22, 1931; David Marx to Newfield, June 23, 1931; Joseph Kornfeld to Newfield, June 30, 1931; and William Rosenau to Newfield, September 8, 1931, all in author's files.

9. Melvin I. Urofsky, *American Zionism from Herzl to Holocaust* (Garden City: Anchor Press, 1975), p. 1, 119–33.

10. Ibid., p. 31.

11. Ibid., p. 2.

12. Morris Newfield, "Passover," p. 1 (1898); "Zionist Movement" (n.d.), pp. 3–4, sermons delivered at Temple Emanu-El, American Jewish Archives.

13. Naomi W. Cohen, *American Jews and the Zionist Ideal* (New York: K'tav, 1969), p. 16; and Urofsky, *American Zionism*, pp. 120–23.

14. Melvin I. Urofsky, "Zionism: An American Experience," *American Jewish Historical Quarterly* 63, no. 3 (March 1974), pp. 215–30.

15. Newfield, "Rosh Hashana Eve" (September 16, 1918), pp. 2–3, and "Jews and the Peace Conference" (December 1918), sermons delivered at Temple Emanu-El, American Jewish Archives.

16. *New Orleans Jewish Ledger* (1896–1936), copies at Hebrew Union College, Cincinnati.

17. See Bela Vago and George L. Mosse, *Jews and Non-Jews in Eastern Europe, 1918–1943* (New York: Wiley, 1974).

18. See n. 1.

19. Mervyn H. Sterne in "Proceedings of Pre-Drive Meeting in Campaign of United Jewish Relief," (1926), pp. 40–41.

20. "Rabbi Maximillian Heller Honored at Emanu-El," *Birmingham*

News, April 1, 1928, and "Newfield to Raise Funds for Palestine," *Birmingham News,* November 11, 1928.

21. Morris Newfield, "President's Report to Central Conference of American Rabbis," *Yearbook of the CCAR* 41 (1931):174.

22. Stephen S. Wise to Newfield, March 31, 1932; and Newfield to Wise, April 5, 1932, CCAR Collection, American Jewish Archives.

23. Newfield to Samuel Goldenson, April 25, 1932, CCAR Collection, American Jewish Archives.

24. Newfield to Members of the Executive Board of CCAR, May 2, 9, 1932, CCAR Collection, American Jewish Archives.

25. Newfield to Goldenson, October 11, 1932, and Goldenson to Newfield, October 13, 1932, CCAR Collection, American Jewish Archives.

26. Morris Newfield, "President's Message to CCAR," *Yearbook of the CCAR* 42 (1932):149–52.

27. See "Report of Contemporaneous History and Literature," "Report of the Committee on the President's Message," and "Report of Committee on Resolutions," *Yearbook of the CCAR* 42 (1932):86–90, 126–36, 136–45.

28. Samuel Goldenson to Newfield, November 30, 1932, in CCAR Collection, American Jewish Archives.

29. Newfield, "Report of the President," *Yearbook of the CCAR* 43 (1933):127. Jacob R. Marcus, personal interview, April 1981.

30. Samuel Goldenson, "Report of the President," *Yearbook of the CCAR* 44 (1934):122–23.

31. See "Resolution of CCAR Regarding Zionism," *Sentinel of Chicago* (June 21, 1934), CCAR Collection, American Jewish Archives. Also see Newfield to Edward L. Israel, December 13, 1934, and Goldenson to Newfield, December 10, 1934, CCAR Collection, American Jewish Archives.

32. Arfa, "Attitudes of the American Reform Rabbinate."

33. Urofsky, *American Zionism,* pp. 402–403; also see Arthur D. Morse, *While Six Million Died: A Chronicle of American Apathy* (New York: Random House, 1968); David Wyman, *Paper Walls: America and the Refugee Crisis* (Amherst: University of Massachusetts Press, 1968); and Henry L. Feingold, *Politics of Rescue: The Roosevelt Administration and the Holocaust, 1938–1945* (New Brunswick: Rutgers University Press, 1970).

34. Harry Schneiderman to Newfield, October 10, 1938; John Buchanan to Newfield, October 13, 1938; William B. Bankhead to Newfield, October 18, 1938; and Cordell Hull to John Bankhead, October 19, 1938, in author's files.

35. A. H. Reed, Mediator of Birmingham Baptist Association to Franklin D. Roosevelt, n.d.; Ewart H. Wyle to Roosevelt, n.d.; Newfield to Solomon Goldman, October 14, 1938, all in author's files.

Conclusion

NOTES TO CONCLUSION

1. "Goodwill Memorial Planned," *Birmingham Age-Herald,* May 17, 1940.

2. See John Higham, *Strangers in the Land: Patterns of American Nativism* (New Brunswick: Rutgers University Press, 1955); and Oscar Handlin, "Historical Perspectives on the American Ethnic Group," *Daedalus* (Spring 1961):231.

3. For a further discussion of this point, see Jonathan D. Sarna, "The Spectrum of Jewish Leadership in Ante-Bellum America" (paper presented at the annual meeting of the New York American Historical Association, December 1981).

4. See Mark K. Bauman and Arnold Shankman, "The Rabbi as Ethnic Broker," *Journal of American Ethnic History* 2, no. 2 (Spring 1983):51–68.

BIBLIOGRAPHY

Unpublished Manuscript Sources

There are three collections of Morris Newfield Papers that I consulted in writing this biography. One is located at the Alabama State Department of Archives and History in Montgomery. It contains an autobiographical sketch that Newfield wrote in 1913 and various papers concerning his social welfare activities in Birmingham and Alabama. A second, in the American Jewish Archives at Hebrew Union College, Cincinnati, Ohio, was donated by Mayer Ullman Newfield and contains not only many of his sermons and papers that he delivered in Birmingham but also assorted correspondence between the rabbi and other Jewish leaders. A third, consisting of material that I discovered in the attic of Temple Emanu-El, contains a large part of the correspondence that Newfield conducted with his wife in the years 1896–1914, correspondence between Newfield and other Jewish leaders on important events for his temple, and correspondence between Newfield and other social welfare leaders in Alabama in the years 1909–1940. These materials will be accessible to scholars at the American Jewish Archives of Hebrew Union College and at the Department of Archives and Manuscripts, Birmingham Public Library.

Alabama Children's Aid Society. Scrapbooks. Alabama Children's Aid Society, Birmingham.

Alabama State Child Welfare Department. Reports, 1919–28. Manuscripts Division, Alabama Department of Archives and History, Montgomery.

Alabama Tuberculosis Association. History. Jefferson-Shelby Lung Association, Birmingham.

Ayers, Harry M., Collection. William S. Hoole Special Collections Library, University of Alabama Library, Tuscaloosa.

Birmingham Board of Education. Minute Books. Board of Education, Birmingham.

Bowron, James. Autobiography. Typescript. 3 vols. William S. Hoole Special Collections Library, University of Alabama Library, Tuscaloosa.

Central Conference of American Rabbis Collection. American Jewish Archives, Cincinnati.

Children's Aid Society. Milestones. Children's Aid Society, Birmingham.
Edmonds, Henry M., Collection. Department of Archives and Manuscripts, Birmingham Public Library.
Elyton Land Company. Papers. Department of Archives and Manuscripts, Birmingham Public Library.
Hebrew Union College. Grade Books, 1895–1900. American Jewish Archives, Cincinnati, Ohio.
Hill Ferguson Historical Collection of Birmingham, Jefferson County, and Alabama. Scrapbooks. Department of Archives and Manuscripts, Birmingham Public Library.
Jefferson County Community Chest. Minutes, 1923–40. Birmingham United Appeal, Birmingham.
Jefferson County Red Cross. Minutes, 1910–40. Jefferson County Community Chest, Birmingham.
Newfield, Morris. Papers. American Jewish Archives, Hebrew Union College.
———. Author's Private Files. Cincinnati, Ohio.
———. Manuscript Department. Alabama State Department of Archives and History, Montgomery.
Parke, Thomas D. Diaries. Department of Archives and Manuscripts, Birmingham Public Library.
Pastors Union. Minute Books, 1911–17. Collection of D. R. Price, Birmingham.
Temple Emanu-El of Birmingham Collection. American Jewish Archives, Cincinnati.
Temple Sinai of Chicago. Records. American Jewish Archives, Cincinnati.
U.S. Children's Bureau Collection. Department of Archives and Manuscripts, Birmingham Public Library.
Ward, George B., Collection. Department of Archives and Manuscripts, Birmingham Public Library.

Published Primary Sources

Edmonds, Henry M. *A Parson's Notebook*. Birmingham: Independent Presbyterian Church, 1960.
Gladden, Washington. "Baccalaureate Address." In *Seventeenth Annual Commencement Exercises of the University of Cincinnati*. Cincinnati, 1895.
Independent Presbyterian Church. *The Other Side of the Recent Case of Dr. Henry M. Edmonds and the North Alabama Presbytery*. Birmingham: Independent Presbyterian Church, 1915.
Jahresbericht der Landes-Rabbinerschule in Budapest für das Schuljahr 1884–5, 1885–1886, 1888–1889. Budapest: Buchdruckerei des Atheneum, 1885–89.

Jefferson-Shelby Lung Association. *Lung Health News, 1914–1974.* Birmingham: Jefferson-Shelby Lung Association, 1974.

Marcuson, Isaac, ed. *Yearbooks of the Central Conference of American Rabbis.* Vols. 41–46. Cincinnati, Ohio, 1931–36.

Newfield, Morris. "A History of the Birmingham Jewish Community." *Reform Advocate,* November 4, 1911, pp. 6–33.

Office of the Alabama Conference of Social Work. *Reports of the Alabama Conference of Social Work.* Montgomery: Alabama Conference of Social Work.

Presbytery of North Alabama. *A Review and an Exposition of the Case of Dr. Henry M. Edmonds and the Presbytery of North Alabama.* Birmingham: privately published, 1915.

Southern Sociological Congress. *Proceedings of the Southern Sociological Congress: The Coming Democracy.* Birmingham: Southern Sociological Congress, 1918.

Secondary Sources: Monographs

Abell, Aaron I. *The Urban Impact on American Protestantism, 1865–1900.* Cambridge, Mass.: Harvard University Press, 1943.

Armes, Ethel. *The Story of Iron and Coal in Alabama.* Reprint. Birmingham: Bookkeepers Press, 1972.

Atkins, Leah Rawls. *The Valley and the Hills: An Illustrated History of Birmingham and Jefferson County.* Woodhills, Calif.: Windsor Publishing, 1981.

Avery, Mary Johnston. *She Heard with Her Heart: Life of Mrs. R. D. Johnston.* Birmingham: Birmingham Publishing, 1944.

Bailey, Hugh C. *Edgar Gardner Murphy: Gentle Progressive.* Coral Gables: University of Miami Press, 1968.

———. *Liberalism in the New South: Southern Social Reformers and the Progressive Movement.* Coral Gables: University of Miami Press, 1969.

Bailey, Kenneth K. *Southern White Protestantism in the Twentieth Century.* New York: Harper and Row, 1964.

Berman, Myron. *Richmond's Jewry, 1869–1976: Shabat in Shockoe.* Charlottesville: University of Virginia Press, 1979.

Bernstein, Irving. *The Lean Years: A History of the American Worker, 1920–1933.* Boston: Houghton Mifflin, 1960.

Blakely, Hunter B. *Religion in Shoes: Brother Bryan of Birmingham.* Rev. ed. Birmingham: Birmingham Publishing, 1953.

Braham, Randolph L., ed. *Hungarian Jewish Studies.* Vols. 1 and 2. New York: World Federation of Hungarian Jews, 1966 and 1969.

Bremner, Robert H. *American Philanthropy.* Chicago: University of Chicago Press, 1960.

———. *From the Depths: The Discovery of Poverty in the United States.* New York: New York University Press, 1956.

Brooks, Bessie. *A Half Century of Progress in Family Welfare in Jefferson County.* Birmingham: Roberts, 1936.

Bruno, Frank J. *Trends in Social Work as Reflected in the Proceedings of the National Conference of Social Work, 1874–1956.* New York: Columbia University Press, 1948.

Carter, Dan T. *Scottsboro: A Tragedy of the American South.* New York: Oxford University Press, 1969.

Carter, Paul. *The Decline and the Revival of the Social Gospel: Social and Political Liberalism in American Protestant Churches, 1920–1940.* Ithaca: Cornell University Press, 1954.

Chalmers, David. *The History of the Ku Klux Klan.* New York: Franklin Watts, 1981.

Cohen, Naomi W. *American Jews and the Zionist Ideal.* New York: K'tav, 1969.

Corley, Robert G. *Paying Civic Rent: The Jews of Emanu-El and the Birmingham Community.* Birmingham: A. H. Cather Publishing, 1982.

Cross, Robert D., ed. *The Church and the City, 1865–1910.* Indianapolis: Bobbs-Merrill, 1967.

Cruikshank, George M. *A History of Birmingham and Its Environs.* 2 vols. Chicago: Lewis Publishing, 1936.

Daniels, Roger. *Concentration Camps, USA: Japanese Americans and World War II.* New York: Holt, Rinehart and Winston, 1971.

Davis, Allen F. *Spearheads for Reform: The Social Settlements and the Progressive Movement, 1890–1917.* New York: Oxford University Press, 1967.

Davis, Allison, Burleigh B. Gardner, and Mary R. Gardner. *Deep South.* Chicago: University of Chicago Press, 1965.

Dinnerstein, Leonard, and Mary Palsson, ed. *Jews in the South.* Baton Rouge: Louisiana State University Press, 1973.

Elovitz, Mark H. *A Century of Jewish Life in Dixie: The Birmingham Experience.* University: University of Alabama Press, 1974.

Evans, Eli N. *The Provincials: A Personal History of Jews in the South.* New York: Atheneum, 1973.

Feingold, Henry L. *The Politics of Rescue: The Roosevelt Administration and the Holocaust, 1938–1945.* New Brunswick: Rutgers University Press, 1971.

Garraty, John A. *The Nature of Biography.* New York: Alfred A. Knopf, 1957.

Gaustad, Edwin Scott. *Historical Atlas of Religion in America.* New York: Harper and Row, 1976.

Gladden, Washington. *Applied Christianity: Moral Aspects or Social Questions.* Reprint. New York: Arno Press, 1976.

Glazer, Nathan. *American Judaism.* Chicago: University of Chicago Press, 1972.

Goldman, Eric F. *Rendezvous with Destiny.* New York: Alfred A. Knopf, 1952.

Gordon, Milton M. *Assimilation in American Life: The Role of Race, Religion, and National Origins.* New York: Oxford University Press, 1964.

Graham, Otis L., Jr. *An Encore for Reform: The Old Progressives and the New Deal.* New York: Oxford University Press, 1967.

Grantham, Dewey. *Hoke Smith and the Politics of the New South.* Baton Rouge: Louisiana State University Press, 1958.

Hackney, Sheldon F. *Populism and Progressivism in Alabama.* Princeton: Princeton University Press, 1969.

Hamilton, Virginia V. *Alabama: A Bicentennial History.* New York: W. W. Norton, 1977.

Handlin, Oscar. *Adventures in Freedom: 300 Years of Jewish Life in America.* New York: McGraw-Hill, 1954.

Handy, Robert T. *The Social Gospel in America, 1870–1920.* New York: Oxford University Press, 1966.

Harris, Carl V. *Political Power in Birmingham, 1871–1921.* Knoxville: University of Tennessee Press, 1977.

Heller, James G. *Isaac M. Wise.* New York: Union of American Hebrew Congregations, 1965.

Hero, Alfred O. *The Southerner and World Affairs.* Baton Rouge: Louisiana State University Press, 1965.

Higham, John. *Strangers in the Land: Patterns of American Nativism, 1860–1925.* New Brunswick: Rutgers University Press, 1955.

———, ed. *Ethnic Leadership in America.* Baltimore: Johns Hopkins University Press, 1978.

Hill, Samuel S., ed. *On Jordan's Stormy Banks: Religion in the South, a Southern Exposure Profile.* Macon: Mercer University Press, 1983.

———. *Religion in the Southern States: Essays on the History of Religion in the Southern United States.* Macon: Mercer University Press, 1983.

Hirsch, David Einhorn, ed. *Theology of Emil G. Hirsch.* Wheeling, Ill.: Whitehall Company, 1977.

Hirsch, Emil G. *My Religion and the Crucifixion Viewed from a Jewish Standpoint.* 1955. Reprint. New York: Arno Press, 1973.

Hofstadter, Richard. *The Age of Reform: From Bryan to FDR.* New York: Alfred A. Knopf, 1955.

Hopkins, Charles. *The Rise of the Social Gospel in American Protestantism, 1865–1915.* 1940. Reprint. New Haven: Yale University Press, 1957.

Hopkins, Charles, and Ronald White, eds. *The Social Gospel: Religion and Reform in Changing America.* Philadelphia: Temple University Press, 1976.

Hornady, John R. *The Book of Birmingham.* New York: Dodd, Mead, 1921.

Hudson, Alvin W., and Harold E. Cox. *Street Railways of Birmingham.* Birmingham: Privately published, 1976.

Jackson, Kenneth T. *The Ku Klux Klan in the City, 1915–1930.* New York: Oxford University Press, 1967.

Kaganoff, Nathan M., and Melvin I. Urofsky, eds. *Turn to the South: Essays on Southern Jewry.* Charlottesville: University of Virginia Press, 1979.

Karff, Samuel E., ed. *Hebrew Union College–Jewish Institute of Religion: At One Hundred Years.* Cincinnati: Hebrew Union College Press, 1976.

Knee, Stuart E. *The Concept of Zionist Dissent in the American Mind, 1917–1941.* New York: Robert Speller, 1979.

Kohn, Sylvia Blascoer. *By Reason of Strength: The Story of Temple Emanu-El's Seventy Years, 1882–1952.* Birmingham: Temple Emanu-El, 1952.

Kraut, Benny. *From Reform Judaism to Ethical Culture.* Cincinnati: Hebrew Union College Press, 1979.

LaMonte, Edward S. *George B. Ward: Birmingham's Urban Statesman.* Birmingham: Birmingham Public Library, 1974.

Laqueur, Walter. *A History of Zionism.* New York: Holt, Rinehart and Winston, 1970.

Lavender, Abraham D., ed. *A Coat of Many Colors: Jewish Subcommunities in the United States.* Westport: Greenwood Press, 1977.

Leuchtenberg, William E. *Franklin D. Roosevelt and the New Deal, 1932–1940.* New York: Harper and Row, 1963.

———. *The Perils of Prosperity, 1914–1932.* Chicago: University of Chicago Press, 1958.

Lowe, David. *Ku Klux Klan: The Invisible Empire.* New York: W. W. Norton, 1967.

Lowinger, Dr. Samuel, ed. *Seventy Years: A Tribute to the Seventieth Anniversary of the Jewish Theological Seminary of Hungary, 1877–1947.* Budapest: Jewish Theological Seminary, 1948.

Lubove, Roy. *The Professional Altruist.* Cambridge, Mass.: Harvard University Press, 1965.

Lurie, Harry. *A Heritage Affirmed: The Jewish Federation Movement in America.* Philadelphia: Jewish Publication Society of America, 1961.

McCagg, William O. *Jewish Geniuses and Nobles in Modern Hungary.* New York: Columbia University Press, 1972.

McDavid, Mittie Owen. *A History of the Church of the Advent.* Birmingham: Church of the Advent, 1943.

McKinney, John C., and Edgar T. Thompson, eds. *The South in Continuity and Change.* Durham: Duke University Press, 1965.

McMillan, Malcolm C. *Yesterday's Birmingham.* Miami: E. A. Seeman, 1975.

Mann, Arthur. *The One and the Many: Reflections on the American Identity.* Chicago: University of Chicago Press, 1979.

———. *The Progressive Era*. New York: Holt, Rinehart and Winston, 1963.

Manners, Ande. *Poor Cousins*. New York: Coward, McCann and Geoghegan, 1972.

Morse, Arthur D. *While Six Million Died: A Chronicle of American Apathy*. New York: Random House, 1968.

Mowry, George. *Another Look at the Twentieth Century South*. Baton Rouge: Louisiana State University Press, 1972.

Owen, Thomas McAdory. *History of Alabama: Dictionary of Alabama Biography*. 1921. Reprint. 4 vols. Spartenburg: Reprint Company, 1978.

Philipson, David. *Max Lilienthal*. New York: Bloch Publishing, 1915.

Plaut, W. Gunther. *The Growth of Reform Judaism: American and European Sources until 1948*. Vol. 2. New York: World Union for Progressive Judaism, 1965.

Raphael, Marc Lee. *Jews and Judaism in a Midwestern Community: Columbus, Ohio, 1840–1975*. Columbus: Ohio Historical Society, 1979.

Richmond, Mary. *Social Diagnosis*. New York: Russell Sage Foundation, 1917.

Rosenstock, Morton. *Louis Marshall, Defender of Jewish Rights*. Detroit: Wayne State University Press, 1965.

Spotswood, James E. *Crossroad to Service: The Birmingham Area Red Cross, 1917–1976*. Birmingham: Red Cross, 1976.

Strout, Cushing. *The New Heavens and New Earth: Political Religion in America*. New York: Harper and Row, 1973.

Tindall, George B. *The Emergence of the New South, 1913–1945*. Baton Rouge: Louisiana State University Press, 1967.

Trattner, Walter I. *From Poor Law to Welfare State*. New York: Free Press, 1974.

Tulman, Victor David. *Going Home*. New York: Quadrangle, 1977.

Urofsky, Melvin I. *American Zionism: From Herzl to the Holocaust*. Garden City: Anchor Press, 1975.

Vago, Bela, and George L. Mosse. *Jews and Non-Jews in Eastern Europe, 1918–1945*. New York: Wiley, 1974.

Voss, Carl Herman. *Rabbi and Minister: The Friendship of Stephen S. Wise and John Haynes Holmes*. Cleveland: World Publishing, 1964.

Ward, Robert D., and William W. Rogers. *Labor Revolt in Alabama: The Great Strike of 1894*. Tuscaloosa: University of Alabama Press, 1965.

Weiner, Jonathan M. *Social Origins of the New South: Alabama, 1860–1885*. Baton Rouge: Louisiana State University Press, 1978.

Weinstein, James. *The Corporate Ideal in a Liberal State, 1900–1918*. Boston: Beacon Press, 1969.

Wiebe, Robert. *Businessmen and Reform: A Study of the Progressive Movement*. Cambridge, Mass.: Harvard University Press, 1962.

———. *The Search for Order, 1877–1920.* New York: Hill and Wang, 1967.

Wisner, Elizabeth. *Social Welfare in the South.* Baton Rouge: Louisiana State University Press, 1938.

Wyman, David. *Paper Walls: America and the Refugee Crisis, 1938–1941.* Amherst: University of Massachusetts Press, 1968.

Woodward, C. Vann. *Origins of the New South, 1877–1913.* Rev. ed. Baton Rouge: Louisiana State University Press, 1971.

Secondary Sources: Articles

Alston, Wallace M., Jr., and Wayne Flynt. "Religion in the Land of Cotton." In *You Can't Eat Magnolias,* ed. H. Brandt Ayers and Thomas H. Naylor. New York: McGraw-Hill, 1972.

Anderson, Fletcher. "Foundations of a Musical Culture in Birmingham, Alabama, 1871–1900." *Journal of the Birmingham Historical Society* 6, no. 3 (January 1980):2–17.

Armes, Ethel. "The Spirit of the Founders." *Survey Magazine* 27 (January 6, 1912):1453–63.

Baron, W. Salo. "American Jewish History: Problems and Methods." *Publication of the American Jewish Historical Society* 39 (September 1949):207–66.

Bauman, Mark K., and Arnold Shankman. "The Rabbi as Ethnic Broker." *Journal of American Ethnic History* 2, no. 2 (Spring 1983):51–68.

Breedlove, Michael A. "Progressivism and Nativism: The Race for the Presidency of the City Commission of Birmingham, Alabama in 1917." *Journal of the Birmingham Historical Society* 6, no. 4 (July 1980):2–9.

Brownell, Blaine A. "Birmingham: New South City in the 1920's." *Journal of Southern History* 38 (February 1972):22–26.

———. "The Notorious Jitney and the Urban Transportation Crisis in Birmingham in the 1920's." *Alabama Review* 25 (April 1972):105–18.

Burkhardt, Ann M. "Town within a City: The Five Points South Neighborhood, 1880–1920." *Journal of the Birmingham Historical Society* 7, nos. 3 and 4 (November 1982):11–90.

Feldman, Egal. "The Social Gospel and the Jews." *American Jewish Historical Quarterly* 58, no. 3 (March 1969):308–29.

Flynt, Wayne. "Dissent in Zion: Alabama Baptist and Social Issues, 1900–1914." *Alabama Review* (November 1969):523–42.

———. "Organized Labor, Reform, and Alabama Politics, 1920." *Alabama Review* 23 (July 1970):163–81.

———. "Religion in the Urban South: The Divided Mind of Birmingham, 1900–1930." *Alabama Review* 30, no. 2 (April 1977):108–35.

Friedman, Lee M. "An Invitation to American Jewish History." *American Jewish Historical Quarterly* 38 (September 1948):1–21.

Gelders, Esther Frank. "Professor, How Could You?" *New Republic* 94 (1938):96–97.

Goodrich, Gillan. "Romance and Reality: The Birmingham Suffragists, 1892–1920." *Journal of the Birmingham Historical Society* 5, no. 4 (July 1978):4–21.

Gordman, Ethel M. "History of the Juvenile Court and Domestic Relations Court." Birmingham: Family Court, n.d.

Handlin, Oscar. "Historical Perspectives on the American Ethnic Group." *Daedalus* 90 (Spring 1961):220–32.

Harris, Carl V. "Annexation Struggles and Political Power in Birmingham, Alabama, 1890–1910." *Alabama Review* 27 (July 1974):163–84.

LaMonte, Edward S. "The Mercy Home and Private Charity in Early Birmingham." *Journal of the Birmingham Historical Society* 5, no. 3 (January 1978):5–15.

Levine, Daniel. "Edgar Gardner Murphy, Conservative Reformer." *Alabama Review* (Spring 1962):100–16.

Link, Arthur. "What Happened to Progressivism in the 20's?" In *The Progressive Era,* ed. Arthur Mann. New York: Holt, Rinehart, and Winston, 1963.

McCagg, William O. "Jews in Revolution: The Hungarian Experiment." *Journal of Social History* 6 (1972–73):78–105.

Mervis, Leonard. "The Social Justice Movement and the American Reform Rabbinate." *American Jewish Archives* 7, no. 2 (Fall 1955):171–230.

Meyer, Michael. "A Centennial History." In *Hebrew Union College–Jewish Institute of Religion: At One Hundred Years,* ed. Samuel E. Karff. Cincinnati: Hebrew Union College Press, 1979.

Morgan, Roberta. "Social Implications of the Human Side." *Journal of the Birmingham Historical Society* 1, no. 1 (January 1960):11–17.

Reed, John Shelton. "Ethnicity in the South: Some Observations on the Acculturation of Southern Jews." *Ethnicity* 6 (1979):97–106.

Snell, William R. "Masked Men in the Magic City: Activities of the Revised Klan in Birmingham, 1916–1940." *Alabama Historical Quarterly* (Fall–Winter 1972):206–27.

Straw, Richard A. "The United Mine Workers of America and the 1920 Coal Strike in Alabama." *Alabama Review* 28 (April 1975):104–28.

Urofsky, Melvin I. "Zionism: An American Experience." *American Jewish Historical Quarterly* 63, no. 3 (March 1974):215–30.

Whiting, Marvin Y. "True Americans, Pro and Con: Campaign Literature from the 1917 Race for the Presidency of the Birmingham City Commission." *Journal of the Birmingham Historical Society* 6, no. 4 (July 1980):10–23.

Newspapers

Alabama Baptist. 1900–15.
Birmingham Age-Herald. 1900–40.
Birmingham Post. 1920–40.
Cincinnati Enquirer. 1895.
Memphis Jewish Spectator. 1896–1910.
New Orleans Jewish Ledger. 1896–1940.
Reform Advocate of Chicago. 1911.

Government Documents

U.S. Department of Commerce and Labor. Bureau of the Census. *Religious Bodies.* Washington, D.C., 1910.

Unpublished Theses

Ackridge, Susan. "Roberta Morgan." Term paper. University of Alabama, 1973.

Arfa, Cyrus I. "Attitudes of the American Reform Rabbinate toward Zionism, 1885–1948." Ph.D. diss. New York University, 1978.

Atkins, Leah Rawls. "Early Efforts to Control Tuberculosis in Alabama: The Formation and Work of the Alabama Tuberculosis Association, 1908–1930." M.A. thesis. Auburn University, 1960.

Bigelow, Martha. "History of Birmingham, 1870–1910." Ph.D. diss. University of Chicago, 1946.

Buroker, Robert. "From Voluntary Association to Welfare State: The Illinois Immigrants' Protective League, 1908–1926." M.A. thesis. University of Chicago, 1971.

Burrows, John Howard. "The Great Disturber: The Social Philosophy and Theology of Alfred James Dickinson." M.A. thesis. Samford University, 1970.

King, Jere C., Jr. "The Formation of Greater Birmingham." M.A. thesis. University of Alabama, 1935.

LaMonte, Edward W. "Politics and Welfare in Birmingham, Alabama, 1900–1975." Ph.D. diss. University of Chicago, 1978.

Lesser, Charles B. "Principles of Jewish Benevolence as Reflected in the Various Law Codes." Rabbinic thesis. Hebrew Union College, 1935.

Phillips, Marshall. "A History of the Public Schools in Birmingham, Alabama." M.A. thesis. University of Alabama, 1939.

Scroggins, Raymond. "A Cultural and Religious History of Birmingham, Alabama, 1871–1931." A.B. thesis. Howard College, 1939.

Snell, William R. "The Klan in Jefferson County." M.A. thesis. Samford University, 1967.
Spain, Rufus. "Attitudes and Reactions of Southern Baptists to Certain Problems of Society, 1865–1900." Ph.D. diss. Vanderbilt University, 1961.
Sterne, Ellin. "Prostitution in Birmingham, Alabama, 1890–1925." M.A. thesis. Samford University, 1977.
Van DeVoort, Anita. "Public Welfare Administration in Jefferson County." M.A. thesis. Tulane University, 1935.

INDEX

INDEX

INDEX

INDEX